FREE LEGAL MARKETING RESOURCES, CHECKLISTS AND TEMPLATES

Digital marketing is forever changing, so we have created an online resource at our blog on *legalmarketingreview.com* to help you keep up to date. Please check out our downloads and resources to help you get the most out of this book.

legalmarketingreview.com/downloads

Feel free to contact John D. McDougall at McDougall Interactive with questions or help with your legal marketing 877-623-4291 or *www.mcdia.com*

Content Marketing and SEO for Law Firms

How to get consistent website leads by following a highly actionable roadmap

John D. McDougall

INTERA PRESS

Published by Intera Press
12 Riggs Point Road
Gloucester, MA 01930

For information, contact McDougall Interactive at the address above or at 877-623-4291 or *www.mcdia.com*.

Quantity sales: For information on bulk purchases, please contact McDougall Interactive.

First Edition: January 2020
Editor: Kate Victory Hannisian, Blue Pencil Consulting
Proof Reader: Evelyn Howell
Book Layout: Wordzworth
Cover Design: McDougall Interactive
Printing: King Printing Co., Inc.

ISBN: 978-0-9911593-5-2

Library of Congress Control Number: 2019916620

A special thanks to my father for getting me into marketing and for being an ongoing source of help as I grow my agency. And to my late mother for her endless support and creative inspiration.

Without my team and clients at McDougall Interactive, this book would not be possible. The powerful work we do together is how we learn what works and what doesn't.

Thanks to Kate Victory Hannisian, my editor and Evelyn Howell, my proofreader, who tirelessly helped to organize my ideas and meanderings. And to Joe Rubino, Michael Gass and David Baker for helping with my strategy.

Thanks to Vignesh Kumar of Neil Patel's team for outstanding inspiration on marketing and agency growth.

Thanks to Anna Norregaard and HubSpot for her great contribution to the tools section.

Without my wife Ai-Thu and our son, nothing would be as good as it is now.

Thanks to God for keeping me inspired and on track.

Contents

Foreword viii

Why and How to Read This Book x

Introduction xi

Part 1 Before You Dive into Optimization 1

Document Your Roadmap and Strategy 1

Top 10 Reasons Law Firm Content Marketing and SEO Fails 4

How to Do Competitive Analysis in Legal Content Marketing and SEO 6

Part 2 SEO Ranking Factors and Roadmap for Law Firms 29

Overview of SEO Ranking Factors 29

Summaries of the 7 Key SEO Tactics 31

The 7 Key SEO Tactics in Depth 37

1. Build your brand for positive impact on search rank 37
2. Technical SEO Ranking Factors 44
3. On-Page SEO Best Practices for Marketing Your Law Firm 61
4. Create Compelling Content for SEO 77
5. User Experience Optimization Is Key to Your Law Firm Marketing Strategy 77
6. Law Firm SEO Link Building 92
7. Law Firm Social Signals for SEO 101

Additional SEO Considerations: Local SEO for Law Firms 113

Part 3 Content Marketing 126

Overview: How to Do Content Marketing for Your Law Firm 126

Overview: Types of Content for Digital Marketing 142

Types of Content for Digital Marketing and How to Use Them In Depth 140
1. Your Main Website Pages 140
2. Law Firm Blogging 101 148
3. Guest Blogging Opportunities for Law Firms 157
4. Law Firm Video Marketing and YouTube SEO 164
5. Podcast Marketing for Law Firms 168
6. Infographics and Images 176
7. The Benefits of Creating E-books for Your Law Firm 183
8. Law Firm Press Releases 188
9. Benefits of Webinar Marketing 192
10. FAQ Pages and Voice Search Optimization for Law Firms 198
11. Topic Clusters For Advanced Law Firm SEO 203
12. Law Firm Link Bait 214
13. Law Firm Case Studies for Content Marketing 221

Part 4 Increasing Conversions and Tracking ROI in Analytics 228

10 Things Great Law Firm Websites Do Right 228
Top 9 Things Law Firms Should Track in Google Analytics 233
11 Top Digital Marketing Tactics and How They Fit Together 239
Final Thoughts! 245

Part 5 SEO and Content Marketing Resources 247

Checklists and Resources for Legal Marketing with the "On All Cylinders" System 247
The Big Dog Authority Marketing Checklist for Lawyers 249
10 Ways to Meet Ethical Obligations in Online Marketing for Law Firms 255
Top Digital Marketing Tools for Law Firms 258
9 HubSpot Tools That Can Help Law Firms Rev Up Their Digital Marketing 263
Top Digital Marketing Blogs for Law Firms to Follow 267

About the Author 270

About McDougall Interactive and Our Services 271

Foreword

Marketing for law firms has undergone radical changes because of the internet, and it's not always easy to know what is effective and what is a waste of time.

Most attorneys have a sense that blogs and various forms of digital marketing can help position them as experts and get them more leads, but they are not always clear on exactly how to implement and use these tactics consistently.

Marketing law firms is one of the most competitive niches to do marketing in, which only complicates matters because your efforts must be precise.

When I was working at *The National Law Review* as the lead publications manager, I was entrenched in terms I never thought would matter to me in law school: metadata, search engine optimization, content marketing, conversion, data analytics, and more. *The National Law Review* publishes hundreds of legal news articles per month and cares deeply about the success of each one of them.

Before things started to crystallize for me, I met John McDougall of McDougall Interactive at a Legal Marketing Association conference in Boston, where I experienced at least half a dozen SEO-related revelations during his talk. From then on, John and his team were integral in my continued learning and understanding of content marketing and SEO. I learned an incredible amount about the inner workings of things like podcasting and running webinars from McDougall Interactive.

If you ask several attorneys if they know what a podcast is, most will say yes. Yet when it comes time to produce one, most will have no idea about the finer details of successful podcasting, such as how to come up with the topics, the mechanics involved in audio engineering, and the value of the content and words surrounding the audio itself.

Likewise, most will have watched and listened to a webinar, but few will have the right strategy and checklist of steps to create one of their own that helps with sales and marketing for their law firm.

Content marketing and search engine optimization work more effectively when these nuanced principles are applied toward raising a law firm's profile and successfully attracting prospective clients. These fine details are what distinguish the savvy legal marketers from the average, and the renowned attorneys from the simply known.

Having been on the front lines of content marketing and producing massive volumes of content, it was a delight to have someone to turn to for the technical side of things like solving Google penalties, which requires a level of detail many writers and attorneys would not care to dig into deeply.

I've seen firsthand how John McDougall and his team think, both about creative content and the technical aspects of implementing it; they think in a way that leads to significant and trackable new business.

Perhaps you wonder whether this book will go too far into the weeds or if it is worth investing your time to read it. Let me tell you that the time you will save by having the right information to avoid making mistakes will easily make it worth reading.

This book was created with great care and thoughtfulness. Knowing that attorneys may not read all of it, the critical sections for "C-Suite" and high-level attorneys are marked with a gavel icon. The rest of the material can be shared with your marketing staff or read later, if you are intrigued.

Launching or promoting a website that looks nice and has an in-depth blog can quickly turn into a disaster without the right technical details and strategy behind it.

If you want to understand how to develop content that is seen at the very top of the search engine results and gets people engaged on social media, then get this book for yourself, your marketing staff, and the top attorney(s) at your firm.

Carpe Diem!

Nicole Minnis

FORMER LEAD PUBLICATIONS MANAGER, THE NATIONAL LAW REVIEW
STAFF ATTORNEY AT DEPAUL UNIVERSITY COLLEGE OF LAW

Why and How to Read This Book

If you have ever had any anxiety over your website and digital marketing, you are not alone.

This book will help you understand why legal marketing is so hard and how to beat the competition.

You will learn about using search engine optimization (SEO) and high-quality content marketing, both in terms of strategy and execution. Which level of detail you read and which you hand off to your marketing team is up to you.

Partner and C-Level "must reads" are designated with the gavel symbol. If you miss those, you might go down a long and dusty road and get lost.

We will lay out a roadmap that has a lot of details and may seem overwhelming, but it is truly what it takes to make digital marketing effective.

Once you have the roadmap and get a team to help you with it, you will start seeing results and get excited to hit the gas pedal!

Introduction

Why Content Marketing and SEO Has Become as Important to Law Firms as Getting Referrals

When I started selling websites in 1995, I had no idea I would still be building them and marketing them 25 years later.

My father owned the sixth-largest ad agency in New England, and so I was lucky enough to be tasked with switching from being a media planner to selling digital marketing.

I got mocked by more than one company that thought I was the latest version of a snake oil salesman when I pulled out my laptop and dialed up over AOL in their office. Yet here we are, with digital marketing accounting for about half of marketing budgets and much more than that for businesses with sales revenues under $25 million.

Because of the vast amount of helpful information on the internet, prospective customers are now nearly 75% of the way through their decision-making process before they ever engage with a sales representative.

- "57% of the purchase decision is complete before a customer even calls a supplier." (*CEB*)[1]
- "67% of the buyer's journey is now done digitally." (*SiriusDecisions*)[2]
- "B2B customers are more than 70% of the way through the decision-making process before ever engaging a sales representative." (*Demand Gen 7th Annual B2B Buyer's Survey*)[3]

---

1 *http://www.executiveboard.com/exbd/sales-service/challenger/new-decision-timeline/index.page*

2 *http://www.siriusdecisions.com/blog/three-myths-of-the-67-percent-statistic/*

3 *https://www.demandgenreport.com/resources/research/2017-b2b-buyers-survey-report*

That means people and businesses know what they want, and they know the handful of law firms that they might consider working with. They have read those law firms' blogs, bought their books, downloaded their white papers, and are receiving their automated email sales messages with intriguing content and occasional offers.

If you are focused solely on sales tactics and are not getting in front of prospects with a steady diet of your content, you lose to other lawyers, some of whom may even give new meaning to the phrase "criminal lawyers."

For example, one law firm showed me a network of sites built by an attorney who had a criminal record and yet was great at SEO. He was eating his competitor's lunch despite his own infamy.

When I was working on a mesothelioma law SEO and Google ad project, a client shared how one meso marketer made fake veterans hospital websites to get leads. It doesn't get any more unethical than that. Sadly, though, Google can't always sort the good from the bad law firms and sometimes rewards great content, regardless of who created it (or how legitimate it is or isn't).

Let's look at Google for how people can find legal counsel and advice.

Search Google for "How to file a patent" and Nolo, Legal Zoom, Forbes, Inc., and ipwatchdog.com all come up as sources of information on that topic.

Search Google for "What to do if I get pulled over for drunk driving," and the search results will include lawyer videos, law firm websites, and the Huffington Post site.

Search Google for "Is an LLC or trust better to protect my business?" and LLC Wizard, Legal Zoom, Investopedia, and a couple of law firm websites show up in the search results.

The experts who are doing the writing and thinking like publishers are winning the business these days, not those with the largest Yellow Pages ad or the most TV commercials. Very often, you will see legal directories, big media sites like Forbes, and then niche sites like LLC Wizard or Birth Injury Guide that have a lot of content on niche topics.

If you let others own the searches for what makes you money, you and your firm lose.

People are so bombarded by marketing messages, and even now by content, that you really need to get in front of them with just the right message that solves their pain right when they are ready to pull the trigger.

So you need to have content available and visible when they are researching, when they are considering what company to choose, and finally when they are ready to buy — at all stages of the marketing funnel, or what people refer to now as the buyer's journey.

Sadly, many attorneys think everyone is always ready for a free consultation and that they are mostly searching for things like "hire Boston business lawyer right now."

While I have a few unkind words to say about some of FindLaw's older practices, I remember seeing a great talk they did about how most law leads actually come from long tail searches, where customers are seeking to solve their problems, not just hire an attorney in xyz city and state.

Some of the most expensive Google ads are legal related and can cost over $900 per click! So long-term, "owning" thousands of non-paid organic Google search terms is critical. You also need to take improving your website to another level. If you only turn 100 website visitors into leads at a 1% conversion rate, it could potentially cost you $90,000 per lead, and that's hardly sustainable.

It must be nice to own Google... If they can get nearly $1,000 per click in extreme cases and it just takes a second to click, they could theoretically make $60,000 per minute.

Just to help illustrate this further, here's how much it would cost advertisers, on average, to buy Google ads for the ten most expensive Google keyword concepts:

Term	**Cost per click***
Business Services:	$58.64
Bail Bonds:	$58.48
Casino:	$55.48
Lawyer:	$54.86
Asset Management:	$49.86
Insurance:	$48.41
Cash Services & Payday Loans:	$48.18
Cleanup & Restoration Services:	$47.61
Degree:	$47.36
Medical Coding Services:	$46.84

**To get this data, WordStream examined the top keywords between June 1, 2016, and June 12, 2017, and categorized them by core intent.*

As mentioned, there are individual keywords with much higher costs than these, but WordStream's research was specifically looking at related keywords with extremely high costs per click on average. This data gives you the broad sense of hot and expensive topics online.

Now let's look at a few more fun examples to freak out you and your wallet completely.

If you use SEMrush to search for the single word "lawyer" and filter keywords by the highest estimated cost per click in Google ads, you get the following:

Accident and Injury

Indianapolis Semi Truck Accident Lawyer:	$905
Car Accident Lawyer Elite:	$872
Mesothelioma Lawsuit Lawyers:	$756
Albany Ga Personal Injury Lawyer:	$750
Los Angeles Uber Accident Lawyer:	$733
Car accident lawyers Colorado Springs CO:	$732
Iron Horse Motorcycle Lawyers Greenville SC:	$728
Offshore Lawyers In Louisiana:	$680
Birth Injury Lawyer Pittsburgh:	$666
Car Accident Lawyer Decatur GA:	$665

Mesothelioma

Stage 4 Peritoneal Mesothelioma Life Expectancy:	$889
Mesothelioma Lawsuit Lawyers:	$756
Mesothelioma Attorney Pittsburgh:	$740
Best Mesothelioma Attorneys:	$648
Mesothelioma Lawyers In Michigan:	$625
New York Mesothelioma Lawyer:	$566
Mesothelioma Lawyer Near Me:	$561
Cases of mesothelioma:	$534
Mesothelioma Attorney Seattle:	$523
Mesothelioma Net:	$503

DUI and Criminal Defense

DUI Lawyers in San Antonio:	$348
Cheap DUI Lawyers Los Angeles:	$344
Best Criminal Defense Lawyers in Fort Myers FL:	$237
Jewish Criminal Defense Lawyers:	$155

Business Law

Business Tax Lawyer:	$87
Small Business Lawyer Maryland:	$73
Business Tax Lawyer Near Me:	$69
Business Partnership Dispute Lawyers:	$64
Business Lawyers In Cincinnati Ohio:	$56
Medical Marijuana Business Lawyers LLC:	$55
Business Mediation Lawyer:	$54
Home And Business Lawyer Software Download:	$52
Business Lawyer Colorado:	$50
Business Lawyer For Small Business:	$47

Misc.

Real Estate Litigation Lawyers Near Me:	$141
Real Estate Lawyer Fairfax VA:	$54
Intellectual Property Lawyer Long Island:	$35
Intellectual Property Lawyer San Diego:	$26
Estate Planning Lawyer:	$20
Estate Planning Lawyers Near Me:	$18
Immigration Lawyer NYC:	$19
Immigration Attorney:	$12
Family Lawyer Near Me:	$19
NY Whistleblower Lawyer:	$77
Whistleblower Lawyers:	$41

Digital marketing works. Otherwise, people would not have spent years bidding up the cost of these ads. Therefore, showing up in the search results without paying for Google ads has a tangible value.

For example, FindLaw has 3.4 million keywords that rank organically in Google. Based on Google's estimated costs per click, those keyword ranking positions would have cost $29 million per month, if they had to buy them as Google ads!

And how many people are searching?

Here is the monthly volume for some top terms that come up when you search SEMrush for just the word "lawyer."

Keyword	**Volume**
Lawyer	135,000
Attorney	110,000
Immigration Lawyer	74,000
Donald Trump Jr Russian Lawyer	40,500
Lawyer Salary	40,500
Rocket Lawyer	40,500
Divorce Lawyers	33,100
Lawyers Near Me	33,100
Personal Injury Lawyer	33,100
Bankruptcy Lawyer	27,100
The Lincoln Lawyer	27,100
Bankruptcy Lawyers	22,200
Car Accident Lawyer	22,200
Disability Lawyers	22,200
Divorce Lawyer	22,200
How Much Do Lawyers Make	18,100
OJSimpson Lawyers	18,100
Real Estate Lawyer	18,100
Accident Lawyer	14,800
Divorce Lawyers Near Me	14,800
Immigration Lawyer Near Me	14,800
Injury Lawyer	14,800

Pro Bono Lawyers	14,800
Stormy Daniels Lawyer	14,800
Bankruptcy Lawyers Near Me	12,100
Family Lawyer Near Me	12,100
Lawyers Guns And Money	12,100
Workers Comp Lawyer	12,100
Average Lawyer Salary	9,900
Child Support Lawyers	9,900
Dog Bite Lawyer Vancouver	9,900
How To Become A Lawyer	9,900
Malpractice Lawyers	9,900
Medical Malpractice Lawyers	9,900
Trump Lawyer	9,900
Trump Lawyers Mueller	9,900
Ask A Lawyer	8,100
Attorney Vs Lawyer	8,100
Criminal Defense Lawyer	8,100
Free Lawyer Consultation	8,100
Probate Lawyer	8,100
Trump Jr Russian Lawyer	8,100
Ty Cobb Lawyer	8,100
Wrongful Termination Lawyers	8,100
Child Custody Lawyer	6,600
DUI Lawyer	6,600
Family Lawyers Near Me	6,600
Find a Lawyer	6,600

Here is just one example of customers searching on their pain points, who may appreciate an attorney's thought leadership content on this immigration law-related topic:

Keyword	**Volume**
How To Get A Green Card	8,100
How Long Does It Take To Get A Green Card	4,400
How To Get A Green Card In USA	2,900

How To Get Green Card In USA	1,900
Getting A Green Card	880
How Do You Get A Green Card	880
How Long To Get Green Card	720
How Much Does It Cost To Get A Green Card	720
How To Get A Green Card Through Marriage	720

So there is immense potential to getting leads from organic SEO that could otherwise cost a fortune if a firm tried to get the same visibility through buying Google ads. Despite that, so many law firms half-bake their SEO and blogging efforts. Then they change digital marketing agencies like the wind, and wonder why they are frustrated with their content marketing efforts.

Because you're reading this book, that should not happen to you. That's because you will gain much greater confidence that you are strategically on the right path and are using a time-tested roadmap, instead of notes on a napkin, to maximize your digital marketing efforts.

You will learn what you might do yourself, what you would be better off outsourcing (like technical SEO), and how to think about marketing as a team effort.

Hiring Versus Outsourcing

I recently made a list of the things you might do in order to embrace digital marketing fully. Wait, let me rephrase that: Here is a list of things we (as a digital marketing agency) actually do with our in-house team and extended team of highly specialized subcontractors.

This list may help you realize the importance of having your own team versus having a "webmaster" or even one or two people at your firm to handle all the various tactics and software tools needed.

Marketing Tasks

"Before You Start" Tactics

- Marketing Plan
- Strategy Development (Business, Digital, Traditional)
- Market / Target Audience Research
- Competitive Analysis
- SWOT Analysis
- Persona Development
- Buyer's Journey Mapping
- Positioning / Messaging / UVP Development
- Mission Statement Writing
- Assigning Roles, Timing and Project Management System
- Budget Setting (5% to maintain, 10% to grow, 7% is the average according to *cmosurvey.org*)
- Business and Marketing Goals / KPIs Documentation
- Logo, Font and Color Guideline Documentation

Content Marketing

- Blogging
- Podcasting
- Videos
- E-books
- Infographics
- Photo Galleries
- Webinars
- Surveys

Content Promotion

- Email Outreach
- Paid Promotion

Digital Ads

- Paid Search
- Paid Social
- Display Ads
- Retargeting
- GEO Fencing

SEO

- Tech SEO
- On-Page SEO
- Off-Page SEO (Links and PR)
- Local SEO
- Topic Cluster Strategy
- Voice Search Strategy

Social Media

- Social Media Policy
- Facebook
- YouTube
- LinkedIn
- Twitter
- Google My Business
- Instagram
- Pinterest
- Snapchat
- Social Graphics
- Social Writing
- Social Ads
- Influencer Marketing

Analytics/ROI Tracking

- Dashboard Development
- Monthly Analysis
- Attribution Modeling
- Setting Up Goal Conversions
- Phone Tracking
- Live Chat
- Thank-You Page Development

Public Relations

- PR Strategy
- Press Releases
- Media Outreach

Graphic Design

- Logo Design
- Print Design
- Web Design
- UX Design
- Infographic Design
- E-book layout
- Book and E-book Cover Design
- E-book Kindle / Digital Formatting

Web Design — Front End

- Wireframing
- Photoshop
- Design to HTML Conversion
- HTML
- CSS
- WordPress

Web Development — Back End

- PHP
- Python
- ASP

Server Administration

- Updating Server Platform
- Handling 301 Redirects

Conversion Rate Optimization

- Marketing Psychology
- Principles of Influence
- A/B Testing
- Landing Pages

Writing

- Taglines
- Headlines
- Web Page Text
- Blog Posts
- White Papers
- Technical Writing
- Editing
- Proofreading
- Landing Page Copy
- Text Ads
- Social Ads
- Social Profile Updates
- Email Newsletters
- Editorial Calendar Development
- Topic Cluster Writing

Email

- Email List Development
- Email List Segmentation and CRM
- Email Marketing Design
- Email Marketing Text
- Marketing Automation Workflows
- Outreach to Buy Sponsored Email Placement

Book Marketing

- Book Concept for Sales and Positioning
- Writing, Editing, Proofreading
- Cover Design, Layout, Digital Version
- Book Promotion, PR, Backlinks, Awards

Sales and MarketingAlignment

- Lead Scoring
- Account-Based Marketing
- Social Selling
- Content For Sales Outreach
- CRM Setup and Training

Public Speaking

- Booking Speaking Gigs
- Coaching
- Recording and Repurposing

Affiliate Marketing

- Affiliate Program Management
- Make a Page / Program for Referrals

Reputation Management

- Handling Negative Online Reviews and Press
- Building Personal and Business Brands via Content

Did you know that magazines have full-time headline writers? That is because they know that writing effective headlines is a skill that can make the difference between someone walking past the magazine and being engaged enough to pick it up.

I am not saying you need a different person for each of the different tasks listed above, but in my experience having your marketing staff wear too many hats can cost you years of wasted time.

It's not just the number of skills and tasks involved — there's also a crazy number of tools that go with these skills.

Have you heard of chiefmartec.com? This year's graphic, where they show all the tools you can use for digital marketing, has 6,829 marketing technology solutions from 6,242 unique marketing technology vendors.

[4]

---

4 *https://cdn.chiefmartec.com/wp-content/uploads/2019/03/marketing-technology-landscape-2019-slide.jpg*

The good news is that finding the right resources is half the battle.

Here are some of my favorites:

1. SEMrush
2. HubSpot
3. Google Analytics
4. HotJar, Crazy Egg, or Clicktale
5. Google Optimize, Optimizely, or VWO
6. Unbounce
7. Hootsuite
8. Smartsheets
9. Wordpress
10. Ahrefs
11. Photoshop
12. Buzz Sumo

Later on, in the tools section of this guide, I will describe a little bit of what each resource does.

Marketing has made great progress in the past 20 years in terms of generating customers and has improved beyond such methods as cold calling. It will get even better as artificial intelligence gives us tools to deeply understand and interact with potential customers.

Grammarly, the world's best spelling and grammar software, just got $110 million in venture capital, in part to make a writing assistant to guide your writing that uses huge amounts of data from the social media profiles of your ideal customer, massaged by artificial intelligence.

Imagine you want to reach young female technology entrepreneurs, and the words they are known to share and like are highlighted for you to use! So much better than guessing when trying to enter the conversation in their heads.

Who says robots can't write? Well, not so fast, but they will be helping smart marketers radically improve their conversion rates and therefore the volume of leads they get from the web.

If you still think you can make your website drive leads consistently with just your gut instincts, think again.

Marketing technology, fused with people who know how to use it and can dovetail it with your internal team's efforts, is where it's at, in my opinion.

SEO without techies who keep your site loading fast and error-free, bloggers who are just writing weekly because someone told them to, web designers who rely merely on the highest-paid person's opinion of what will matter to a customer, and people running paid ads who have no clue about marketing psychology — all of these will produce neither hot nor cold results.

Back in 1995, 2000, or even 2010, maybe you could have gotten away with such indifferent tactics, but not now, when law firms are all blogging, using social media, and running digital ads. Not when someone referred to your firm searches for your brand name, looks at your site to gauge your level of thought leadership, and pores over your online reviews.

To get consistent and high-quality leads, you can't let referrals slip away unnoticed, rely on one channel, ignore how channels work together, or just dip your big toe in the water. Not when clicks from law-related Google ads cost more than they do for almost any other industry (and can cost $1,000 each). Not when doing content marketing and SEO could supercharge your business development outreach efforts.

If you want to jump in headfirst and learn how to avoid the failures of so many other legal marketing projects, then this book is for you.

If you want to learn to use a roadmap that will help you to get more leads and still let you get home in time for dinner, then read on, my new friends. For you are the true heroes, and I am merely a guy who has a bit of information to guide you on your journey to many successful projects.

PART 1
Before You Dive into Optimization

Document Your Roadmap and Strategy

Here's how to create a simple legal marketing plan that will put your lack of strategy to bed once and for all.

A roadmap that is unfinished is useless. In my first book, *Web Marketing on All Cylinders*, I went a bit wild on the strategy chapter. I even built a piece of marketing planning software at plansprout.com, which you can give a try if you like.

The problem is that I provided so many details on each tactic and how they went together that many people got lost in the weeds and didn't get their marketing plan done.

So instead of creating a long and overly detailed marketing plan that might work for a large enterprise or a marketing geek, the idea I want to focus on here is for you keep it small and get it done relatively fast. The plan has two parts, briefly described below.

First, start with writing one paragraph for each of the items on this list.

1. Executive Summary and Marketing Strategy Synopsis: Write this last, but put it first in your written plan.
2. Business / Marketing goals: Key progress indicators (KPIs) are used to track progress. List the #1 and #2 things you want to see happen both short and long term.

3 Your Competitors: List at least four and identify what they do better than your firm.

4 SWOT: Write one sentence for now on your strengths, weaknesses, opportunities, and threats.

5 Budget for marketing: Set a realistic number (5% of revenue to maintain, 10% to grow, 7% average according to cmosurvey.org).

6 Timing: For now, just list a few key dates. Later you can assign each task a date.

7 Project Management Tool: Make sure you and your team are clear on how you will keep organized, and commit it to writing.

8 Roles: Who will implement which parts of the plan? For now, just list the key players and the agreed-upon tasks they are responsible for.

Second, list some of the key digital marketing and sales tasks that will be part of your plan. These include attracting prospects, converting prospects, closing prospects, and delighting customers. Let's take a quick look at each of these.

Attracting Prospects

1 Who we are targeting and why. List key personas such as "business owner Barbara," "marketing manager Mark," etc.

2 Your message and unique selling proposition. Explain why customers should buy from you versus the competition.

3 List the marketing tactics you will use.

Here's a quick list of specific tactics to spark your thinking, if you want to do this in a way that gives more detail across channels:

Branding – What is our firm's core message, unique selling proposition (USP), and mission?

SEO – What are example keywords people might use to search for our firm?

Content Marketing – What types of content will resonate most with our customers?

PPC & Paid Advertising – What keywords will most likely lead to direct conversions?

Conversion Rate Optimization (CRO) – How will split testing show which creative works best?

Email and Marketing Automation – How can we grow our list and nurture leads?

Online Public Relations – What part of our story or sizzle will attract journalists?

Social Media – What social media sites are our prospects most likely to use?

Persuading Referrals – How will we persuade referrals to hire us after they have searched for our firm?

Design – What design projects should we work on and why?

Development – How can we avoid technical issues and improve mobile user experience (UX) / page speed?

Converting Prospects

What calls to action will we use to get calls and leads? These might include unique web phone numbers, live chat, e-book downloads, contact forms for those who know what they want and those who do not, "buy now" buttons, etc.

Do we have content for each stage of the marketing funnel (awareness, consideration, decision), such as e-books, white papers, case studies, and contact forms?

Closing Prospects

How we will nurture our leads using tools such as HubSpot, Marketo, or Infusionsoft marketing automation?

What is our sales conversion strategy?

Delighting Customers

Once people decide to hire us, how we will wow our customers and stimulate referrals?

Conclusion

A marketing plan is a rare bird for a small law firm, as far too many just wing it and dive right into the shiniest new tactics.

Now that you have created a quick basic marketing plan, review this checklist to sort out what *not* to do.

Top 10 Reasons Law Firm Content Marketing and SEO Fails

Before you begin to flesh out your legal SEO and content marketing plan and then implement it, please review this important list of key things to avoid. These are the most common reasons why SEO and content marketing programs fail, and we want to see you succeed.

1. **Tech issues:** These are just some of the technical reasons that your terrific blog content might go to waste: slow page load, not having a secure site even if you don't do ecommerce (SSL), broken links, pages that result in a 404 error, lack of 301 redirects from old URLs, improper use of redirects, and poor site folder architecture. SEO is not dead, and it's essential to get tech nerds to help you fix these issues before you blindly plod along with a content strategy.
2. **Bad links:** If you have bad sites linking to you that an SEO firm got (thinking they would help you), get them removed or use the disavow tool. Google Search Console is where you upload your list of admittedly bad links to the disavow program.
3. **Lack of links:** Google still admits that content, links, and RankBrain (basically artificial intelligence) are the three big ranking topics you need to address. If you just have average content, you won't get links. If you don't promote your content, you likely won't get links.
4. **Doing regular content but not properly using keywords:** The average writer says they "know SEO" but do they really know how to craft a careful keyword strategy? If not, you fail. You also need to understand how to add related keywords (LSI) that give more depth to your content and help make it more relevant to users' intent.

5 **Focusing only on keywords and not also on topics:** Do you know what topic clusters are? You need to because they are crushing it in terms of making content rank highly. If you want to rank for "birth injury lawyer," for example, either on your practices area page or on a resource page/post, write some long page content — like 1,600 to 2,000 words or more. Make it all about the topic and have a short paragraph on the 12 or so most important aspects of birth injury lawsuits. Then link from each general paragraph about each topic to another shorter post of say 750 or 1,000 words that dives deep into that aspect of the content. Link back and forth from the cluster subpages to the pillar mother ship pages and voilà, your pages will kick ass (in terms of search engine results) over one page about the topic — even if it that one page has lots of keywords in it.

6 **Reducing high bounce rate:** Go into Google Analytics to discover how often people bounce off your site if they land on one of your pages and never go to another. If potential customers hate your site, why should Google love it? Add better headlines, better images, more information for the customer, a video, and/or links to supplemental information. When people stay longer and visit more pages on your site, Google will factor that in when deciding if your site deserves to rank in the top 10 search results.

7 **Having a poor click-through rate:** Make sure when people see your listing in the search results that it entices them to click to your site. When possible, don't just add keywords to title tags, but add a value proposition or some emotional hot button.

8 **Getting ranked anywhere below the top 10:** The top five results get 67% of the traffic, while six to ten only get another 3%. So if you do SEO half-heartedly, do not expect to get leads. Go onto SEMrush and check what terms you rank for on pages 2 and 3 of search results. Then make even better the pages that cause those ranks. Add more content on those topics to take advantage of being within striking distance of having your SEO actually matter.

9 **Doing the tactics but not being a true thought leader:** Google will sniff out if you are respected on LinkedIn and if your content is shared, liked, and loved. Think you can game the system? Go to Google headquarters and smell the fresh black ink on the hundreds of whiteboards burning with the math of algorithms designed to stop "black hats" and spammers.

10 **Not having strong brand signals:** Do people search thousands of times a month for a firm you compete with but only hundreds of times for you? Try adding your

brand name as a search in SEMrush to see what the monthly search volume is on your brand. We will get deeper into the various brand signals elsewhere in this guide, but know that you need to be respected in order to be ranked. This is not just checking a bunch of SEO items off your list.

Don't make these mistakes, or you will fail to get real leads from your law firm's new SEO strategy.

If you need help on some of them, hire an SEO agency (like us) that specializes in law firms or anyone who leads with quality content and knows how to address these key issues.

How to Do Competitive Analysis in Legal Content Marketing and SEO

Before you even begin to work on your SEO and content strategy for your law firm, it's important you conduct a competitive analysis. To me, this is really fun because it is where your path becomes crystal clear.

You might be in a rush to start looking into keywords, optimizing your content, or even attempting link building.

However, if you do this without first conducting an SEO competitive analysis, you will hinder your law firm's efforts.

Competitive analysis allows you to understand not only who your competitors are, but to see where they are positioned in relation to you. Doing the analysis will give you a comprehensive understanding of what goals you should be working toward and will present you with opportunities to rank for specific keywords.

Think about it. If you don't know which law firms are dominating organic search, which keywords are most valuable, or what the best backlink strategy is, how do you expect to grow your own organic traffic through SEO?

In this section, you'll learn the components that go into a competitive analysis and which tools you can use to make it as effective as possible.

Find your competitors

The first step of an SEO competitive analysis is to identify your competitors. When you do this, you'll be able to:

1 Discover what they're doing well
2 Find your strategic advantages
3 Help you find link opportunities

If you don't know who your competitors are, use a tool like SEMrush or SearchMetrics to identify them.

You should be looking out for a combination of your search competitors and business competitors (law firms offering services similar to yours). Search competitors are firms that are also ranking for the terms you hope to rank for.

Once you've identified these competitors and analyzed them, you'll have a clearer idea of which tactics do and do not work within your industry. You'll have a number of different tactics to improve your own keyword rankings, and you can prioritize which tactics should take precedence.

Once you have the competitor data overview, it's time to start looking in more detail at certain aspects of what makes your competitors' sites great. These are in the list below.

It's okay to skip to the next section on SEO ranking factors if you don't want to get into the weeds. Just be aware that underestimating your competitors can be a main reason for having weak results.

Competitor Analysis Considerations

1 Number of monthly brand searches via SEMrush
2 Average visit duration, pages per visit, bounce rate via Similarweb.com
3 Channels driving traffic via Similarweb.com
4 Competitor search metrics overview
5 Google top 10 SERPs (search engine results pages) and what is in them that matters to you

6 Keywords and keyword gap
7 Competitor top website pages (that drive SEO rankings)
8 On-page optimization levels
9 Backlinks and commonly occurring links
10 Social media followers, engagement, and frequency
11 Swipe files of competitors' top-performing headlines
12 Topical authority – Screaming Frog SEO Spider or MarketMuse, etc.
13 Calls to action, navigation, and trustworthiness via user tests
14 "Spy" (legally) on how competitors get leads with Nacho Analytics

Here's a brief explanation of each of these list items.

1. Number of monthly brand searches via SEMrush

Sometimes we have a client who imagines they are the number one firm or company in their niche, but it is a good idea to get a reality check on your brand power. This is something Google can see and that can be used as a signal of trust.

Below are examples of specific ways people search each month, with brand names included, for large legal sites. Sometimes you need to add up the variations of your brand name that get searched on to get the total monthly branded search volume.

Term	**Monthly Searches in Google**
Above The Law	40,500
FindLaw	12,100
Bloomberg Law	9,900
Mass Lawyers Weekly	2,900
FindLaw.com	1,900
Lexology	1,600
JD Supra	1,000
National Law Review	720
Mondaq	320
Lexblog	260

2. *Average visit duration, pages per visit, bounce rate via Similarweb.com*

Google has patents on judging if a site is able to retain visitors and get them to take an action. They use the term "dwell time" and the idea of a "long click" in some of these patents that they have filed over the years.

Does that mean that what they call "dwell time" is a ranking factor?

The head of Google Brain, Nick Frost, at a conference in 2017, said this:

"Google is now integrating machine learning into [the process of figuring out what the relationship between a search and the best page for that search is]. So then training models on when someone clicks on a page and stays on that page, when they go back or when they and trying to figure out exactly on that relationship."

That still doesn't guarantee it is a direct ranking factor, but I would argue it's a great reason to improve your website, even if it is a supportive ranking signal.

And SEO authority Neil Patel says *"an optimal bounce rate, a healthy session duration, and a strong SERP CTR are all factors that improve dwell time."*

So it's important to make sure you are in the ballpark of what your competitors are doing in terms of the metrics below. This way your website is as good as theirs is for users and potentially will address newer ranking signals.

My big takeaway from this small list below is that Above The Law has a stronger hold on people's imaginations than the other sites. People visit longer, click more pages, and bounce less.

Name	Avg. Visit Duration (minutes)	Pages Per Visit	Bounce Rate
AbovetheLaw.com	4:15	2.42	68.51%
Bloomberg Law – BNA.com	1:54	2.15	69.13%
FindLaw.com	1:35	2.18	76.53%

(Note: The lower a site's bounce rate is, the better, because it means visitors are staying on a site longer before they leave.)

Here is a breakdown of what is a good or bad bounce rate.

0-40% bounce rate: Good
41-60% bounce rate: Fair
61-100% bounce rate: Poor

Just be aware sometimes people bounce because they found what they wanted, like a mortgage rate.

Your job is to find sites that appear to be doing something better than your firm, based on easily scannable metrics. Then try to figure out what they are doing specifically, so you can improve your own site's engagement.

3. Channels driving traffic

Google respects you more if you have traffic from various channels, because they have seen spammy SEO-driven sites kill it with SEO in the past, only to discover they are not actually great companies.

Similarweb.com has a useful traffic sources graph that gives you a rough idea of what other ways a site is getting love.

In the examples, on the next page, Above The Law has a greater variety of channels driving significant traffic to them than Lexology.com has.

Lexology

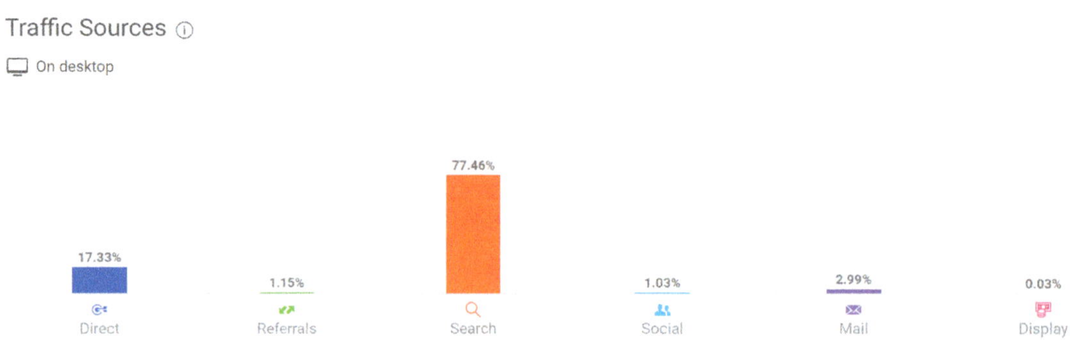

Above The Law

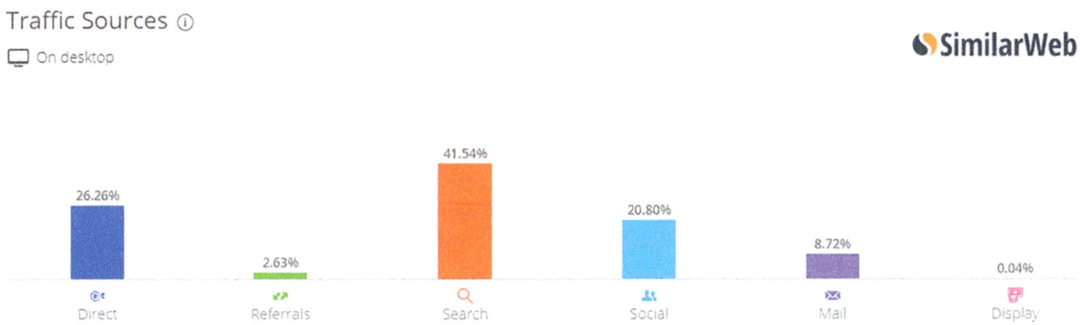

4. Competitor search metrics overview

The competitor data overview provides you with a holistic view of what your competitors are currently doing in a broader sense.

It goes without saying that you'll need the name and URL of the sites in question. How many sites you choose to analyze is up to you, but we recommend five to ten in order to get a real understanding of what your competitors are doing. SEMrush lets you add four in the keyword gap tool in addition to your own, so that is a good number to start with.

Using tools like SEMrush, or Ahrefs, you want to look at how many of your competitors' pages are indexed in Google, how many referring domains they have, the number of organic keywords they rank for, how much their traffic costs, whether they're mobile friendly, and how fast their page loads.

Set up an Excel spreadsheet using these columns to make comparison easy.

Name | URL | pages indexed | referring domains | organic keywords | traffic cost | speed

It will look something like this.

Company Name	Web Address	Pages Indexed in Google	# of Referring Domains	# of Organic Kys	Traffic Cost	Page Speed
Ropes & Gray LLP	*www.ropesgray.com/en*	8900	1.6K	20.3K	$19.2K	4.0s
Goodwin	*https://www.goodwinlaw.com/*	12,100	902	13.9K	$54.6K	6.8s
Mintz Levin	*www.mintz.com*	3,390,000	1.8K	46.6K	$70.6K	4.1s
Wilmer Cutler Pickering and Dorr LLP	*http://www.wilmerhale.com/*	20,800	2.9K	15.0K	$7.5K	2.8s
Foley Hoag LLP	*http://www.foleyhoag.com/*	5,090	1.2K	10.2K	$4.0K	2.8s
Choate Hall & Stewart LLP	*http://www.choate.com/*	1,580	447	3.6K	$9.1K	2.4s
Goulston & Storrs PC	*http://www.goulstonstorrs.com/*	7,090	392	4.6K	$685	4.3s
Nutter McClennen & Fish LLP	*http://www.nutter.com/*	4,670	508	9.3K	$9.5K	3.0s
Nixon Peabody LLP	*http://www.nixonpeabody.com/*	10,900	2K	19.3K	$44.9K	35.7s
Holland & Knight LLP	*http://www.hklaw.com/*	16,400	3.2K	23.3K	$9.5K	2.0s

Pages indexed

For pages indexed you can start by using the "site:" advanced operator in Google search. Type site:yourdomain.com and hit enter like you would when doing any other search. Then you will see how many pages Google has in its index for your site. Do the same with your competitors.

To really get the pages indexed that matter, use a web crawler like Screaming Frog. You can put a site's URLs into Excel and delete unimportant things like tag and category pages.

Number of referring domains

I prefer to use Ahrefs for this because it has the best link database, but you can use SEMrush if you do not have Ahrefs access. Just add the URL into the tool and go to referring domains on the left navigation panel.

Number of organic keywords

SEMrush gives you this under the "organic search positions" link in the left navigation panel. It is how many keywords SEMrush sees as appearing in the top 100 search results in Google. It is not everything because very local variation would be astronomical, but it's extremely robust.

Traffic cost

SEMrush calls this traffic cost, but I call it traffic value. This is the value of the organic keywords if you had to buy them as Google ads.

Page speed

You can get this from GTmetrix or Think With Google / Google mobile page speed tools. A search in Google should bring these up easily.

When you have access to all this information, you'll quickly be able to see *why* the websites on the first page of Google rank for the keywords they do. You also might find some anomalies, namely websites that seemingly have poor SEO efforts, but still manage to rank for the keywords you're trying to target. This presents you with a really good opportunity to outrank your competitors with better content and better SEO optimization.

5. Google top 10 SERP

One of the best ways to find your top competitors is to look at which websites show up within the top 10 search results on Google. These top results show you the websites that rank for the keywords you're trying to target.

I use the following items in my overview. (I've broken this into two segments for easier viewing in book format.)

Here are the top pages that come up in a search for "high interest cds":

- *nerdwallet.com/blog/banking/nerdwallets-best-cd-rates*
- *nerdwallet.com/rates/cds/best-cd-rates*
- *magnifymoney.com/blog/earning-interest/best-cd-rates967994263*
- *bankrate.com/cd.aspx*
- *ally.com/bank/cd-rates*
- *thecollegeinvestor.com/21693/best-bank-cd-rates*
- *usatoday.com/story/money/2018/06/05/how-find-best-rates-cds-cash/663924002*
- *depositaccounts.com/cd*
- *synchronybank.com*

Here are the primary factors for each of the above pages:

Word Count	Insite Related Pages	InBound Links - Page	InBound Links - Site
1876	13,100	159	3.56M
1703	13,100	557	3.56M
20912	1,720	1.51K	698K
712	15,700	112K	19.9M
2430	5	1.12K	1.98M
2141	117	750	94.1K
1213	2,750	745	170M
1124	3	3.61K	182K
1032	240	57.1K	57.1K

Next, let's look at the secondary factors. Keep in mind that page speed is quickly becoming a dominant ranking factor. Google won't highly rank a content-rich long page with lots of links to it if the page itself doesn't load in a reasonable time.

Keyword inTitle	Keyword inHeading	Page Type	Page Speed		Mobile Friendly	Secure Protocol	MultiMedia	Have Comments
			Page Speed	Yslow				
No	No	Blog	E (56%)	E (55%)	Yes	https	No	Yes
No	No	WebPage	E (56%)	E (55%)	Yes	https	No	No
No	No	Blog	B (83%)	C (73%)	Yes	https	No	No
No	No	WebPage	D (61%)	E (56%)	Yes	https	No	No
Yes	No	WebPage	E (52%)	E (51%)	Yes	https	No	No
No	No	WebPage	D (62%)	F (48%)	Yes	https	Yes	No
No	No	WebPage	F (14%)	F (43%)	Yes	https	No	Yes
No	No	WebPage	F (47%)	E (52%)	Yes	https	No	No
Yes	No	WebPage	C (72%)	B (80%)	Yes	https	No	No

Below are some tools to help you get these metrics.

- **Word Count** – wordcounter.net
- **Related Pages on a Website / Insite Pages** – Type (*site:yourfirmsdomain.com*) in Google and add a space and then a key phrase. Example: (***site:mintz.com patents***) and hit search. Google shows you pages indexed with that term on them, but it's only a quick way to get a very rough idea. We crawl sites with Screaming Frog and then go through the URLs in MS Excel and add a column for the topic of each page. Or use the expensive tool MarketMuse for time-saving topical authority research.
- **InBound Links for a Page** – Ahrefs
- **InBound Links for a Site** – Ahrefs
- **Keyword in Title** – SEMrush
- **Keyword in Heading** – SEMrush
- **Page Type** – Manual Review
- **Page Speed** – GTmetrix or Google Page Insights
- **Mobile Friendly** – Google Mobile Friendly Tool
- **Secure Protocol** – Manual Review
- **MultiMedia** – Manual Review
- **Have Comments** – Manual Review

6. *Keywords and keyword gap*

You can get new ideas for your own digital marketing campaigns by looking at the keywords your competitors use.

I like to make a spreadsheet with multiple tabs. Tab one has the search rankings overview from SEMrush from all the main competitors we are looking at.

You can use the number only for the number of organic keywords in the top 100 and what the traffic would have cost if you had to buy it as Google ads. (See that chart below.)

Note that I usually ignore the traffic number because most research sites do not have great accuracy in getting that information, which is normally only accessible if you are logged into a website's Google Analytics account. That said, I am evaluating a new tool called Nacho Analytics that claims to have deep competitor analytics.

Or you can use this information with the multiyear tracking chart to see where a competitor is going up or down.

The full chart is below. You can see that FindLaw.com had a dip in total keyword volume starting around January 2018 but then came back even stronger. Their traffic is now worth $29 million a month if you bought the keyword search terms as Google ads.

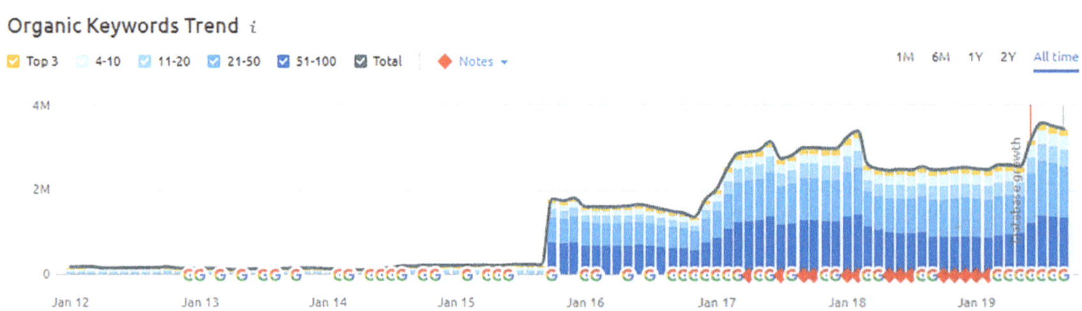

Next, you want to export the total keywords for your site and those of your competitors and have all of those keywords in separate tabs in Excel. I like to add filters so I can re-sort by the largest amount of monthly search volume, then by highest cost per click (CPC) and the percentage of traffic driven by each term.

You'll end up with a nice graphical overview tab of who is getting the most from organic search, then tabs with all of the search terms, so you can pick and choose what might also work well for you.

In order to make finding golden nuggets easier, you can select the "domain vs. domain" or "keyword gap" feature in SEMrush. It gives you five slots to add your site and four competitors. It lets you sort by keywords unique to the first domain, unique keywords, and common keywords.

Below is a Venn diagram that SEMrush displays when I sort by unique keywords. It looks like FindLaw.com is crushing it.

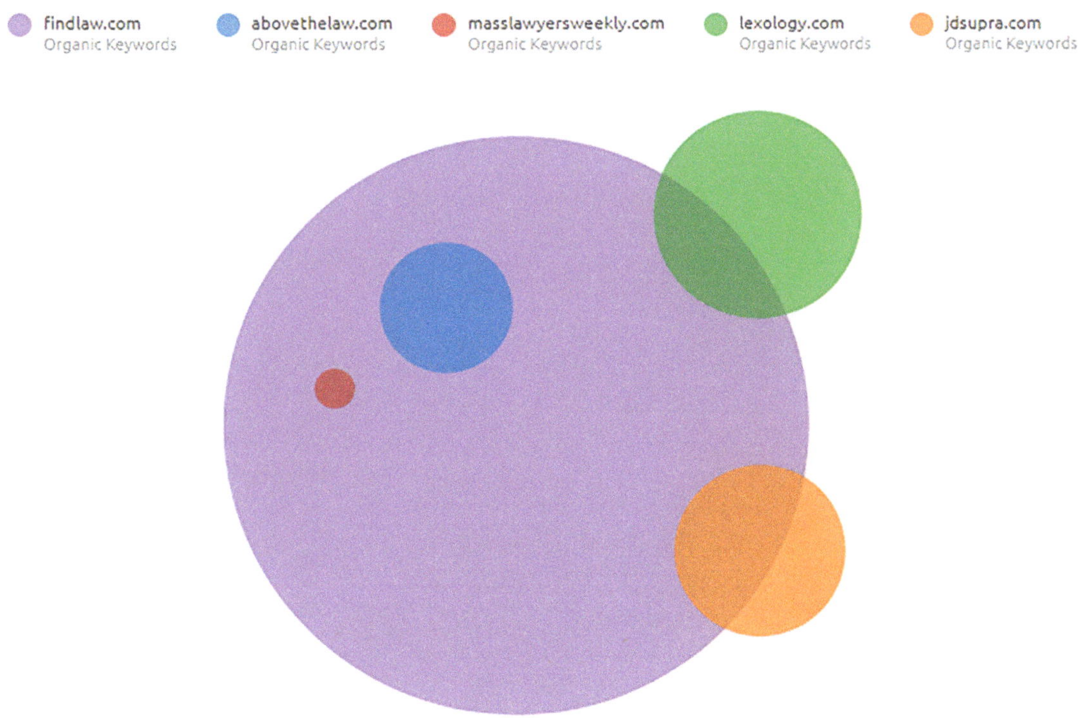

When I sort by cost per click, it shows how dominant FindLaw is for expensive terms. If other competitors had ranking positions in the top 100, their search position number would show up in their column. This type of analysis is critical when you want to choose the right keywords.

Keyword	findlaw.com	abovethe law.com	masslawyers weekly.com	lexology.com	jdsupra.com	Search Volume	CPC
car accident lawyer charleston sc	2	0	0	0	0	70	647.16
mitch burns attorney	3	0	0	0	0	50	633.15
auto owners insurance st cloud mn	30	0	0	0	0	50	628.48
la car accident lawyer	6	0	0	0	0	30	627.36
george sink injury lawyers myrtle beach	11	0	0	0	0	20	609.34
truck accident attorney dallas	4	0	0	0	0	90	605.28
sysco union	65	0	0	0	0	70	600.65
car accident attorney savannah	1	0	0	0	0	50	596.53
birth injury attorney chicago	7	0	0	0	0	320	585.46
miami auto accident lawyer	2	0	0	0	0	20	581.91

7. Competitor top pages

A "top pages" report shows the pages that drive the most organic keyword traffic to you or your competitors' sites. Look at this for new page and keyword ideas. It is easily accessible from SEMrush. It will simply be a list of the pages on the site sorted by the ones that have the highest number of organic keyword positions in Google.

It looks like this on the next page.

URL	Traffic (%)	Number of Keywords
https://constitution.findlaw.com/amendments.html	2.68	2755
https://constitution.findlaw.com/amendment1.html	0.92	1260
https://criminal.findlaw.com/criminal-charges/racketeering-rico.html	0.74	192
https://criminal.findlaw.com/criminal-procedure/what-is-an-indictment.html	0.73	259
https://litigation.findlaw.com/going-to-court/what-is-a-subpoena.html	0.67	521
https://family.findlaw.com/emancipation-of-minors/how-do-you-get-emancipated.html	0.63	735
https://constitution.findlaw.com/amendment5.html	0.57	327
https://criminal.findlaw.com/criminal-charges/extortion.html	0.55	186
https://criminal.findlaw.com/criminal-charges/homicide-definition.html	0.53	358
https://blogs.findlaw.com/blotter/2011/08/difference-between-first-second-degree-murder.html	0.52	147

Clearly the amendments pages are doing a lot for FindLaw, as well as a page on exempt versus non-exempt employees. The first example — https://constitution.findlaw.com/amendments.html — is ranking for 2,755 keywords in Google. It also drives 2.68% of the organic search site traffic to their site.

It is well worth using this tool to dig up great ideas for content. All it takes is a few heavily detailed new pages on your site to show solid SEO progress. Just writing lots of super-basic blog posts doesn't do much anymore for your site's Google rankings.

8. On-page optimization

Now let's look at an example of a top-ranking page and how the site is optimized, and then take this data and apply the keywords and content to your own site. Please note, you can't do this in a vacuum, because each industry has its own ranking factors and optimization levels.

If you did a Google search for "Law Firm New York," you'd see results like these.

Most Prestigious Law Firms In America - Business Insider
https://www.businessinsider.com/most-prestigious-law-firms-in-america-2013-7
18 Jul 2013 - #4 Skadden, Arps, Slate, Meagher & **Flom** LLP and Affiliates. "Endless training resources" "The work is top-notch" "Global presence of the firm"

Best Law Firms in New York, NY
https://bestlawfirms.usnews.com/new-york/new-york-city
Practice Area. **Aaronson Rappaport Feinstein** & Deutsch, LLP. of National Rankings: 1. **Abigail Pessen** Dispute Resolution Services. Abrams, **Fensterman, Fensterman, Eisman**, Formato, Ferrara, **Wolf & Carone**, LLP. **Akerman LLP**. **Akin Gump Strauss Hauer & Feld LLP**. ALL Counsel P.C. Allen & Overy LLP. Alston & Bird LLP.

Best companies to work for|Best Law Firms in New York|Vault.com
www.vault.com/company-rankings/law/best-law-firms-in-each-us-region/?sRankID...
Cravath, **Swaine** & Moore LLP. Cravath, **Swaine** & Moore LLP has been known as one of the nation's pre-eminent law firms for nearly 200 years.

New York Law Firm & Office | Alston & Bird
https://www.alston.com › Offices › New York
Alston & Bird's **New York** office represents a number of prestigious Wall Street institutions and other leading publicly traded and privately held entities, both U.S. ...

List of largest law firms by revenue - Wikipedia
https://en.wikipedia.org/wiki/List_of_largest_law_firms_by_revenue
This is a list of the world's largest **law firms** by revenue. The combined revenue of the world's ... Skadden, Arps, Slate, Meagher & Flom, $2.41b, United States (**New York, NY**) (4 Times Square), 23, 1948, 51%, $727,000, $3,125,000. 6 Decrease ...

Category:Law firms based in New York City - Wikipedia
https://en.wikipedia.org/wiki/Category:Law_firms_based_in_New_York_City
Pages in category "**Law firms** based in **New York** City". The following 74 pages are in this category, out of 74 total. This list may not reflect recent changes (learn ...

The Blanch Law Firm
https://www.theblanchlawfirm.com/
The Blanch **Law Firm** focuses on criminal investigations and cases from **New York** to California. Our White Collar Criminal Division represents those accused of ...

It's useful to analyze each of these pages to see what the total word count is and which other sites link to them. This will give you a clear idea of what sort of content you need to include on your own website in order to compete for the same keywords.

If you're looking for an easy way to measure word count without copying and pasting the entire text on the page, you can use WordCounter.net. All you need to do is enter the URL in question and the tool will tell you how many words appear on that page.

So if we take the number one search result, we see the following:

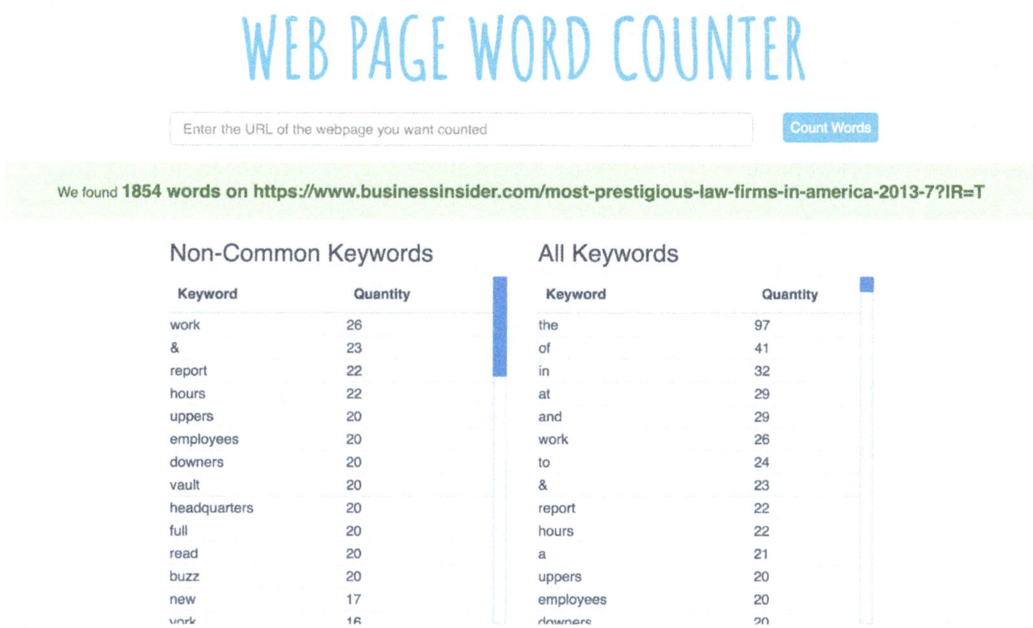

Not only does it tell how you many words in total are on the page, but it tells you exactly what keywords are used throughout the page, too.

Do this analysis for at least your top five to ten key phrases; otherwise, you might use the right keywords but have the less-than–optimal word count.

Analyze competitors' site optimization

When you first begin to analyze your competitors' SEO, what you might find is that many don't have a strategy at all. You'll wonder how they were able to rank on the first page, despite not having everything in complete order. If this is the case, you'll easily know what you can do to improve your own marketing efforts.

Keyword density

Take some time to look at their keyword density. You want to know how many times your top competitors are using keywords throughout their best-ranking pages in order to know how aggressive you'll need to be.

Note: Google is very intelligent, and keyword stuffing will be penalized. If you notice that one site uses the keywords 50 times on the page and still ranks, don't take heed of this site as it's an anomaly and eventually Google will penalize them for it.

If we take one of the law firms from the top 10 SERP results and put their URL into the Internet Marketing Ninjas *keywords density analyzer*, [5] we'll find a wealth of data.

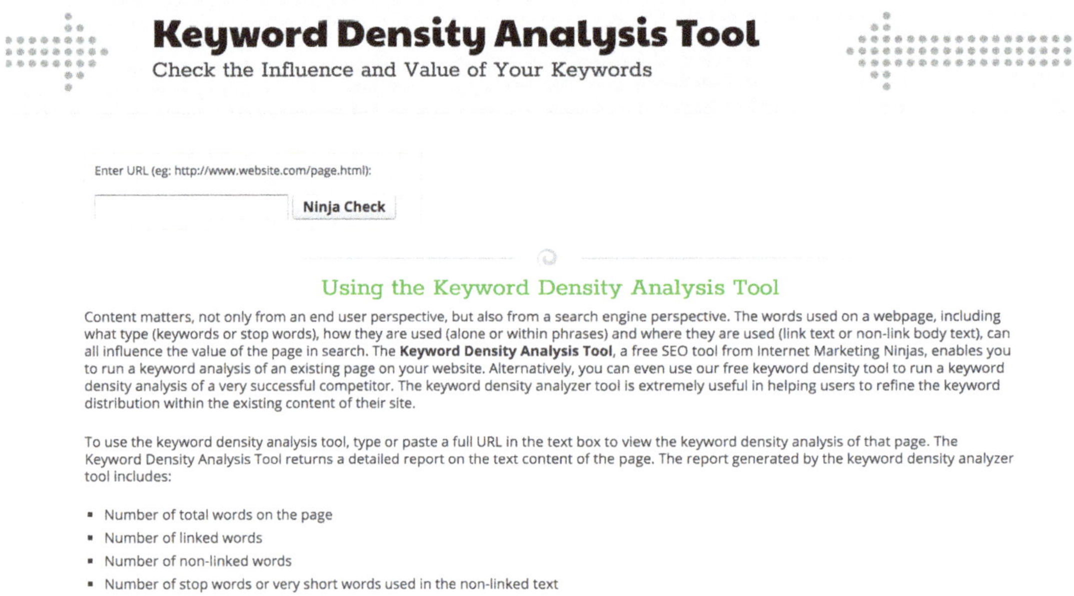

Keyword Density Analysis Tool

Check the Influence and Value of Your Keywords

Enter URL (eg: http://www.website.com/page.html):

Ninja Check

Using the Keyword Density Analysis Tool

Content matters, not only from an end user perspective, but also from a search engine perspective. The words used on a webpage, including what type (keywords or stop words), how they are used (alone or within phrases) and where they are used (link text or non-link body text), can all influence the value of the page in search. The **Keyword Density Analysis Tool**, a free SEO tool from Internet Marketing Ninjas, enables you to run a keyword analysis of an existing page on your website. Alternatively, you can even use our free keyword density tool to run a keyword density analysis of a very successful competitor. The keyword density analyzer tool is extremely useful in helping users to refine the keyword distribution within the existing content of their site.

To use the keyword density analysis tool, type or paste a full URL in the text box to view the keyword density analysis of that page. The Keyword Density Analysis Tool returns a detailed report on the text content of the page. The report generated by the keyword density analyzer tool includes:

- Number of total words on the page
- Number of linked words
- Number of non-linked words
- Number of stop words or very short words used in the non-linked text

5 *https://www.internetmarketingninjas.com/seo-tools/keyword-density*, we'll find a wealth of data

Results for https://www.mandellawfirm.com/

- There are 1735 words on this page
- Of those 1735 words 694 words are linked ones
- Of 1735 words 1041 are not linked
- Of 1041 non linked words 480 words are either stop words or have less than 3 characters
- This tool only shows keyphrases with **three or more** occurrences

Below you can see words from the entire text ranked by their occurrence

Word	Count	Percent	2 Word phrases	Count	Percent	3 Word phrases	Count	Percent
law	43	2.47%	family law	26	1.49%	mandel law firm	10	0.57%
family	33	1.9%	mandel law	11	0.63%	family law attorneys	7	0.4%
divorce	22	1.26%	law firm	10	0.57%	ui wpengine netdna-ssl	4	0.23%
custody	20	1.15%	york city	9	0.51%	sxrjr ui wpengine	4	0.23%
mandel	17	0.97%	law attorneys	8	0.46%	png class wondercarousellightbox	4	0.23%
york	17	0.97%	child custody	7	0.4%	https yefn sxrjr	4	0.23%
child	16	0.92%	child support	6	0.34%	yefn sxrjr ui	4	0.23%
support	15	0.86%	milo meed	5	0.28%	class wondercarousellightbox wondercarousellightbox	4	0.23%
attorneys	13	0.74%	liz fried	5	0.28%	peer review rating	4	0.23%
firm	10	0.57%	angel reed	5	0.28%	problems take care	4	0.23%
Show/Hide			Show/Hide			Show/Hide		

Below you can see words from the non-linked text ranked by their occurrence

Word	Count	Percent	2 Word phrases	Count	Percent	3 Word phrases	Count	Percent
law	32	3.07%	family law	20	1.92%	mandel law firm	10	0.96%
family	21	2.01%	mandel law	11	1.05%	family law attorneys	7	0.67%
divorce	14	1.34%	law firm	10	0.96%	problems take care	4	0.38%
york	13	1.24%	law attorneys	8	0.76%	peer review rating	3	0.28%
mandel	13	1.24%	york city	7	0.67%			
attorneys	11	1.05%	take care	4	0.38%			
firm	10	0.96%	nassau counties	4	0.38%			
problems	7	0.67%	problems take	4	0.38%			
city	7	0.67%	real solutions	4	0.38%			
martindale-hubbell	6	0.57%	review rating	3	0.28%			
			Show/Hide					

And by looking at the home page the keyword phrase "Family Law Firm New York" doesn't even show up, despite the company ranking on the first page for this term. However, despite this, there are instances of "New York" dotted around the site, although these are not "match terms." This means that you *don't* need to overfill your website with "Family Law Firm New York" in order to rank well for this specific phrase.

Further research on this website will be able to provide reasons for why this company is able to rank on the first page, despite there being so many search results for the keyword phrase.

Don't just do this for one competitor; do it for at least four good ones, and track the data in a spreadsheet. Keep a note if there are other keywords that repeatedly pop up that you perhaps haven't considered using on your own site.

You'll also want to look at the following:

1. Meta descriptions. Do they use keywords within their meta descriptions to increase the click-through rate? Are they using LSI keywords, which are basically related keywords, and is there a strong call to action for what a user should do next? Ideally, you're looking for *why* a user would click onto their site.
2. Do they link internally? Here you want to see what model of internal linking they're using to see if you could make changes to your own link architecture.

On-page optimization is likely the first thing people think of when they think SEO, and many writers will claim they can do it. However, I am shocked by how we have to burn through testing four or five writers for every one person we can find who can even be trained properly to get this job done.

It takes a writer's finesse, but it also takes an engineer's mindset and strategy. Much as in sales, the salespeople who make the most money are often both technically knowledgeable and also have strong relationship-building skills.

9. Backlink analysis

Backlinks are still one of the top three ranking factors. Doing backlink research is not optional if you want your SEO and content marketing to actually work.

When it comes to backlinks, look at two things. The first is what backlinks your competitors get. The second is your common backlinks, meaning the links that are common to you and your competitors. These can sometimes spur ideas about who to reach out to for links.

To analyze your competitors' backlinks, you can use a range of tools from Ahrefs, Majestic, or Open Site Explorer. Analyzing their links tells you whether there are opportunities to generate links from sites you haven't considered, or whether you should try to mirror their approach.

Mirroring their approach assumes that if you're getting the same links, your site should perform in a similar way. However, if you notice some of your competitors are generating links from irrelevant sites, it's best to ignore those. But if you see they're getting links from industry journal websites, these would be great to target within your own backlink campaign.

When it comes to backlink opportunities, you want to see what sites are linking to your top competitors but not to your site. You may notice that there is one particular site that links to all your top competition but not to you, and if so, there's a good chance they'll link to you too with the right outreach message.

If you can also get links that your competitors don't have, that is even better.

10. Social media competitive analysis

Social media has a positive impact on SEO, even though it may be more of an indirect factor. Many people debate the use of social media for SEO results, but the fact of the matter is, the more people who share links to your content on social media, the more people are likely to link to and visit your law firm's website.

If you produce a solid social media campaign, you'll be able to foster relationships with industry experts, interact with your current and new customers, and discover where your content fits in the market.

Look at what your competitors' social media strategy is. What types of content do they post and share? What is their engagement like? Are people actively and consistently sharing links to their website, their content, or their other marketing assets? If the answer is yes, then it gives you an idea of what you should be doing with your own social strategy.

Amazingly, several social media "experts," whom we have hired in-house and/or used as subcontractors, don't have a good system for social media competitive analysis.

Do keep in mind that social sites like Facebook prefer you don't send people via a link to your site because they are "greedy" and want people to stay on their site. They may also decrease engagement to "punish" you for sending people to your own site and off of theirs.

So, if organic social engagement is your key metric, then don't share a link to your site. Rather, get insights about what people love to share from your best content pieces you used in your social profiles, and find a way to get those same topics on your site. And then you will have to use other means to promote your website and blog content.

Set up SEMrush to do a social media audit of your site against a good number of competitors. It will show you, in a bar graph format, numbers of social media followers, engagement, and frequency.

Here's how it looks in action.

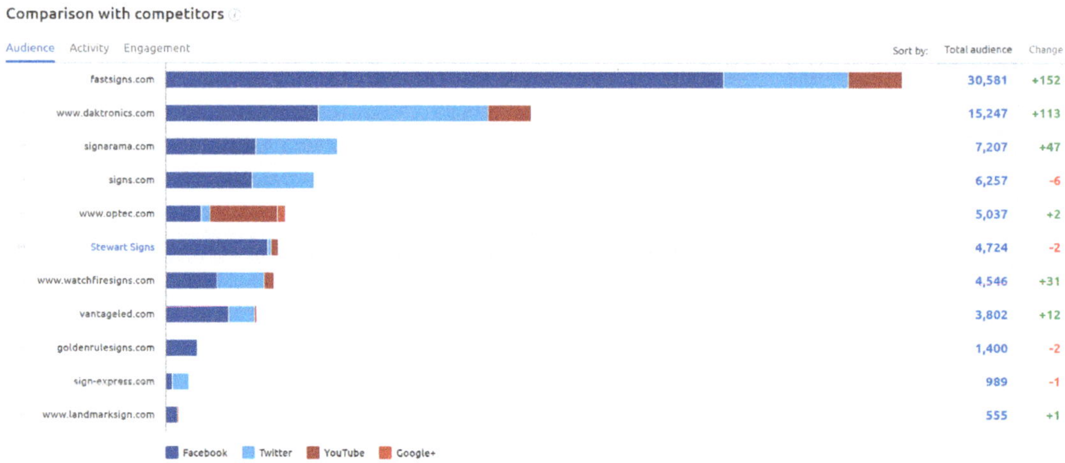

11. Keep swipe files of competitors' top-performing headlines

Keeping a swipe file is a copywriting technique where you gather the best headlines from your competitors and use them to generate ideas.

Ahrefs is a great tool for this because you can assess both the top pages on your competitors' sites by the number of links but also by the number of social shares.

Simply make a spreadsheet with a tab for each of your best competitors and add the top 25 pages on their website sorted by links, and then in another tab, add the top 25 sorted by social shares.

You can turn to these swipe files when you are generating ideas for blog posts and/or more powerful content like pillar pages, "link bait," and social media contests.

The topic research tool in SEMrush gives you lists of top headlines by backlinks and the top questions people ask about the topic.

12. Topical authority: Screaming Frog SEO Spider or MarketMuse

Being a topical authority is critical if you really want to dominate the organic search results in your industry. You can't just put keywords in a page and expect to rank highly if your competitors have dozens or hundreds (or in some cases, thousands) of pages on a single niche topic.

What you need to do is use a "crawling" tool like Screaming Frog and put all of your URLs into a tab and organize them by type. You will have the main pages like home, about, and contact, and then all of the practice area pages and blog posts organized in a logical flow.

Then add a column to the right side of your spreadsheet entitled "topic." Look at the URL and if necessary go to the page and decide what the topic of the page is. Type that into the column.

Let's say you want to rank well in search results for "estate planning attorney" and you find that your website only has one practice area page and a couple of blog posts about the topic, but a couple of your top-ranked competitors have dozens or hundreds of pages. The work that you have to do becomes obvious after you see what your competitors are doing.

13. Calls to action, navigation, and trustworthiness via user tests

Google understands and can potentially track when a user completes an action on a website like buying a product or filling out a free consultation form. You need to make sure that your calls to action — whether it's your phone number, an invitation to a live chat, consultation forms, or e-book downloads — are easy for your site visitors to find and act on.

Your website must be easy to navigate and create a sense of trust in the visitor who doesn't know you or your firm well, especially if they found you through search engines or social media. Even if people come to you through a referral, you still want to have these things under control on your site. Bonus: It will help your search engine optimization.

A great way to figure out how to correct these things is to run user tests with the tool at UserTesting.com. You can ask users to go to your website and then to one of your best competitors' websites and compare the experience. Fixing these things will also give you more leads, so it's well worth the effort.

14. Spy (legally) with Nacho Analytics

As I write this guide, I am testing Nacho Analytics, software that's supposed to allow you to look at your competitors' website analytics. The software developers claim to have figured out how to get the data similar to what your competitors have in their Google Analytics accounts so you can see how they get leads and sales. If it works, it will be very exciting — but also a little bit creepy.

With the advent of Google looking more and more at user signals and user experience factors, understanding a range of factors, from your competitors' bounce rate and time on site, to the number of pages visited and even deeper elements, could be a game changer for law firm SEO and marketing.

Takeaways

In the introduction, we mentioned the growing competitiveness in paid advertising (for such items as pay per click — PPC — ads for popular keywords) and as a result, the increasing cost of PPC. However, if you conduct a thorough competitive analysis, you can find opportunities to rank for specific keywords at a fraction of the cost.

Keep in mind that when you buy Google ads, you mostly buy positions 1 to 3 in the search results, and so your SEO must mimic that in order to be effective.

When you conduct an SEO audit of your top competitors, you put yourself in a position whereby you have access to some really important insights. You can use these insights to help drive your own SEO strategy, knowing what you should and shouldn't do for success.

Putting the reports together with the data from all your competitors will take time, but it's important to actually *do* something with this data. The audit tells you what you need to do right away in order to get ahead. For example, if you know that all your competitors have double the number of backlinks that you have, then you should focus on a backlink campaign, creating new assets to generate more backlinks.

If you do decide to conduct an SEO competitive analysis, you'll have a resource that will allow you to develop your law firm's marketing in a strategic way, based on real data from your market.

Following "top 10 SEO tips" is no longer enough, and will lead you down a road where you try everything and hope something sticks. Follow the process and blueprint outlined in this guide -- we tell you exactly what you need to do and why.

PART 2

SEO Ranking Factors and Roadmap for Law Firms

Overview of SEO Ranking Factors

In this section, we share an overview of law firm search engine optimization (SEO) ranking factors and how they go together. What used to work in SEO just a few years ago won't work today. In this guide, we outline the action steps you need to follow to develop an effective SEO action plan for your law firm.

What's more, other methods of marketing (such as paying for PPC ads) is becoming increasingly competitive, meaning increasingly expensive. So although PPC and social media are great marketing approaches to add to your arsenal, they don't drive as much traffic as SEO and should be used as a supplementary strategy, rather than the entire thing.

Studies from leading enterprise-level SEO software companies Conductor and Bright Edge showed that only 2% to 5% of traffic comes from social media, but as much as 64% comes from organic search. This means it's never been more important to have an active presence in search results for the keywords you're hoping to rank your law firm for.

There are an estimated 3.5 billion searches per day on Google and 1.2 trillion worldwide. Although this might sound overwhelming, we're going to use this opportunity to look at the SEO landscape, what sort of websites or pages rank for specific keywords, and how you can implement these strategies to help your own law firm gain extra visibility on search engines like Google. Throughout this section, we'll delve deeper into each strategy to provide you with a framework for success.

Before we begin to learn about SEO, here's a quick glimpse of how ranking factors have changed and will continue to change. I won't try to document everything, but rather am offering a casual, not perfectly historical, sketch.

A super-brief history of ranking factors

1996 – 1999	On-page keyword usage, meta data
1999 – 2002	PageRank, On-page
2002 – 2005	Anchor text, Domain name, PageRank, On-page
2005 – 2009	Domain authority, Diversity of links, Topic modeling, Anchor text, Domain name, PageRank, On-page
2010 – 2011	Entry of social signals from Facebook and Twitter
2011 – 2011	Google Panda makes sure sites have high-quality original content
2012 – 2012	Google Penguin penalizes sites with bad links
2014 – 2014	HTTPS becomes a ranking signal
2015 – 2015	Mobile usability becomes a ranking signal
2016 – 2016	Content development shifts as RankBrain looks beyond keywords
2017 – 2017	HTTPS becomes a near-requirement
2018 – 2018	Mobile page speed becomes emphasized
2019 – 2019	Relevance and user intent are critical
2020 – 2020	Customer engagement with your brand getting easier for Google to analyze

Search engines have evolved dramatically, and in order to do the work of a quality SEO person, you need the stamina of an Olympian and the plan below to keep you on track.

Now let's look at the steps we're going to cover.

When considering all the facets of SEO for your law firm, you should focus on the following ranking factors. It's as if you are building a house – you will see how the pieces all fit together. If you skip a step, the house crumbles.

Ranking factors and important tactics

1. Building Your Brand for SEO: Designing your house
2. Technical SEO: Laying the foundation
3. On-Page SEO Optimization: Framing the rooms
4. Content: Designing the rooms
5. User Signals and User Experience: The flow of your floor plan
6. Link Building – Off-Page Optimization: Having the equivalent of an ocean view
7. Social Signals: Engaging with guests

Now let's get started mapping out your new action plan and look more closely at each of these seven ranking factors and tactics.

Summaries of the 7 Key SEO Tactics

1. Branding for SEO: Design your house

In order to judge websites, Google uses three factors that go by the acronym "EAT," which stands for expertise, authority, and trustworthiness. If your firm is a thought leader and people search frequently for your brand name, you are more likely to rank well in Google.

Having social mentions, PR placements, and high branded-search volume sends a signal to Google of trust and authority.

While social media isn't necessarily a direct ranking factor, we know that Google looks at your level of expertise and good standing in your niche.

In 2008, Google CEO Eric Schmidt said, "Brands are the solution, not the problem" and "Brands are how you sort out the cesspool."

If you have checked all the SEO boxes like having good backlinks, keyword placement, and blogging, etc., but people don't search for your brand, Google will place you in the search rankings below someone with the same or less "optimization" if they are seen as the go-to company for that topic in other detectable ways.

So you should make sure that you tie your SEO into your broader marketing plan and build your brand with "Mad Men style," as opposed to winging it.

Your house can be made of the best materials, but if no one wants to come over or live there, it's all for nothing.

2. Technical SEO: Lay the foundation

For many, the technical side of SEO is confusing and a world away from what they're used to.

Fear not; in this guide we'll provide you with a checklist you (and/or your SEO team) can use each time you need to perform a technical SEO audit.

Focus on things like having a secure site by using HTTPS:// rather than HTTP://. Make sure you've included H1 and H2 title tags to give your content some clarity as well. Also be sure the file sizes of your images and videos are compressed as small as they can be without losing quality, to ensure your site loads as fast as it can. You can use Google Search Console to help you improve the technical aspects of your site.

3. On-page SEO: Frame the rooms

Adding keywords into text and code is one of the most misunderstood things in SEO. Maybe because I have been doing it since the 1990s, I think of it as fairly simple. Yet our agency has hired, from the best agencies in Boston and beyond, top writers who failed to "get it." Bloggers and writers working for our clients claim to know it, yet fail to pick logical keywords for each page and then don't optimize the title and meta tags or the text on the existing pages.

While it is less important than it once was, when you could slap in some keywords and make clients millions, proper keyword use is still a prerequisite for most sites to rank well.

Back in the day, your old-school "SEO guy" or "SEO girl" could do it. Now you want a writer to do it with finesse, because Google is not so forgiving as they used to be.

But you also need the keyword strategy done in a way the average writer may not understand. You may even need more related keywords and other factors only an SEO geek could muster, such as tying your keyword strategy into a topic cluster strategy. More on that later.

Like technical SEO, it's one of those things that gets mocked for being "fluff" until your search rankings drop off the map. So get your hammer and be prepared to frame up the walls of your digital mansion.

4. Relevant Content: Design an "interior experience"

You know that if you want your law firm to show up in search results, you need to create relevant content that engages people's emotions and minds.

But what you might not know is that search engines, especially Google, are becoming exponentially smarter about determining relevance rather than simply just recognizing keywords. Gone are the days where you could write content and stuff your keyword in every sentence.

Now, Google understands content in much greater detail and can understand the relevance of a piece of content regardless of whether you've used keywords in the body of the content or H2 tags. This is not to say that these things aren't important. They are, and we'll look further at on-page SEO later in this guide.

Create deep content

You'll notice many of the chapters within this guide have a heavy focus on content. That's because if you want your law firm's SEO strategy to be successful, you need to get better at creating content. That includes what's known as "deep content."

Deep content is often defined by its length — the pages in the top 10 results on Google have on average 1,633 words — but it's so much more than that. Writing deep content involves more than just writing length; it's also about focusing on depth. The idea is to cover a topic in detail so the reader no longer needs to seek out further information elsewhere.

However, you might not consider this a viable strategy. You may feel there are few readers who would appreciate a law firm practice page of this length, but it's still worth considering making those pages -- not just your blogs and resource pages -- at least 1,000 words.

Remember though, if you are thinking about changing your current law firm practice pages into deep content, use the opportunity to focus on your user's needs, as opposed to your own sales pitch.

Create content for specific user intent

We've already mentioned that Google is getting smarter at understanding what type of content will resonate with what type of person. Because of this, you need to make sure you're creating content with specific user intent in mind.

Although the importance of keywords has declined over the years due to improvements in Google's machine learning algorithms, you should still look at the text on a topic level and ensure you've included enough context for Google to understand what content you're producing and who it's for. That's not to say you should ignore keywords completely. In the on-page SEO section of this guide, we'll look at some of the best-use cases for keywords within your law firm's content.

Think like a publisher

Although you're running a law firm, you should still think about your business like a publisher. Why? A recent study found that bloggers are spending more time creating content, and an increasing number are publishing once a week, or even monthly, compared to recent years where the common practice was to publish sometimes as often as daily.

This might be due to bloggers focusing on writing deeper pieces of content that take more time to produce.

On the other hand, bloggers who publish content frequently reported higher search rankings. What this means is that you should publish as much in-depth content as you can, making sure you don't sacrifice quality for quantity.

Thinking like a publisher involves thinking about promotion, too. Many bloggers use a combination of social media, SEO, email marketing, and influencer outreach to market their content, and your firm can, too.

5. User Signals and User Experience Optimization: Create the flow of your digital floor plan

User signals and user experience optimization work together to make it easier and smoother for visitors to move around your site and find what they're looking for.

User signals

User signals show you how a reader interacts with your site. These include click-through rate, time on site, and bounce rate. Your bounce rate refers to users who enter your site and leave without clicking through any further.

If you want users to click through to your website from search results, you need to make yourself stand out with more interesting titles and meta descriptions, along with short and easy-to-read URLs. We call this click-through rate optimization.

It's good to know that the web pages in positions 1 through 3 on Google (in the search results) have an average click-through rate of 3%. However, converse to that, the average bounce rate for URLs on the first page is 4%.

This means there is plenty of opportunity to take the winning spot on the first page of the search results simply by producing better, more relevant content on your site and creating more engaging titles that show up in the search results.

Improve your user experience

User experience is as much about SEO as keywords are. You should make a conscious effort to improve the user experience of your website by setting text in a readable font size, including a number of images, and providing users with internal links to your other content to help them navigate around your site. Using internal links helps improve the user experience by connecting one comprehensive article to another, so readers spend more time on your site.

6. Backlinks: Like having an ocean view

Backlinks should never be ignored in your SEO strategy. Such links have been an important part of SEO since their first few years in existence.

Although questionable "black-hat" SEO tactics have meant that Google has slightly reduced the power of backlinks over time, it's still a good idea to improve the number and the quality of the inbound links your site generates. You can use various tools to sort your backlinks from best to worst.

You should also use the Google "disavow" tool to disassociate with any bad backlinks that might be hindering your efforts.

7. Social Signals: Engage with guests

Social media platforms like Facebook, Twitter, LinkedIn, and Youtube should be a part of your overall SEO strategy.

You can use tools like LinkedIn and Twitter to share and improve your own thought leadership. Keep in mind that longer content is more likely to be shared across social media.

You can use a tool like Ahrefs to understand what pages on your law firm website generate the most shares.

Set up ROI and campaign tracking first

If you don't tie your success to overarching company goals, it's unlikely you'll feel inspired to set the budget needed to do SEO at the advanced level required to see serious results.

This involves making sure you look at specific metrics, such as where your law firm currently ranks in the search engines results; the search volume for the keywords you want to target; the traffic you're targeting from search engines; and the conversions you're hoping to get from search engines, as well your website's ability to retain customers by bringing them back to your website again and again.

Later, in the tools section, we'll look at some of the tools you can use to help you do this. If you haven't already, make a note of SEMrush, Advanced Web Ranking, and Google Analytics.

Now that you've reading this overview on how SEO ranking factors work together, feel free to skip directly to the section most relevant to you and your law firm. Just make sure you cover all of the SEO ranking factors eventually.

The 7 Key SEO Tactics in Depth

1. Build your brand for positive impact on search rank

The first thing that comes to mind for most of us when we think of branding is the visual identity of a firm. However, your logo, website, fonts, and colors are just a few elements of branding.

Your advertising and communications, your products or services, pricing, reviews, thought leadership, content, and the experience you give your customers are all also a part of branding. Even your sponsorship agreements, support of charitable causes, and partnerships impact the perception of your brand.

However, as Intuit co-founder Scott Cook says, "A brand is no longer what we tell the customer it is — it is what customers tell each other it is."

The traditional idea of branding has shifted because of the internet, but at the same time, your off-line brand, and the perception of your company in general, affects your digital branding capabilities.

Google is starting to give higher importance to businesses that receive the maximum engagement, and if people don't engage with you, it may be because you don't have a strong brand.

Your content is one of the primary ways that you can build a strong relationship with your customers in an age where customers don't want to talk to you until after they've done their research online.

Reviews are essential because customers like to know that they can kick your tires, so to speak, without you noticing them sizing you up.

Customers may be turned off by your brand if you cold-call them and advertise too much, so you need your digital experience to be much more personal and engaging than you did in the days when you could dominate the search engine rankings by hiring someone to manipulate results.

Google is very sophisticated. Here are some insights about the ways that they can determine if a brand is strong.

Let's start with local rankings, since that is so important for law firms. According to tidings.com: "Google's goal in local search has always been to mirror the real world as closely as possible with its digital results. The engagement signals they now have access to as a result of the firehose of data coming from Chrome, Gmail / G Suite, Google Maps, Waze, Android, and soon Google Home, has finally given them the ability—at least in Local—to make the algorithmic shift so many of us have long yearned for: to stop using backlinks as their primary ranking factor."

This graphic from Tidings.com makes it much clearer in terms of where they expect Google to put the emphasis moving forward.

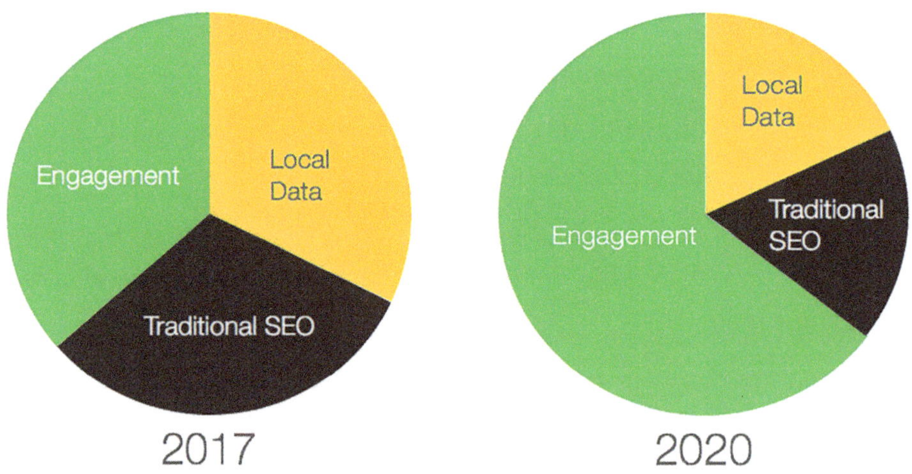

The bottom line? The absolute top experts in local search are strongly buzzing about the engagement factor.

We have been talking about the idea of "pogo sticking" (when users hit the back button after clicking from search results to your site) at least since 2014, when SEO expert Rand Fishkin wrote about how Google may be using it as an important ranking signal.

The click-through rate from search results to your site as a ranking factor has also been discussed since 2014 or before.

Larry Kim of WordStream posits that "dwell time" is already having an impact on rankings. He shares how Google has filed patents on "dwell time," which essentially looks at how long a customer stays on your website.

These are merely speculative topics for SEO-obsessed people like me if Google can't incorporate them in a practical way into their search algorithms. However, you have to take them seriously, now that Google is gaining traction on putting them into practice.

Here is a list of brand signals:

1. Branded searches – People search frequently on your firm name
2. Brand + keyword searches – People look for your brand and specific topics
3. Brand name anchor text – People link to your site using your brand name
4. Known authorship by authors listed on your about us and bio pages
5. Brick and mortar location as seen on contact page
6. Site has Facebook page with lots of likes
7. Site has Twitter profile with followers
8. Site has LinkedIn company page
9. Legitimacy of social media accounts
10. Brand mentions on top stories
11. Brand mentions without getting linked to

Check out this post by *Brian Dean of Backlinko*,[6] where some of these came from.

Entity popularity

People discussing you and your firm on forums, in communities or articles, and mentioning you online, builds you into an entity that can be put into a database by Google. Once again, Google has filed patents on the idea of tracking entities and authors.

Here's an *example of such a patent.*[7]

6 *https://backlinko.com/google-ranking-factors#brand*

7 *https://patents.google.com/patent/US20180046717A1/en*

These are important Google ranking factors today, and a strong brand entity will help with most if not all of them:

- Links
- Organic click-through rate
- Mobile usability
- Dwell time
- Content quality
- On-page SEO

We have already discussed how Google admits that brands help them to sort through the cesspool of the web.

In 2013, Google CEO Eric Schmidt noted that verified people get better ranks.

> *"Within search results, information tied to **verified online profiles** will be ranked higher than content without such verification, which will result in most users naturally clicking on the top [verified] results."*

We know Google's algorithms look at expertise, authoritativeness, and trustworthiness to judge who the true thought leaders are. So if you want your brand to be strong, you should work on building authority — for your company, your locations, and your individual attorneys.

In addition to the other elements in this guide, as well as your traditional branding activities, here are some ways that you can improve your thought leadership and further build your brand.

7 Ways to Become a Thought Leader in Your Practice Area

Thought leadership is one of those concepts that can raise hackles when used in certain circles. Yes, it's business jargon. Yes, the term has been thrown around indiscriminately by people who don't have a clear grasp of what it means.

However, none of those negatives have any effect on its core value. Thought leadership still remains one of the best ways to build a law firm's brand and effectively differentiate that brand from the competition. Not to mention that Google explicitly says it ranks websites better that have clear expertise, authoritativeness, and trustworthiness (EAT).

What is thought leadership? A thought leader is someone who has the knowledge and experience to be seen as an authority in their industry. It follows then that thought leadership involves using that knowledge and experience to answer the questions that your target audience is asking and doing so in ways that differentiate you from your competition.

Typically, thought leadership is demonstrated through content. However, this is not content designed to sell. Rather, it is content designed to convince and to educate. Oftentimes, a thought leadership article will explore a subject in depth, laying out background, diverse approaches, choices, and potential outcomes from a client's point of view. Think of it as one-stop shopping for information on a subject.

The whole point of thought leadership is to build a brand. Authority and confidence build trust with a target audience. Once that trust is established, it becomes much easier to convert prospects into paying customers.

So what does it take to effectively utilize thought leadership to build a firm's brand? Here are seven things to consider when utilizing a thought leadership approach as a part of an overall law firm marketing strategy.

1. Have a clear intention

The initial part of any thought leadership strategy is to have a clear understanding of what you're trying to achieve. Make your intentions as narrow and as focused as possible. This means that brand promotion is not an adequate intention. Determining the exact purpose behind promoting your brand is a far better definition of your intention.

2. Understand who you are talking to

It's important to have a message. But it's far more important to have a message that connects with the people who are viewing your content. In order to accomplish this, you must not only know who those people are, you must also tailor your message to fit their needs. As we will see, the most well-researched and authoritative content will be ignored unless it is designed to tackle subjects that interest the target audience the most.

3. *Understand your audience's needs*

Once you know who your audience is, the next step is to zero in on what they want. Far too many firms take blind stabs at guessing what their audience's needs are. Worse yet, they simply mimic another's firm's content and hope for the best. In order to have a productive conversation with your audience, you must be prepared to engage them. The only way to effectively do this is to put yourself in their shoes. What motivates them? What itch do they need you to scratch? Your audience's needs — as *they* perceive and define them — are paramount, not what you think they need.

4. *What's your angle?*

Face it. There are dozens of firms in any given location that practice in the same areas of law as your firm. How do you stand out in the crowd? How do you clearly communicate to potential clients the things that set your firm apart from the competition? How do you differentiate your message from the dozens of similar messages available to your audience? The answer to these questions is actually deceptively simple. Your message doesn't have to be revolutionary. It doesn't have to be unique. All it has to do, from a thought leadership perspective, is answer their questions more thoroughly, more effectively, and more convincingly than your competition.

In short, differentiate when necessary, but don't make the mistake of trying to always differentiate. A simple and clear demonstration of your knowledge and experience will win the day every time.

5. *The medium is an important part of the message*

You know your angle. You know your audience and you know their needs. What next? In a word, delivery. You could have the most complete and convincing answers to the questions troubling your audience. However, if you don't deliver those answers in a way that the audience expects and, more importantly, in a way that appeals to them, the whole thought leadership process derails.

The manner in which you deliver your message matters as much as the message itself. So, when it comes to content delivery, mix it up. The written word is fine. However, don't neglect audio, video, and graphics. Some of your biggest thought leadership gains can come from taking existing content and repurposing its message in another medium.

6. *Expose your message to the masses*

Too many firms neglect the content delivery platforms that different segments of their potential client base prefer. That means that their message is muted and will not be heard by important segments of their target audience. In order to be a thought leader, you must reach out to your audience through multiple channels. This means that your leadership pieces need to be in multiple media formats, being pumped out on the popular platforms that match the specific media.

Use blogging, social media, print and online magazines, live speaking engagements, podcasts, and YouTube videos in order to effectively demonstrate your knowledge and expertise. A best-selling book on a niche subject is the ultimate way to get exposure and to be the clear leader.

7. *Finally, you've got to stay the course*

Developing a reputation as a thought leader takes consistent effort and time. If you keep the message on point in terms of audience appeal, maintaining a steady volume through multiple channels, your efforts will yield results.

The target audience will begin to see your firm as the leader in your practice area for your location. It is at that point that the role of thought leader will begin to pay dividends in terms of increased client volume and revenue.

Platforms: Deliver your content in the channels your audience prefers. The many different platforms for content delivery include blogs, social media, newspapers, magazines, conferences, podcasts, webinars, YouTube, radio, and television.

Plan: The next step to attaining thought leadership is to come up with a strategic plan that puts all the pieces together. The plan should include your audience, their needs and objectives, your theme, your content, and how you will deliver your content. A great way to start on your plan is to create an editorial calendar. This calendar will enable you to map out your content strategy during the year and will ensure that you stay committed to the plan you develop.

Connect: As previously mentioned, you will need help in becoming a thought leader. Once you have your plan, your next step should be to identify influencers and other thought leaders who can help you attain your goal. Reach out to them and develop a strategic relationship with them. Tell them what your goals and objectives are and ask them for help.

If you are genuine about your efforts and humble in your approach, most thought leaders will be happy to lend a hand and help you to connect with their peers and their audience.

Learn: A true thought leader never stops learning. In order to become a true authority, you must continue to enhance your knowledge and learn from others. Watch and learn from other thought leaders, do research, and read voraciously within your area of interest. Keep up with the latest trends and explore new ideas and new methods. Stay on top of your game.

Execute: As I mentioned above, attaining thought leadership takes a significant amount of time, effort, and determination. Thought leadership is not something you can buy or take shortcuts with. You need to hone your knowledge and skills, execute your plan, and be relentless in your pursuit of greatness.

Sadly, many great law firms and their websites have lots of content, but never land at the top of the search results due to technical issues. The next section will help you avoid those pitfalls.

2. Technical SEO Ranking Factors

Technical SEO is like laying the foundation of your house. Not super-sexy, but nothing else happens without it and the house will crumble if it fails.

Technical SEO is different from on-page SEO (which deals with how the content on the site is optimized) and off-page SEO (which deals with how popular a page is through building relationships with other websites).

Technical SEO is more about the things like how a search engine can "crawl" the web or find your site, and it's more about website load time and coding competency than on- or off-page optimization.

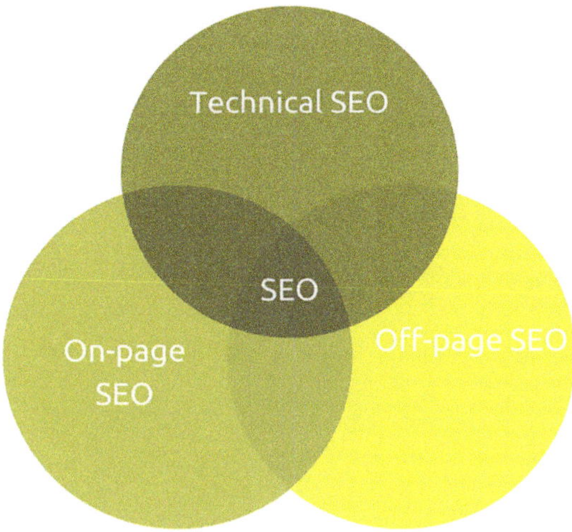

With the constant updates from Google including Hummingbird and RankBrain, these technical aspects are forever changing and are often complex.

So while you can perform a technical SEO audit yourself, it may be helpful for your law firm to seek help from an experienced digital marketing agency. Without technical SEO in the right state, you won't have the proper base for your on-page SEO or links to grow from.

Technical Analysis Overview

I'm giving you two lists, so that you can start with the most important elements and work your way up to being a more comprehensive technical SEO expert or hand it off to someone else.

If you really want to dive in deeper, you can set up a tool like SEMrush with an SEO site audit.

It will give you the errors, warnings, and notices and then show you your progress as you correct errors over time.

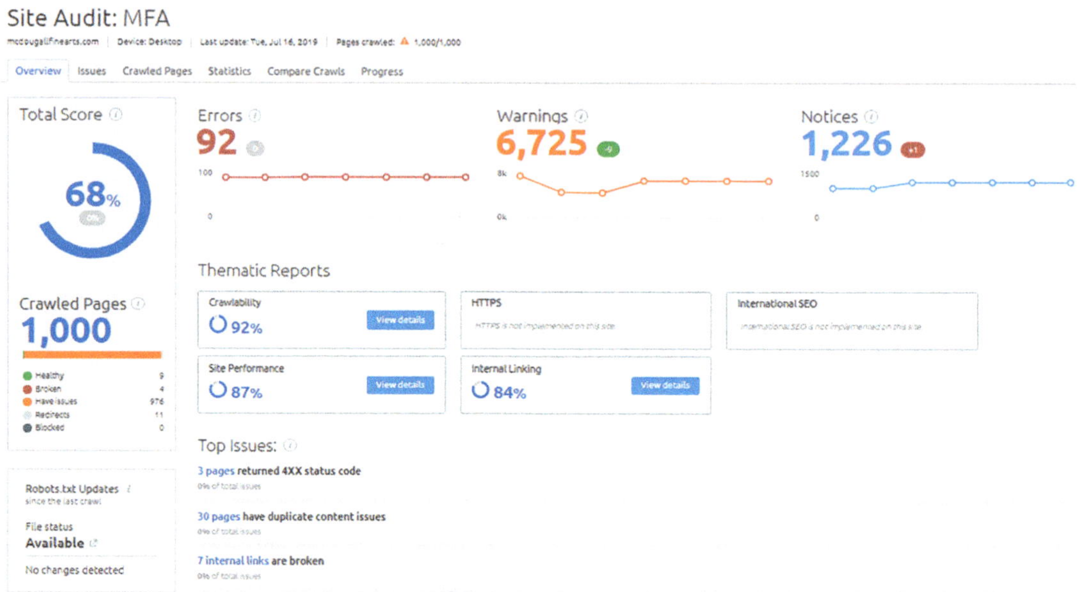

The Mega Technical SEO Action List

First, I will give you the mega list, so your eyes bleed. Just kidding, I mean, so you know how deep this stuff can get. Then I will give you a more manageable list you can take action on.

The second list is the one that's more actionable for C-level folks and partners.

Site Architecture – URL Structure – Getting Pages Indexed

- Make sure your pages and assets are crawlable (don't add a Noindex tag by mistake)
- Make sure your content is actually indexed (Use Google Search Console)
- Test your robots.txt file for "typos" and make sure you are not disallowing, or blocking, good content
- Use an XML sitemap and keep it updated
- Review blocked resources (hashbang URLS) with the Fetch as Google tool
- Optimize your crawl budget (See Search Console >Crawl > Crawl Stats)
- Set up permanent 301 redirects (not temporary 302's) when launching a new website

- Do not use meta refresh for moving a site
- Use hreflang for language and regional URLS
- Use HTTPS, so your site is secure
- Make your URLs simple for users and search engines vs. "index.php?p=367595."
- Add breadcrumbs for better navigation and indexing
- Fix 404 errors, and fix broken links (internal and external)
- Avoid indexing multiple versions of homepage (e.g. www. vs. non www.)
- Rel=canonical can be used for multiple versions of the same content
- Use structured data markup / schema.org
- Avoid canonicalizing blog pages to the root of the blog
- Declare the default language of your site

Content Optimization (This is directly related to technical issues)

- Make sure title and meta-descriptions exist, are unique and the right length
- Use H1 tags for main topic heading, H2 for sub-topics, etc.
- Fix broken images
- Add ALT tags to images
- Get rid of duplicate content
- Review pages with low text-to-HTML ratio and add more content

Usability and Links

- Improve poor mobile experience
- Improve website navigation
- Improve the amount of helpful links to internal pages
- Keep a reasonable number of links on each page
- Remove spammy / bad links to your website

Website Loading Speed Time

- Limit the number of resources
- Improve server response time
- Optimize images for size and quality
- Reduce the number of redirects and remove redirect loops
- Make a browser cache policy
- Minimize render-blocking JavaScript and CSS

Need some aspirin? Here is a more manageable list to start with. For many of you who are not digital marketers or technical SEO experts, the first list might have been a lot to take in. That's why we've included this checklist you can use each time you run a technical SEO audit on your law firm's website.

Technical Analysis Checklist: Top 12 Action Items

1. Make sure URLs follow the same format and make them easy to understand.
2. Implement an XML sitemap to get pages indexed.
3. Use a robots.txt file to direct search engines.
4. Set up secure browsing (HTTPS)
5. Use breadcrumbs for improved navigation and indexing.
6. Create a 404 error page to handle broken links.
7. Make sure you use permanent 301 redirects versus temporary 302 redirects.
8. Limit the number of redirects.
9. Check for duplicate content and remove it (including having two home pages indexed).
10. Correct any title and meta-tag issues (missing, duplicate, length).
11. Improve mobile load time.
12. Make your website's user experience mobile-ready and responsive.

Site Architecture

The site architecture tells search engines how your site is put together. In order to make their job easier, you should ensure your law firm website has a clear and consistent URL structure; a sitemap; a robots.txt file; and secure browsing. We'll go into detail about each of those first because no one will see your site in the search engines if the search engines don't even have a chance to index it.

Making clean URLs

One thing both your users and the search engines want to see is a well-organized URL structure. This helps both parties understand what is on the page.
www.yourlawfirm.com/fhdj334hjhjjk/hjfdsdsfjh

Is more confusing than
www.yourlawfirm.com/family-law

You can use your URLs to add targeted keywords to any pages, but do keep in mind, using hyphens in your URL structure will make them easier to understand. Keep the number of characters under 2,048, or the page won't load.

XML sitemaps

XML sitemaps are useful if you want to correctly index your law firm's website. When the search engine crawls your site, having an up-to-date XML sitemap is beneficial. The sitemap is what the search engine crawlers use to check and update their link database, so they can find pages on your website they might not have previously seen.

So if you're currently going through an overhaul of your website content, or you have a load of updated pages, you should consider creating a sitemap.

Creating a sitemap is easy. You just need to follow these steps. XML-Sitemaps.com offers users a free tool to create your sitemap.

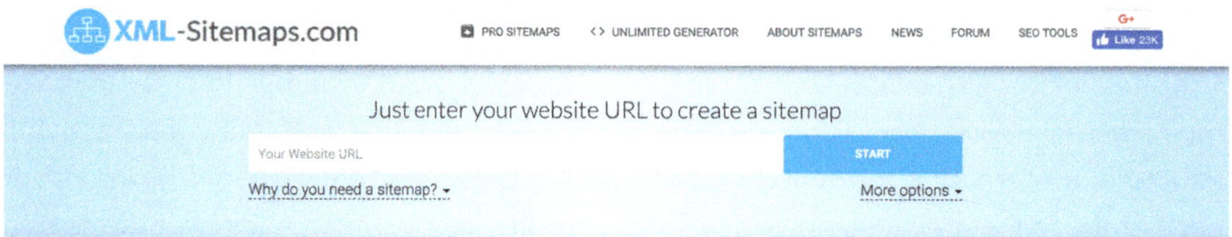

All you need to do is enter the URL of your law firm, and hit "start."

Once you have your sitemap downloaded, you'll need to submit it to Google Search Console.

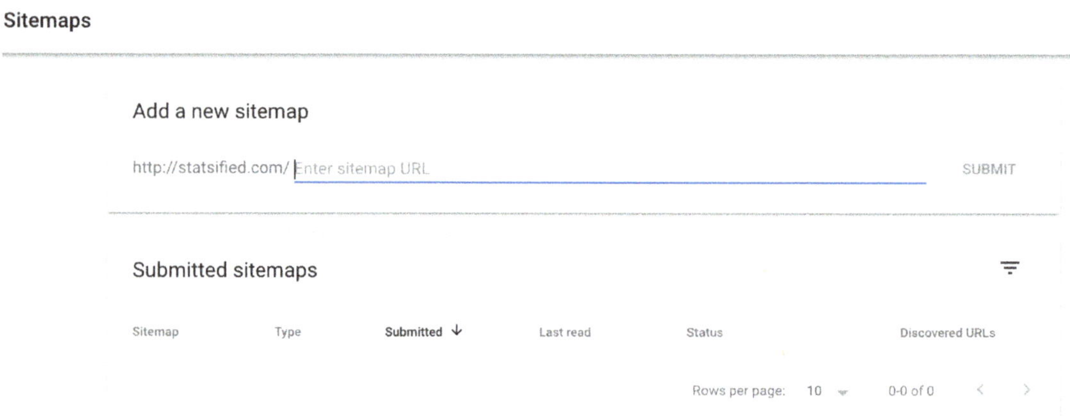

WordPress also has plugins for XML sitemaps. Using *Google Search Console*, you'll be able to upload new sitemaps, as well as see any previous sitemaps you might have created.

If you don't keep your site up to date, you risk indexing old or duplicate content that can cause ranking issues. Google may miss some new content as well.

Robots.txt

A robots.txt file is what webmasters use to instruct web robots (usually the crawlers we mentioned earlier) how they should crawl the pages on their website. In basic terms, a robots.txt file tells robots and crawlers which pages of the website they can and cannot access.

You do this through "allowing" or "disallowing" certain behavior by specific agents, robots, or crawlers. Here's how a robots.txt file might look.

URL: *www.yourlawfirm.com/robots.txt*
Blocking all web crawlers from all content
User-agent: *
Disallow: /

What the above means is that all web crawlers should not crawl any page on *www.your lawfirm.com*

If this seems complicated, don't worry. There are plenty of tools available that can help you generate your own robots.txt file.

SEOBOOK has a free tool that generates the files for you.

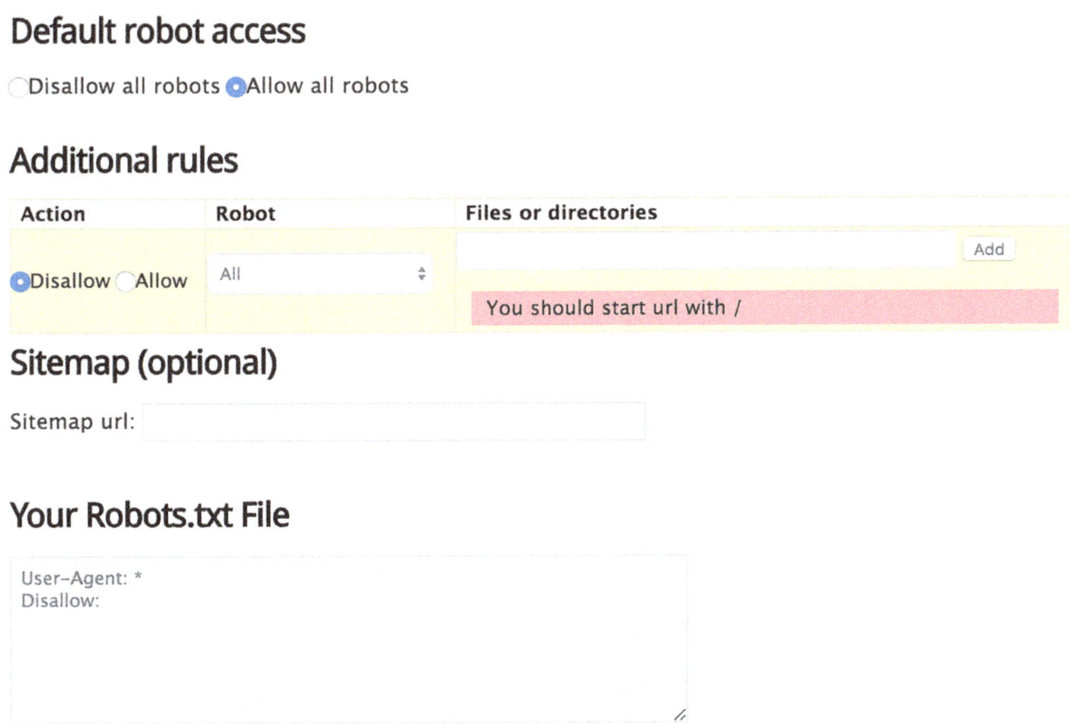

A robots.txt file is also used in situations where you have private or sensitive data you only want certain people to be able to access.

Go to your competitors' websites and add /robots.txt after their domain and you can often see how they're using it.

Set up secure browsing (HTTPS)

Hypertext transfer protocol (HTTP) is the underlying protocol used by the World Wide Web that defines how messages are both formatted and transmitted. It includes letting web servers and browsers know what actions they should take.

But due to safety, you should upgrade your law firm website to the more secure HTTPS rather than just HTTP. Having (or not having) HTTPS on your website is a factor Google takes into account when ranking websites. HTTPS is also a much safer option and reduces the chance of your website being hacked.

Use breadcrumbs for better navigation and indexing

Your website's "breadcrumbs" are a trail of a navigation system that shows where the user is located on your website. Breadcrumbs will be most useful for your law firm if you have a large law firm website with hundreds or thousands of pages.

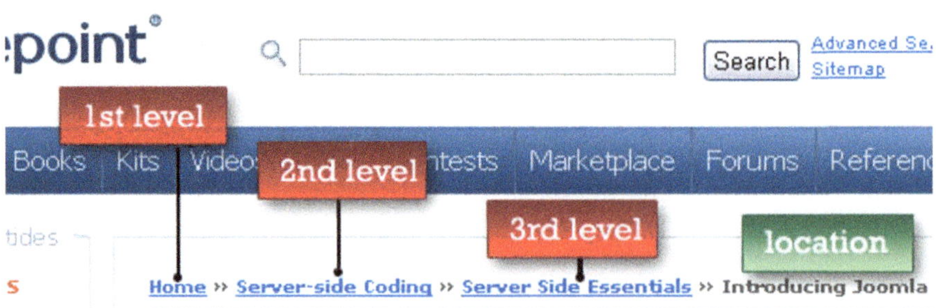

It helps to create a proper structure. However, don't consider breadcrumbs to be your entire navigation system; they should be a secondary extra addition.

Create a 404 error page to handle broken links

Most websites will have 404 error redirect pages that usually occur when a page cannot be found.

To combat users bouncing from your website when they land on a 404 error page, think about making a creative 404 page. Use it as an opportunity to direct visitors back to your home page, or another important service page on your website.

Just because you're a law firm doesn't mean you can't inject some personality into your website, especially when things go wrong.

Fish & Richardson offers a great example of how to design a good 404 page.

And if you want to avoid users reaching the 404 page completely, then you can find your error pages by using Google Search Console.

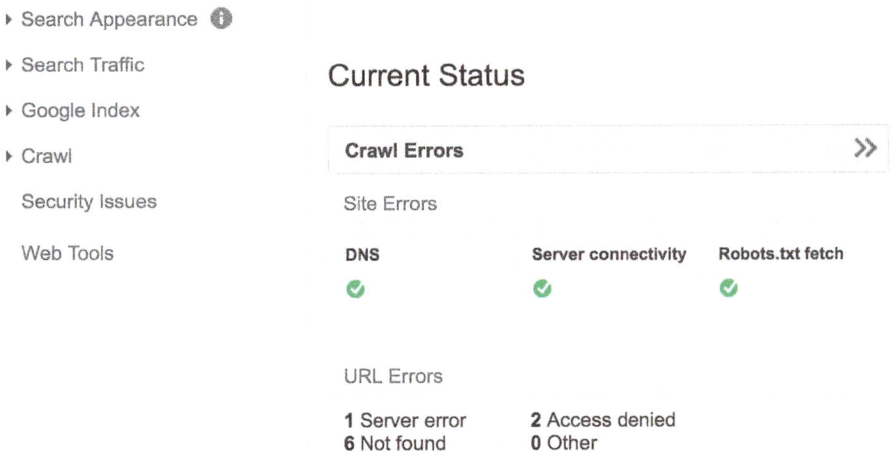

Click "crawl errors" and you'll be presented with a number of pages that might have errors on them.

Use permanent 301 redirects versus temporary 302 redirects

If only I had a dollar for every company that came to me after building a website with massive search engine optimization problems. Advertising agencies, designers and programmers often fail to understand technical SEO, and they either don't set up 301 redirects that permanently tell the search engines that the old pages now have a new name, or they do it improperly.

You need to make an Excel spreadsheet of the old URLs and map them to the new URLs you intend to launch on your new website. Then, using a .htaccess file or by adjusting the server via the admin panel directly, you make this available to Google.

WordPress has some plugins for doing this as well, such as Redirection by John Godley.

You really should direct the search engines on a page-by-page basis, or at the very least, you can redirect an entire URL to the homepage. Simply setting the URL to forward from Go Daddy or a similar domain name registrar is not the same thing and will result in you losing not only a massive amount of revenue if you are getting lots of traffic from the search engines, but you might forever lose the backlinks to the old pages as well.

Improper use of redirects is one of the most common and costly mistakes in all of technical SEO. Getting people to link to your website and its pages is one of the hardest and most expensive things you can do in digital marketing. It is very sad to see companies throwing money and energy away on a regular basis and only employing the help of technical SEO people after the fact.

If you catch mistakes like this within a few weeks, you might be able to get everything back, but if you wait for several months, other websites will stop linking to you because they see that your page no longer exists and doesn't forward properly so they will delete the links.

Limit the number of redirects

Redirects as we just outlined are extremely useful, but they can also slow your website down. The more redirects you have on one page, the longer a user must wait for it to load. Use a redirect tool like *redirect-checker.org* to discover which pages of yours have redirects and consider the necessity of each one.

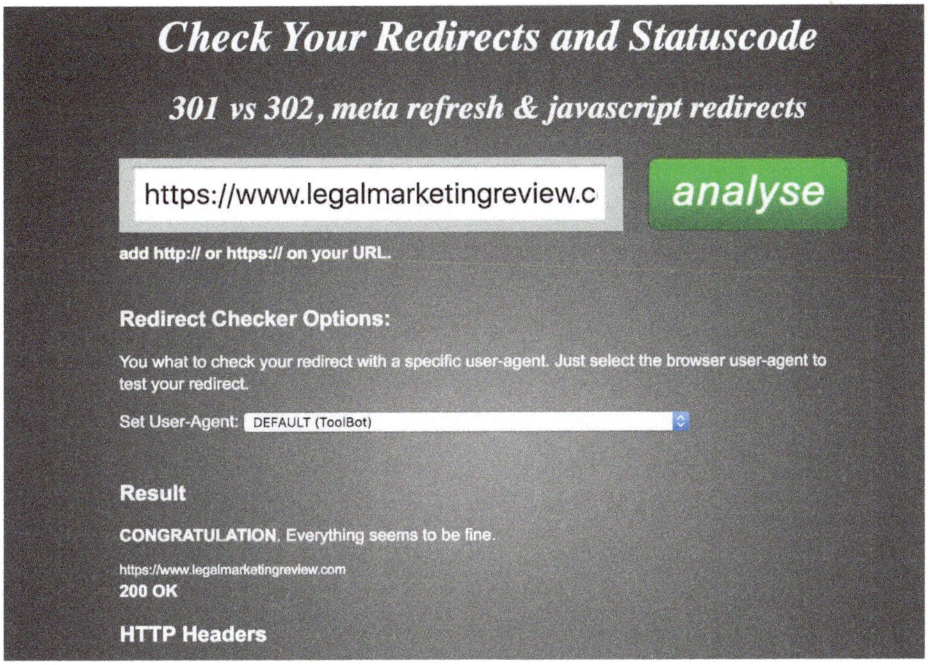

Check for duplicate content and remove it

Duplicate content is when Google sees two or more versions of the same content. Copyscape.com and siteliner.com can be used to diagnose what issues you have.

You can have issues with the following types of duplicate content:

Text that someone let you use on your website but that you didn't realize was already indexed somewhere else on Google. This will get you negative points with Google, so if you want to make use of content from one of your partners, you need to make sure it's not indexed using a "no index" tag.

One way to do this simply with a meta tag is detailed on Google's support pages:

> *"To prevent most search engine web crawlers from indexing a page on your site, place the following meta tag into the <head> section of your page:*
>
> *<meta name="robots" content="noindex">*
>
> *To prevent only Google web crawlers from indexing a page:*
>
> *<meta name="googlebot" content="noindex">"*

If you have a technical issue getting rid of duplicate content on your site, you can use a rel=canonical tag to tell Google which of the pages is the one you want indexed and to get credit for.

You can even have duplicate content in terms of your title and meta-tags. Make sure that your page titles and meta descriptions are unique for each page.

How to correct title and meta-tag issues (missing, duplicate, length)

In addition to having duplicate content in your title and meta description, it is basically considered a technical prerequisite to ensure that you have title tags and meta descriptions that are the proper length.

A title tag should be around 55 to 60 characters, depending on the font styling, which could make the pixel width wider or narrower.

A meta description should be 150 to 160 characters. We shoot for 150.

We will describe in much greater detail how to optimize these in the on-page optimization section. For now, you just need to know that search engine optimization experts consider these factors when looking at the various types of technical SEO issues you may have.

Optimizing website speed for your law firm's website

Internet users have a short attention span. The same can be said for people looking for law firms. In fact, every 100 milliseconds of time it takes your page to load leads to a 1% decrease in potential leads.

In basic terms, the faster the page loads, the better for visitors and also for a site's Google rankings.

Before you begin optimizing your page load time, you should first try to see how quickly or slowly it loads. Our Google rep called me a few weeks ago and pressed the issue of load time for our PPC clients. He suggested using *Test My Site from thinkwithgoogle.com,*[8] *and we also use GTmetrix.*[9]

---

8 https://testmysite.thinkwithgoogle.com

9 https://gtmetrix.com

If you want to improve your page load speed, you should think about the assets you have on your website, as well as where your website is hosted. Page speed optimization is an art usually best done by developers. At the simpler level, it includes enabling compression, optimizing images, and leveraging browser caching.

We will review a few of the basics but know that if you want it done properly, people who specialize in this will get it done quickly, whereas novices will spin their wheels and waste your time and your money. Every day that goes by with a slow-loading website means you are losing money, visitors, and rankings in Google. Here are some important considerations.

Use simpler templates

If you can, limit the number of elements your website template or theme uses. Remember that when a user finds your site, their browser has to load each individual element, and using too many can slow your website down. This includes reviewing what plugins, widgets, or tracking codes your law firm currently uses on your website and considering whether they are all necessary.

Page design is important too, as well as getting important information across to your audience. Don't give up the quality of your law firm website just to reduce the page load speed.

Optimize your images and videos

Images and videos take up a lot of space on your website and are often one of the leading causes for slow website speeds. Ideally, you should be looking to compress your images so that you maintain quality, while still reducing the file size. Use *CompressJPG*[10] to compress your JPEG images.

---

[10] *http://compressjpeg.com*

If you can, save your images in JPEG format (.jpg) when dealing with photographs and PNG format (.png) when dealing with graphics.

Make your law firm's website mobile-ready and responsive

"Mobilegeddon" is a term you might have seen around the internet if you've been looking to improve your own law firm SEO strategy. It refers to how Google ranks websites in the search results, with a preference given to those with mobile-friendly sites.

This is especially true for local mobile results. So when a customer types "Family law firm Illinois," all the results on the first two pages of Google will be responsive and mobile-ready. If your page isn't mobile-ready, there is a huge chance you won't show up in the search rankings at all, and if you do, it'll be so far down, no one will discover you.

Having a responsive, mobile-ready site involves ensuring all the elements load in a way conducive to easy reading.

Look at this example from *Designer websites.*[11] The website on the right is non-responsive and not mobile ready because the text is bunched together and will be difficult for users to navigate. The example on the left shows how the images and text have been spaced out, making it easier to navigate the site.

To see whether your site is ready for mobile, use the *Google mobile test tool.*[12]

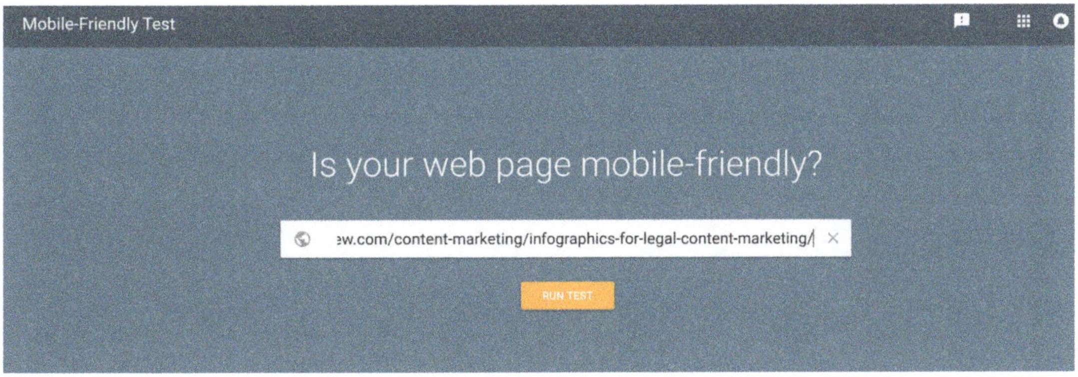

When you click "run test," you'll be presented with a "pass" or "fail."

11 *https://www.designer-websites.co.uk/blog/post/responsive-vs-non-responsive-websites*

12 *https://search.google.com/test/mobile-friendly*

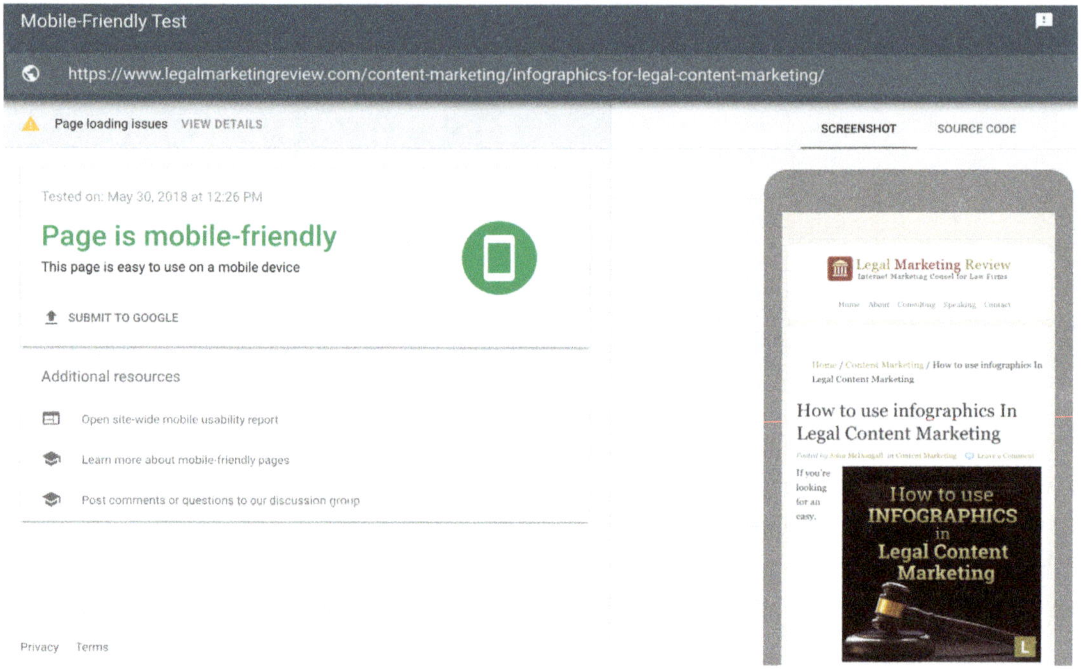

If your page fails the mobile-friendly test, fear not, as Google will outline things you can do to improve it.

Accelerated mobile pages (AMP) are also worth looking into.

Takeaways

In this section of the guide we've walked you through some of the core technical aspects of law firm SEO that you should be concerned with. As we mentioned at the start, if you don't have your technical SEO set up correctly, this will hinder any work you'll do on the on-page and off-page SEO.

Technical SEO, although it might seem confusing, is a process you should follow to ensure your site performs at its highest rate. When performing a technical SEO audit, use our checklist to make sure you have everything covered.

Now it's time to cram your site with repetitive keywords that will destroy the text. Hahaha, just kidding! Let's dig into how to do on-page keyword optimization the right way!

3. On-Page SEO Best Practices for Marketing Your Law Firm

On-page SEO is the bread and butter of SEO marketing tactics for your law firm. However, it's not the entire meal, despite how long it takes to bake the bread and churn the butter.

On-page SEO optimization refers to the techniques you apply to the text of pages on your law firm website to help improve its position in the search rankings. It's very easy to forget elements of on-page SEO. When you first get started, it seems almost as though there is too much to think about.

Keep in mind that Google has capabilities beyond the sci-fi level now, so you can't do only the basics and expect great things. Let's have a quick look at some technology Google uses to understand keywords and text.

Hummingbird

According to Wikipedia, Hummingbird (launched by Google in 2013) is *"capable of understanding the concepts and relationships between keywords,"* and its goal *"is that pages matching the meaning do better, rather than pages matching just a few words."*

RankBrain

Aleh Barysevich, co-founder and CMO of SEO PowerSuite, says, *"There are two parts to RankBrain: the query analysis part and the ranking part. For the former, RankBrain attempts to interpret queries (particularly the rare or completely new long-tail queries) by associating them with other more common queries and concepts, so as to provide better search results in response. For the ranking part, it analyzes the pages in its index and looks for specific features that make them relevant to the query. These pages will not necessarily contain the exact words from the query, but are nonetheless relevant."*

TF-IDF

Google's patents imply TF-IDF is used in ranking. The main purpose of TF-IDF is to sort out the value of a keyword to a page. TF-IDF compares an individual page's keyword usage to lots of other pages. If you use a TD-IDF analyzer, you can look at the top 10 pages ranking for a term and sort out the most important related terms they use. You could then experiment with those terms in ratios similar to those of the winning sites.

If you use a tool like *MarketMuse*[13] or analyze the number of pages on a practice area that a top ranking site has, you can not only match the winning language but improve on the number of relevant sub-pages.

What does it all mean?

Google has tools that look beyond the keyword and, using things like artificial intelligence, can sort out *why* a page should rank. They look at user satisfaction signals, links, and comprehensiveness, as well as on-page elements like headings and body copy.

If you don't want to get really fancy with geek tools, just write very high-quality content that uses lots of related terms that help the page be the best you can find online about the topic.

If you were thinking on-page optimization would be 90% of the work you do in SEO, it's really just the tip of the iceberg.

Below is a synopsis of the latest SEO best practices, aligned with recommendations made by industry authorities such as *Brian Dean*,[14] *HubSpot*,[15] and *our personal favorite, Neil Patel.*[16]

SEO Best Practices for Law Firms

1. Short URLs

Pages should have short, concise, and shareable URLs that let both the user and Google know quickly what the page is about.

---

13 *https://www.marketmuse.com*

14 *https://backlinko.com/seo-this-year*

15 *https://blog.hubspot.com/marketing/new-era-seo*

16 *https://neilpatel.com/what-is-seo*

2. *Keyword in the URL*

URLs should include the primary keyword. This impacts SEO, and users are more likely to click through a URL that contains the keyword they were searching for (or a variation thereof) than one that does not.

3. *Keywords in the Title Tags (Shoot for 55-60 Characters)*

Title tags should include primary keywords, again to help the page rank well in search engines and to quickly convey the primary topic(s) to the user.

4. *Format Title Tag for Click-Through Rate*

Having a strong value proposition or enticing language in addition to keywords in the title tags and meta descriptions where possible will make your search engine results more attractive. User signals are currently a major ranking factor.

Review PPC ads for value proposition ideas and consider using numbers, brackets, and parentheses, which have been shown to improve click-through rates.

5. *Meta Descriptions (Shoot for 160 Characters)*

It's also important to have target keywords and persuasive/enticing language in the meta description to improve click-through rates. Although Google does not give credit for keywords in meta descriptions, if users see the keyword they are searching for or a variation of it in the description, they are more likely to click through.

6. *H1 and H2 Headings*

It's important to have your page structured so Google understands the primary, secondary, and/or tertiary topics of the page. When possible, use at least an H1 with the main topic and an H2 with a subtopic.

If your website's programming does not allow H1 or H2 headlines, at least put headings in bold, since Google will recognize this.

7. Body Copy

It's ideal to use your exact keyword in the first 100 words of text. It's a good idea when possible to use your main keyword several times, but it's not a good idea to over-optimize and focus on keyword density. That said, it can be helpful to look at keyword density for a reality check on what is working for the top five sites in your field. Sometimes in legal SEO, we see over-optimized pages doing well, although that will continue to change as Google gets even smarter.

8. Length of Content

Studies from Search Metrics, Brian Dean, and others show that 1,600 or even 1,890 words is ideal for ranking. Not all of your main website pages will be able to have this much text, but it's an important factor to consider. If a main product or service page can't include this much text, you will need other pages with greater depth, such as blog posts and resource pages, if you want to get your keywords and topics ranking well. *Thin content does not rank well and can hurt your website.*

9. Topic Cluster

Make your page part of a topic cluster. Google appreciates it when you create a "pillar page" that covers a topic broadly and then interlinks with lots of clusters of related content. If you are optimizing the page, you need to think strategically to make sure it is part of a group of related pages to build your topical authority.

10. Scan- and Skim-Friendly

Making your page more readable can have a direct impact on rankings. Having shorter paragraphs and including bulleted and numbered lists is an SEO best practice.

11. Related Keywords/LSI Keywords and TF-IDF

Google has gone beyond keywords. They are now looking at topics and who covers content more comprehensively, also known as topical authority. Your pages will become more authoritative if you include a healthy mix of keywords that are related to your primary keyword. This can help individual pages potentially rank for hundreds, if not thousands, of keywords.

12. Interlinking

Internal Links

It's important to link to two to five or more other related pages or articles on your site from each page. In order to build topical authority, you need to show Google that your site has topic clusters, or multiple pages on the same topic.

Do not use the main key phrase that you are targeting as the anchor text (underlined words) of a link to another page. Anchor text tells Google that you are implying the other page is about the topic more than the page that links to it.

External Links

It's also important to link out on a regular basis to authoritative resources. We've found that using two to five or more external links per page is helpful.

Note: Shorter pages should lean toward having fewer internal and external links and longer pages should have more.

13. Use Multimedia Elements

When possible, use multimedia elements, such as photos, videos, podcasts, etc. "Dwell time," or time-on-site and number of pages visited, is now a ranking factor with Google. Dwell time can be increased by using the above multimedia elements and will also decrease your bounce rate and lead to more conversions.

14. ALT Tags

Every image should have alternative text not only for SEO, but also for disabled users.

Be aware that the following are also important, directly or indirectly:

- How long it takes the page you are optimizing to load
- Inbound links to the page you are optimizing
- Number of social shares the page has
- Additional optimization for ADA disability compliance
- Page author identification using schema markup and links to the author's social profiles
- Make sure to re-optimize and test different best practices on a quarterly or yearly basis, because what works for one site might not work for another,
- Add fresh content over time to keep the page alive.
- Use a striking distance report to figure out where you are coming up on the second and third results pages of Google and take additional action to push yourself into the top ten.
- Pick the right keywords that you have a chance to rank for, or this entire exercise is a waste of time.
- Make sure the keywords you pick for a page match the intent of what someone is looking for when they search for that keyword.

Now that you have a short list, let's dig into some of the details on organizing and creating compelling content.

Organize your content

The first step with any on-page SEO optimization is to get your current content organized. As a law firm, you likely have reams and reams of content already, from category pages for specific practice areas, pages for specific industries you work with, resources pages for downloadable items, and blog posts.

The reason you should optimize each of these pages for SEO is that it will help search engines get a better idea of what content is on each page.

And if the search engines have a good idea of what content is on each page, your rankings on the search engines will be higher.

The overarching theme of on-page SEO optimization is to ensure you have thought about the keywords each page wants to target, as well as building a sufficient site architecture to build topical authority.

In order to organize your content, first, think about the different themes you have present on your website. These themes act as parent categories. Within each parent category, you might also have subcategories. Below is a simple example of how a search engine traditionally would like to see a main category page and subpages.

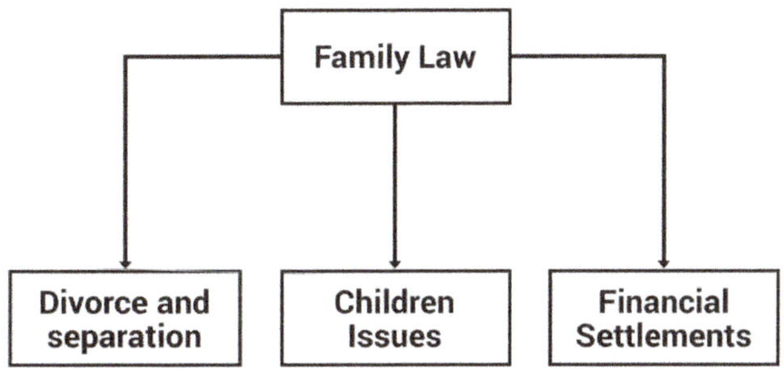

However, our preference for site architecture these days is to use the pillar cluster model instead of the traditional SEO silo model above. Rather than using folder structures, you focus on interlinking powerful general topic pages with subtopic pages, regardless of the folder they are in. Read more about that in the section on topic clusters.

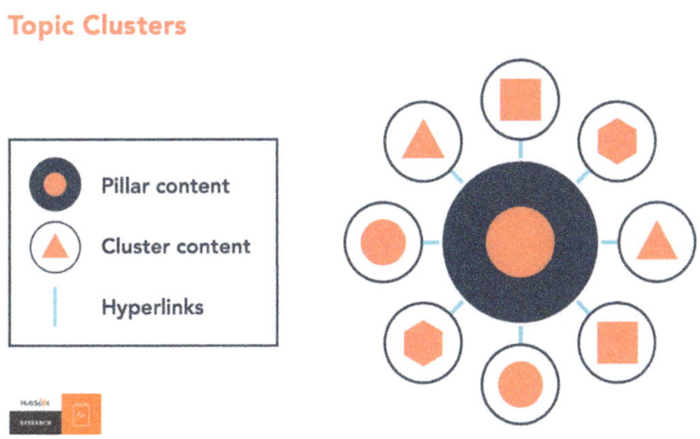

Once you've organized your pages into categories, you can start working on the individual pages. In the following sections, we'll look at optimizing URLs, body content, keywords, meta descriptions, and title tags. Implementing all of these on your site will help you optimize your law firm website to rank better in search engine results.

Content Context and Relevance

When you create each piece of content, think about what keywords you'd like the content to rank for. If we go to our previous example, the top keyword might be: "Family Law."

However, you should delve further and create a series of long-tail anchor keywords too. Long-tail keywords help search engines understand the exact context of what your content is about.

Some examples of long-tail keywords could be:

- "Family law advice"
- "What does the family law court deal with?"
- "What are a man's rights in divorce Vermont?"

These long-tail keywords help give context and intent to your content. If someone is specifically looking for what their rights are, and you include "what are a man's rights in divorce" within your content, the search engines will understand that your content potentially gives a suitable answer to their query.

But you don't want to stuff the page with keywords. Keyword stuffing is where you include keywords so often it appears unnatural.

If you really want to write compelling content, pay attention to keywords, and be sure to include them. But you must make sure your content is also interesting, well-written, easy to share, and that it solves a problem because it's written with the end user in mind.

Keep Your URLs Short

When it comes to your uniform resource locators (URLs), you need to keep them both short and informative. The example below tells the search engine (and the user) nothing about what type of content is on the blog or page.

www.lawfirm.com/jdsfhsjd/jrehtk

Compare that to:

www.lawfirm.com/familylaw/mans-rights

In the second example, you can see we've included some of the keywords we mentioned before. This helps users and search engines alike understand the context of the content on the page.

When you optimize your URLs, you get the opportunity to increase your rankings. However, the rankings aren't the be-all and end-all of optimization efforts. So although it's important to make sure your URLs have a logical structure consistent across the entire website, be mindful that you probably won't see dramatic results.

Short and clear URLs will likely increase your click-through rate, which is another small but positive ranking signal.

Some top URL tips:

1. Keep your URLs short, they shouldn't exceed *2,083 characters.*[17]
2. Make sure the URL represents the content that is on that specific page.
3. Use hyphens to help people and search engines understand what content they're about to read. For example, *www.lawfirm.com/benefitsoflawfirmmarketing* isn't as clear as *www.lawfirm.com/benefits-of-law-firm-marketing.*

If you can, try to use the primary keyword or long-tail keywords within the URL. This is because of user intent. When a visitor looks for a website, they use specific search terms to help them solve their query or problem.

If you can include the primary keyword in a URL, people are more likely to click-through.

Include Keywords in Your Title Tags

As well as the URL, you should understand the importance of a title tag.

[17] *https://helpx.adobe.com/experience-manager/scene7/kb/base/is_protocol-_-forming_is/url-character-limit-get-requests.html*

The title tag gives the viewer the title of the webpage. It appears above your URL in search engines as a clickable link.

Often, when a visitor is looking for a specific search query, they'll read the title to help them decide which of the links to click.

You should optimize your title tags to include keywords, but be careful, you have a maximum pixel size of 600 pixels, which works out to around 60 characters. If you do write more than that, it'll be cut off by the search engines and users won't be able to view the extra characters.

For the same reasons we've already mentioned, you should include keywords in your URL, you should also include them in your title tag, especially if you can match the keyword to direct search intent.

If you want to check how your law firm website's title will appear, use the Moz title tag tool[18] to test it out.

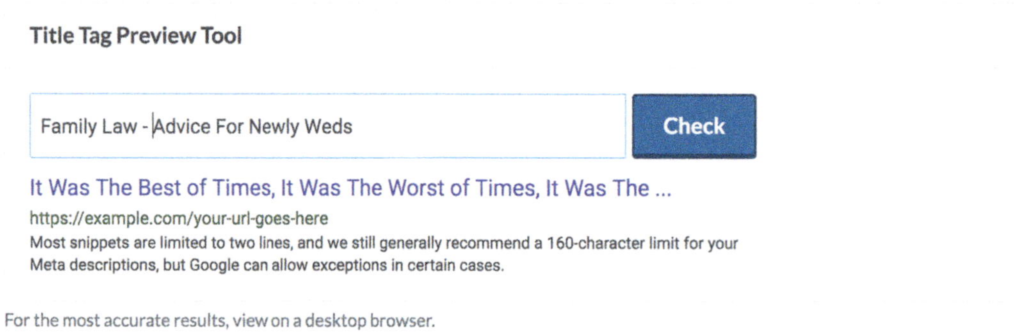

Type in what you think you'd like your title to be and this tool will show you how it'll appear on a search engine and whether or not the text will be cut off.

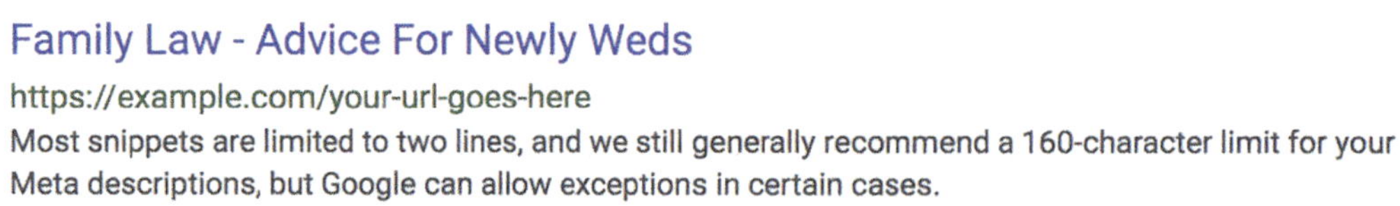

[18] *https://moz.com/learn/seo/title-tag*

When it comes to optimizing your titles, use *Google Search Console*[19] to see your click-through rates for specific keywords people have used to find your site.

Use this data to experiment with the impact that varying your titles might have on clicks. Make sure, however, that each title is unique. Duplicate titles will confuse the search engines as to which piece of content they should show.

When it comes to writing titles, think about the emotional element or think about the practical elements. If you go down the emotional route, you can increase your click-through rate by appealing to your audience's pain points. If you go down the practical route, you give yourself the chance to increase click-throughs by directly adhering to their search query. If you can use emotion and keywords in 60 characters or less, that's even better.

Use a Compelling Meta Description

The meta description (as shown in the image below) is a further indication as to what the content is about. According to a study by *Survey Monkey*,[20] 43.2% click on a search result based on the meta description given.

The meta description should be used to explain what topic the webpage covers and the exact audience who might be interested in it.

It should be descriptive, unique to the page, and shouldn't exceed 160 characters.

Your meta description is where you can show added value. If you offer free law consultations, this is the place you can mention it.

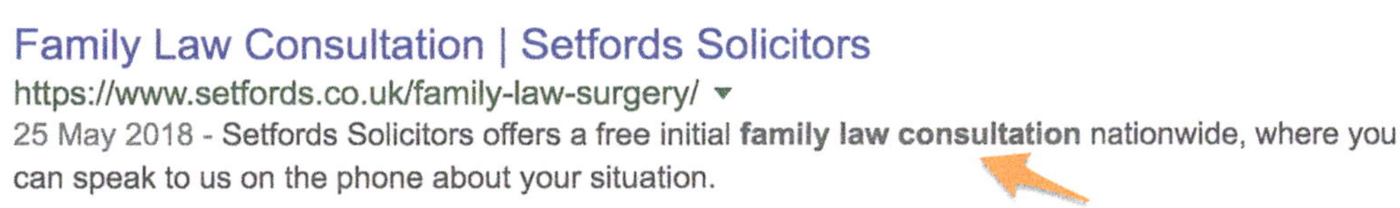

---

19 https://www.google.com/webmasters/tools/home?hl=en

20 *https://newseotechniquesblog.wordpress.com/2017/02/08/how-meta-title-descriptions-affect-seo-ranking/*

Use Structured H1 and H2 Tags

So, once you've convinced someone to click through your website through effective title tags, meta descriptions, and URLs, it's time to work on how to optimize the content on each page.

Each page should have an H1 and H2 tag. These are header tags that help you break up the content. Below is an example of how we use H1 and H2 tags at our own legal marketing review website.

As mentioned, these tags break up the content to help a reader navigate their way through. No one wants to look at a block of text. Just as human readers do, Google uses H1 and H2 tags to understand the context behind the content on the page. The best method is to use the H1 tag as the title and the H2 tags as secondary topics.

Intelligently Use Keywords in the Body of Your Copy

We've already covered the importance of including keywords in the title tags and URL, but they're also important to use within the body copy, too.

However, you don't need to fill your entire webpage with your keyword as often as you can write it. Google's AI is becoming much smarter when it comes to working out what context your copy is written in.

So although you do want to consider keywords and use them sparingly throughout your page, you also should think about phrases that are semantically similar to the main keyword and secondary keywords.

Latent semantic indexing (LSI) means synonyms for your main keyword.

Also, it's important to note that adding keywords in your meta descriptions does not cause rankings to improve. However, you may see a boost in rankings if your meta descriptions generate a lot more click-throughs. For example, if your main keyword was "family lawyer Illinois," here are some LSI keywords that you can use:

- "Best family lawyer Illinois"
- "Most affordable family lawyer Illinois"

If you're struggling to find LSI keywords you can use within your copy, Google will help. Toward the bottom of the search results page, you'll see a range of "searches related to your search phrase."

Searches related to family lawyer illinois

family **law attorney chicago free consultation**

pro bono family **lawyers in chicago**

child custody attorney chicago

best family **law attorney chicago**

top child custody lawyers in illinois

best child custody lawyers in southern illinois

family **law attorney chicago** illinois

lawyer family

How long should my content be?

When it comes to content, size matters, but it depends on the purpose and aim of the specific page. Studies show that content with a longer word count generates better attention. Look at this example below:

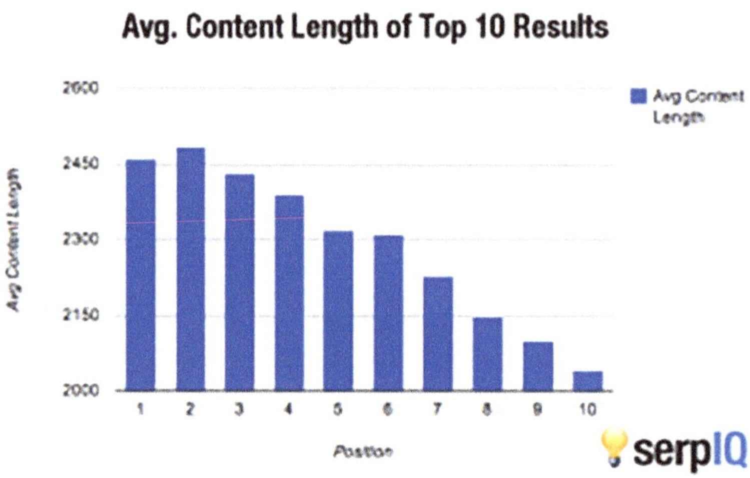

But not every page must have this much text. You might have specific pages for different practice areas that might only need a few hundred words of optimized text. You also might have pages that demand a much more thorough exploration of a topic and therefore need to be longer. Generally, I like longer practice-area pages that lead with engaging and empathetic sentences that summarize the benefits of working with your firm on this topic. Then you can give solid detail on what the practice area is all about, include a video, even an infographic, testimonials, and links to lots of resources you have on the subject.

A user-centric page like that will usually, if not always, outrank and out-convert a few hundred words of dry, "we are great," firm-centric copy.

Make sure your users can scan your pages easily

We already mentioned you should use H1 and H2 tags to break up the content on each page. This helps readers easily scan the content to find exactly what they're looking for. You can also use video and images to ensure the content is easy to understand and easily digestible.

Your website users have a short attention span, meaning you only have a few seconds to capture their attention. In addition, humans have a memory buffer, and we can store only so much information at once. That is why short sentences are better. Long and in-depth content is not the problem, it's how you break it up.

Alongside using your H1 and H2 tags to break up the text, avoid writing paragraphs longer than five lines. Break text up through the use of bullet points and numbered lists.

Always Use Alt Text For Images

We briefly touched upon the concept that you can use images to break up the text within your content.

But the SEO issue with images is that search engines are unable to read text in them the way they do HTML text. The workaround here is to use "alt text." "Alt attributes" tell search engines what the image is of. Just don't use images for keyword-rich headlines or subheads, even if you use ALT tags, because HTML text is better for SEO.

An ALT tag is an HTML element used by web developers and search engines alike.

It's also good to note that for any visually impaired people, if they're using specific browsers or perhaps have their content read to them through voice-to-text, they will be given the alt attribute rather than the image.

If your site fails to load for any reason or is struggling to load, the web browser will opt to show the alt attributes instead.

Not having alternative text attributed to images also may put you at risk of failing to comply with disability laws. If you have a business that is supposed to be fully accessible to the public, like a hotel or a retail store, then you are even more at risk if your website doesn't allow the same degree of accessibility that your physical location does.

Nearly 5,000 ADA lawsuits were filed in federal court for alleged website violations in the first six months of 2018. Even if you don't face potential legal issues, it's a nice thing to do for people who are visually impaired and are using screen readers to "listen" to your website instead of looking at it as they read.

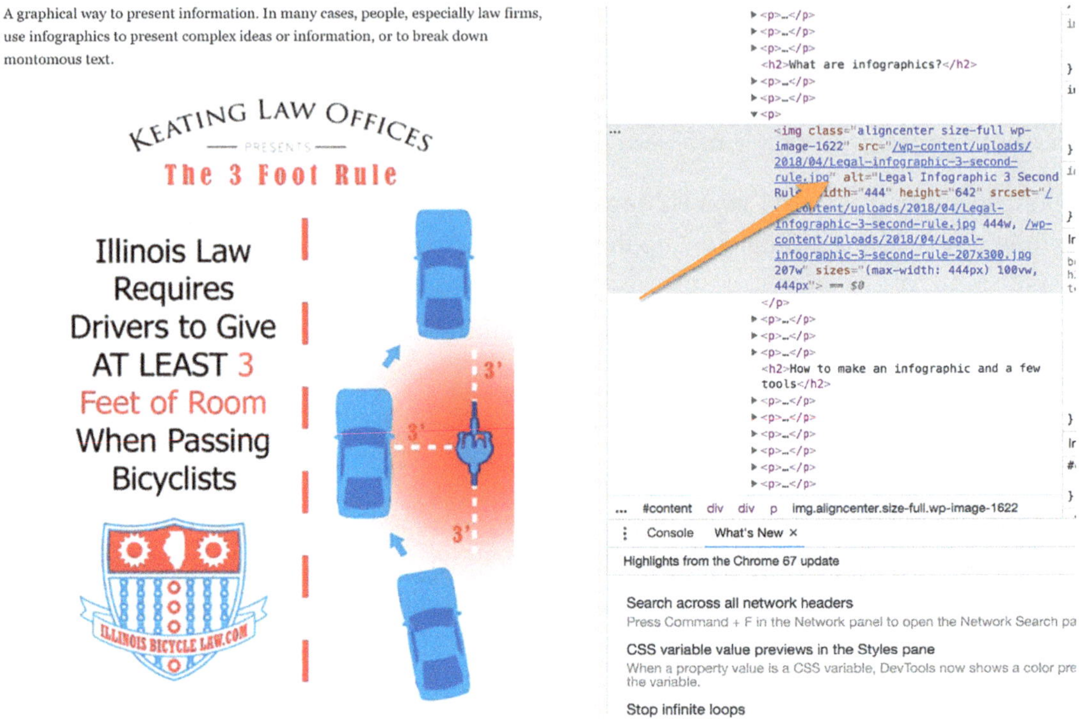

Images are indexed in Google, so describe the image and its use in the best way you can.

Takeaways

Optimizing your law firm website pages for SEO is a difficult task if you don't have this guide and the right people helping you.

It is a task that has to be done by a writer with the exact experience of on page optimization. You also need an SEO expert to map out the keyword strategy, and unfortunately many website copywriters do that wrong.

It's a huge mistake to think that any writer can do this type of work and it's a mistake that is made repeatedly. I personally don't understand why more writers can't get the hang of this, but I can save you a ton of time by promising you that it's better to start with someone who has a proven track record of doing exactly this.

Follow the guidelines listed above and you'll be well on your way to a high-ranking site. Doing so will give you the best possible advantage at ranking with the search engines for your specific topics/keywords and getting more high-quality leads for your law firm.

Back in the 1990s, if you gracefully added keywords and related terms into your pages, you could kick back and relax.

Now you're just getting ready to start the fun part, where you track visitors as they use your site — or bounce away from it — and make it better for them.

4. Create Compelling Content for SEO

Content is already covered in Part 3, so please refer to page 126 in that section for how content fits into wholistic SEO and for what types of content to create.

5. User Experience Optimization Is Key to Your Law Firm Marketing Strategy

Why does your law firm bother having a web presence? Because web traffic generates leads, leads can be converted into clients, and clients keep the lights on.

However, simply having a web presence is not enough.

Your potential clients are internet-savvy. They've seen and interacted with thousands of websites for all sorts of reasons. When it comes to the law, they use the internet to find a firm that can solve a problem they're experiencing, quickly and easily. In fact, legal consumers are among the most motivated customers on the web. According to the National Law Review, 74% of consumers visit a law firm's website to take action.

However, if the website they're viewing doesn't quickly grab and hold their attention, they head for the exits, taking their desire to act with them. In short, it's your competition that's likely to benefit if your website is not up to a visitor's expectations.

This is where UX — short for "user experience" — comes into play. UX is specifically the experience a visitor has (or doesn't have) when visiting a website. The more satisfactory the experience is for the visitor, the longer they will stay on site. The longer they stay on site, the more likely it is that they will become engaged with your brand. The higher their level of engagement, the easier it will be to prompt them to take action and convert them into a paying client.

In today's marketplace, good UX isn't an option. It's a necessity. Not only is it important in generating leads, it is also increasingly important as an SEO element in and of itself.

Google wants the very best results for each search. One of the metrics that's used to determine if a site is a "best result" for a given search is user experience.

User experience encompasses many things, including how long a site takes to load, ease of navigation on the site, and the quality and availability of information on the site. In short, a site that offers good user experience is fast, clean, easy to use, and grabs and holds the attention of the people who visit.

Google increasingly uses UX as a metric to reward sites with good UX and penalize sites with poor UX. In other words, by sacrificing UX you not only are sacrificing potential clients, you're also torpedoing the chances that your website will be seen by anyone at all. And an unseen website is an oxymoron in terms of purpose and function.

In this section, we look at several factors that are important to good UX on your firm's website. Your firm can easily implement these factors to not only raise your website's search ranking, but also to convert a larger percentage of your traffic into clients.

Look to User Signals

Many times, you can get a fairly accurate audit of your site's UX performance simply by looking at the signals being sent by the users on your site. Specifically, you can look at three factors:

1. Click-through rate, or CTR;
2. Time on site; and
3. Bounce rate.

Collectively, the information from these signals will give you a fairly accurate snapshot of the average visitor's experience when using your website. Let's look at each of these user signals separately, so that you can understand what they are and how to use them to improve your site's UX.

1. *Click-Through Rate*

For UX purposes, the click-through rate is the number of visitors who are coming to your site from a third party, in this case from search engine results. These results will be largely, if not totally, from Google and also will be primarily organic traffic. This means that CTR is a metric that is measuring the overall effectiveness of the information contained in the search engine results for your site.

There's an old SEO joke that says the best place to hide a body is on the second page of Google's search results. CTR statistics prove that this old joke is at least partially true. In 2017, the *top 10 search results in Google garnered the best CTR,*[21] with the highest rates going to spots 1 through 3. So, when it comes to CTR, the higher you are in the rankings, the better off you're going to be. However, ranking is not the whole story.

Another thing to consider when discussing CTR is Google's increasing use of paid advertising, carousels, and answer boxes at the top of every search result. These items have a big footprint and take up a lot of geography on the page. As a result, they push organic search results farther down the page. This means that viewers have to wade through more of Google's territory before they get to your result. But don't take my word for it, let's look at the *Moz Google SERP Feature History*[22] over the past 30 days.

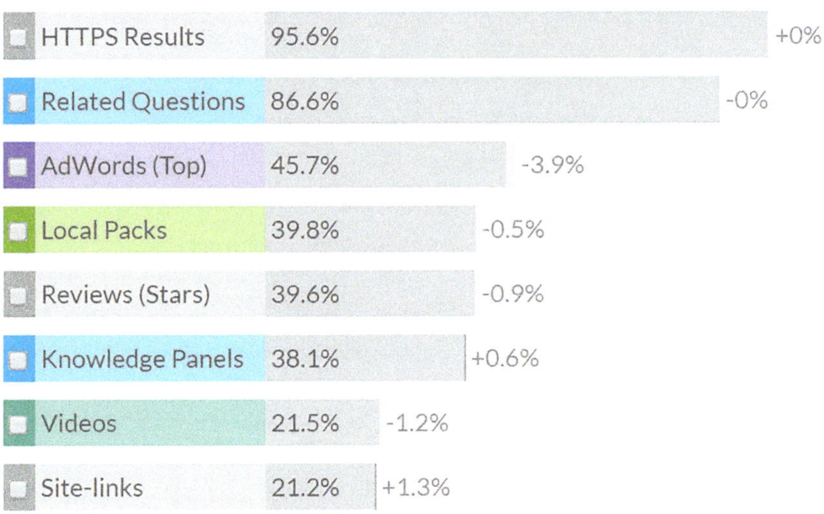

21 *https://ignitevisibility.com/ctr-google-2017*

22 *http://mozcast.com/features*

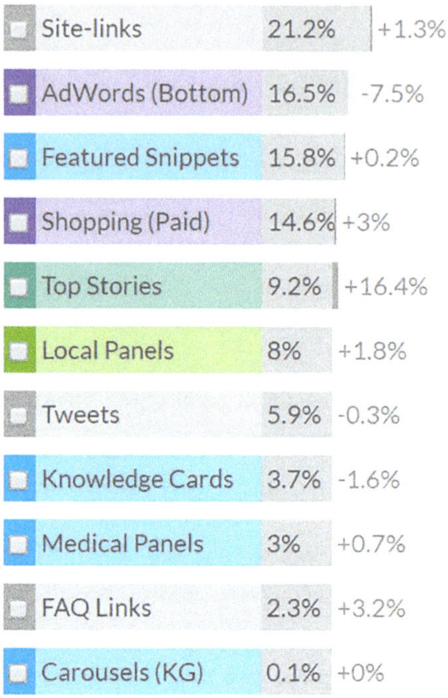

"Data is updated nightly across 10,000 Google SERPs. All percentages reflect unique queries across the 10K (not query volume). Searches link to live queries, and some results may have changed since the last data was captured."[23]

There's a whole lot going on here, but the important statistic to focus on is site links. Site links, the actual links in Google's search result that lead to businesses like yours, only represent 20.5% of matched queries. Even HTTPS results, which include results other than site links, such as external blogs, only account for three-quarters of the search page. The rest of the territory is taken up by Google-related items.

As you can imagine, this means that even if you're in the top ten search results, more of your potential organic traffic is being picked off by Google ads, etc. before someone reaches the organic listing link to your site. Research bears this out.

One industry study[24] showed that the organic CTR has dropped a whopping 37% between 2015 and 2017. Coincidentally, this drop in organic traffic coincides with the rise of Google's increased use of the top of the search results page.

---

23 *http://mozcast.com/features*

24 *https://www.wordstream.com/blog/ws/2017/04/26/google-ranking-click-through-rate*

All of this means that if you want clicks, you'll have to pull out all of the stops. With that in mind, here are some things that you can do to improve your organic CTR in the search results.

To begin with, the search results for your site consist of three elements:

- Title tag
- URL
- Meta description

The graphic below shows all three elements and how they are displayed in a search result.

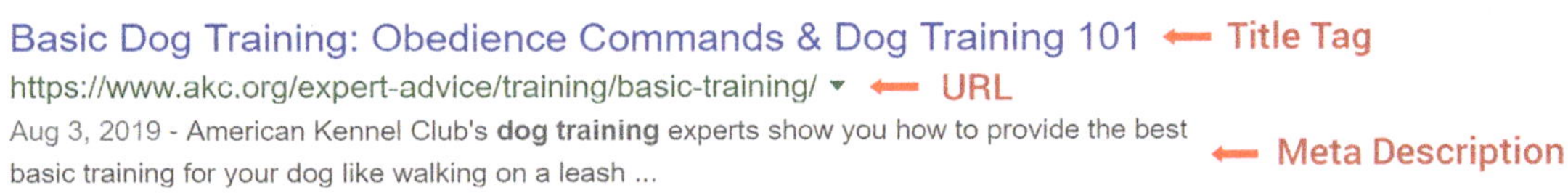

Each of these elements presents an opportunity to boost your CTR, so let's take a closer look at each one.

The Title Tag

The title tag gives the viewer the title of a web page, displayed in search results as clickable links. Titles have a maximum size of 600 pixels. Anything larger than that will be cut off by Google and be unviewable by a potential user.

As such, every title tag should describe a page's content as precisely and concisely as possible. In general, titles of 60 characters or less will generally be fully viewable in the results. Title tags are not only used in search results, they also are displayed in web browsers at the top of tabs, as well as in shared posts in social media.

Therefore, it's important that every title tag you use is as compelling as possible. A good title consists of a number of different factors:

- Always be aware of character length. When composing a title, less is more. Aim for brevity. Remember that capital letters will take up more space than lowercase letters. The last thing that you want to do is exceed the 600-pixel limit and have your carefully crafted title tag become useless because it's been cut off. *Moz offers a neat Title Tag Preview Tool*[25] that can tell you if you're in the ballpark.

- Lead with a title that attracts viewers. For example, people love numbers in titles. Studies have shown that *titles with numbers are 36% more likely to result in a click.*[26] But, not all numbers are created equal. As the graph below shows, it turns out that *people prefer round numbers, ending in zero, in titles far more than any other.*[27]

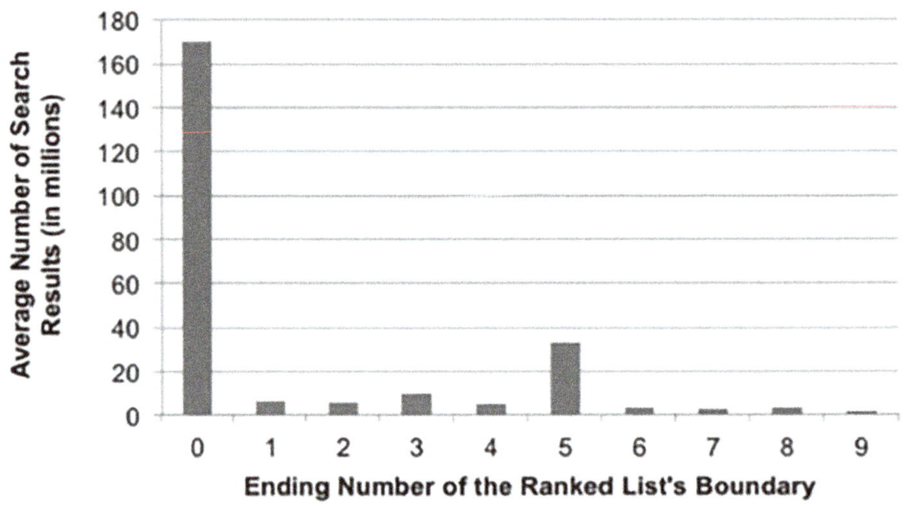

Credit: Via Journal of Consumer Research, DOI: 10.1086/674546

- Don't be afraid of using emotion. Human beings are emotional. This means that *viewers are more likely to click on a title that contains an emotional appeal.*[28] This use of emotion doesn't have to be in-your-face. Simple words like "important," "best" or "effective" speak strongly to a viewer's pain points.
- A good title foreshadows the content to come, so that a viewer doesn't have to guess what's coming next. So make sure that you tell the viewer the format of your content. For example, "tips," "strategies" or "steps" all clearly communicate the format to a viewer.

---

25 *https://moz.com/learn/seo/title-tag*

26 *https://moz.com/blog/5-data-insights-into-the-headlines-readers-click*

27 *https://www.fastcodesign.com/3024538/why-we-love-top-10-lists*

28 *https://searchengineland.com/5-brilliant-headline-hacks-crazy-high-organic-click-rates-249320*

- Use brackets [ ] and parenthesis ( ) as HubSpot has shown them to be effective for *increasing CTR*.[29] Example: Internet Ad Spend Is About to Surpass TV Ad Spend [New Report]
- Finally, use your topic in the title. This can be keyword-driven, an evergreen subject, or a newsworthy event. Again, the point is to let the viewer know up front what's going on.

The URL

The URL (or Uniform Resource Locator) is the web address of the page being viewed in the search results. A URL can have up to 2,083 characters. However, because a URL is more than an address in terms of CTR, you never want to get anywhere close to having one that long. Like your title tag, the shorter and more descriptive your URL is, the better.

The idea is that a potential visitor to the page will know what the page is about just by looking at the URL. This means that the URL should be clear and concise enough so that even if the title tag were hidden or missing, someone looking at the URL would still know what the site is about. If your URL is readable by human beings, you're on the right track. Rand Fishkin formerly of *Moz*[30] has summed this issue up nicely with the graphic below.

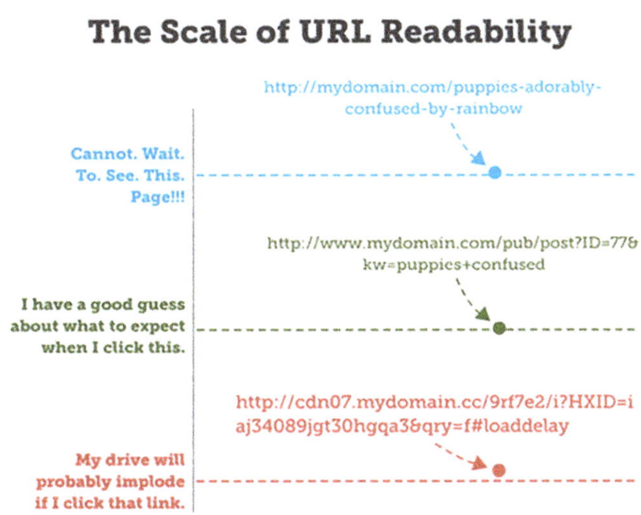

29 *https://blog.hubspot.com/marketing/a-simple-formula-for-writing-kick-ass-titles-ht*

30 *https://moz.com/blog/15-seo-best-practices-for-structuring-urls*

Also, make sure that you're using a top-level domain, or TLD. Both .com and .net are TLDs.

The Meta Description

The meta description is found under the title tag and the URL in a search result. In general, meta descriptions have a size limit of about 150 characters.

When it comes to meta descriptions, you want to reinforce the information that's already contained in the title tag and URL in regard to the nature of the page in question. Because you have a little more wiggle room in terms of length, this is a perfect opportunity to create a good value proposition for your user.

If your firm offers free consultations, this is the place to let the user know that. This is also the perfect place for your phone number, giving a user the opportunity to call you directly without having to click through to your site. That may decrease CTR but calls are worth the small risk.

Full-length, well-thought-out descriptions can give you more real estate in search engine results pages (SERPS) and finally, any starred reviews should be added to them.

2. Time on Site

Time on site, as the name implies, is how much time the average visitor spends on your site after they click through. The average time on site for the top 10 URLs in a given search is 3 minutes and 10 seconds. Given that the average attention span on the internet is now 8 seconds, that 3-minute and 10-second time on site is enormous. It means that the person using the site is having a quality experience and finding relevant and interesting information that solves a problem or meets a need they are experiencing.

It's important that you have a clear idea of how much time visitors are spending on your site. There are three main ways to get this information — analytics, user experience testing, and heat mapping.

In Google Analytics you can look at the average number of pages visited and average visit duration.

User experience testing allows you to watch a video of a typical user interacting with your site and giving feedback about likes, dislikes, and problems. *Usertesting.com* is a platform that allows you to easily set up UX testing at a very affordable rate.

Heat maps are graphic tools that use color-coded values to help you understand how visitors use your site. Areas where users click more frequently, scroll or, in some cases, even look become more brightly colored, while less-frequented areas are duller or not colored at all. Because of this, heat maps can give you a more in-depth understanding of how visitors behave on your site and what pages and content engage them. *CrazyEgg,*[31] *HotJar*[32] and *Clicktale*[33] are all platforms that provide heat mapping services for your website.

3. *Bounce Rate*

Bounce rate is the percentage of total visitors who visit only one page on a site and then leave. Bounce rate is not only indicative of bad UX, it also has a direct correlation to time on site. The higher the bounce rate, the lower the overall time on site will be.

User Signals and Google

It's impossible to talk about user signals without talking about RankBrain, Google's artificial intelligence/machine learning system that helps sort and rank search results. RankBrain has been in place, in one form or another, since 2015. However, since then, Google has revealed that RankBrain is the third most important search ranking factor, after content and linking. Google continues to refine its search algorithm, which means that RankBrain will continue to grow in importance.

Basically, what RankBrain does is look at the number of people who click on your site in the search results and how much time people spend on your site once they click through. In other words, Google is measuring your CTR and time on site (dwell time). The higher both are, the higher your site may rank in the search results.

---

31 *https://www.crazyegg.com/*

32 *https://www.hotjar.com/*

33 *https://www.clicktale.com/solutions/reflect-true-experiences/heatmaps/*

Google is using these metrics as a way of measuring what user experience is like for the average visitor. This means that sites that get great time on site and click-through rates will continue to outperform sites that don't, irrespective of content and backlinks. Google will often use these metrics as the deciding factor between two competing sites that are tied when it comes to content and backlinks. So, if you fail to optimize your site for user experience, specifically looking to user signals, you do so at your own peril.

Important UX Factors

If you've looked at your site's user signals and discovered that your UX needs work, it's not the end of the world. In this section, we offer some proactive steps you can take to improve your UX and, as a result, your ranking and traffic conversion.

Internal Links

Internal linking is one of the easiest ways to give your website a fairly significant UX boost. Despite this fact, many websites often fail to optimize their opportunities to link internally.

An internal link is a link that connects one part of your website with another part of your website. To put it another way, with an internal link, the source and the target domains are the same. Compare this with an external link where the source and target domains are different.

In terms of UX, the primary purpose of internal linking is to help a user navigate around a site more easily. However, smart internal linking also has an important side effect — in terms of SEO, it distributes authority throughout the website. By spreading authority throughout different pages and areas, the ranking power of the site is increased.

Here are several tips to help you increase the effectiveness of your internal links:

- Use descriptive anchor text, the highlighted area of the source that contains the link to the target. When creating anchor text, make sure that you use language that describes the nature of the link target accurately. Descriptive anchor text should establish the relevance of the link target to the content that contains the anchor. This relevance is important to the user because it lets them know why clicking the link will be helpful. It is also important to Google because it establishes the authority of the link.

- Don't use phrases like "Read More" or "Click Here." They're simply not descriptive enough. The same goes for creating an exact match between the anchor text and the title of the link target. Insufficient description equals insufficient relevance, which equals no clicks and no authority.
- Don't use more than one sentence as anchor text. Too much information is as bad as too little information when it comes to link relevance.
- Link to pages on your site that have high conversion numbers. If one part of your site is converting well, you want to make sure that you are funneling users to that area.
- Remember to link deep. This means that you want to link to parts of your site that are deep within the structure, for example blog content that might otherwise be harder for the average user to find. Conversely, you want to avoid shallow links to the top-level pages on the site, places that are already linked by the navigation bar.
- Use links that provide value to a user. The primary purpose of internal linking is to give every visitor a positive UX. Showcase top-notch content and watch your user signals improve.

External Links

External links are the opposite of internal links. Instead of linking from anchor to target within the same domain, the target of an external link is on a different domain. External links are generally a positive thing for the same reasons that apply to internal linking, as long as you follow a few simple rules:

- As with internal links, you want to keep your external links relevant to both the source and the target.
- You also want to use the same kind of descriptive anchor text that you use when doing internal linking. Not too short and not too long.
- It's important that the external link provides real value to the user. So you want to make sure that your external link target is enhancing whatever source content contains the anchor text. External links to authoritative resources are excellent examples of this.

- There's also plenty of evidence that shows *external linking makes your site more relevant in the eyes of other sites,*[34] increases your site's authority, and can even boost your ranking.

Video

In ever-increasing numbers, visitors to your site are expecting video content. Take a look at some of these statistics:

- By 2021, *video will account for 82% of all global consumer internet traffic.*[35]
- Over *500 million people watch over 100 million hours of video*[36] on Facebook every day.
- *YouTube has over one billion users.*[37] (That's almost one third of the internet.)

Clearly, video is the medium of choice for a large percentage of all internet users. That means that it's likely that a large percentage of your site's users will also prefer video over any other medium. In terms of UX, failing to give them what they want could be a serious mistake, one that affects your reach, your brand, and your bottom line.

In order to optimize your video content to improve UX, here are a few tips:

- Don't rely exclusively on video content. Yes, video is increasingly popular as an informational medium. However, even people who prefer video will still explore a website before watching video content. There are also people who *don't* want to watch videos. Make sure that all of the information contained in the videos on your site is also available in text format as well.
- Don't use autoplay. It's annoying and it universally detracts from your site's user experience. Not convinced? *Google has started to block autoplay videos*[38] and will only allow their use under specific, user-controlled circumstances.

---

34 *https://moz.com/blog/linking-internally-externally-from-your-site-whiteboard-friday*

35 *https://www.cisco.com/c/en/us/solutions/collateral/service-provider/visual-networking-index-vni/white-paper-c11-741490.html#_Toc484813971*

36 *http://tubularinsights.com/500-million-watch-facebook-video/*

37 *https://www.youtube.com/intl/en-GB/yt/about/press/*

38 *https://arstechnica.com/tech-policy/2017/09/google-chrome-block-auto-play-video/*

- Keep your video content short. As the chart below demonstrates, users like to watch videos that are of shorter lengths.

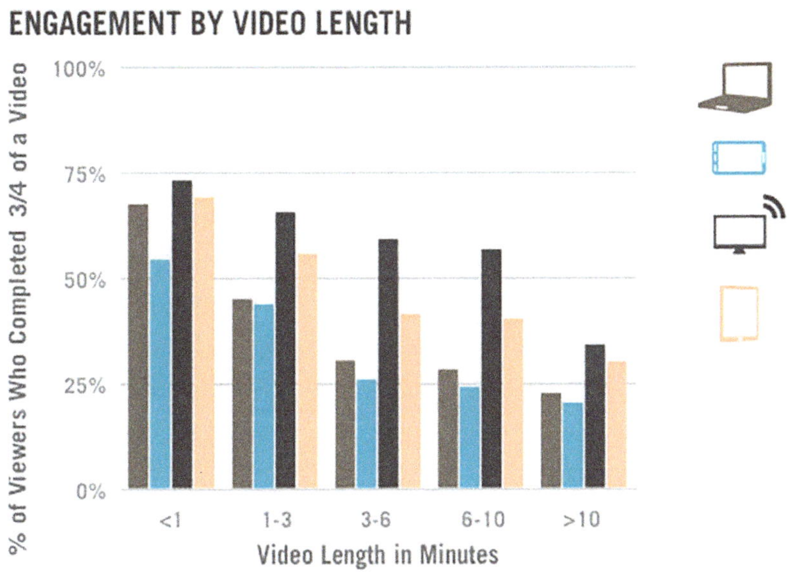

[39]

- Don't leave your viewers hanging. Many videos simply end, leaving the user wondering what they should do next. In terms of UX, a confused user is one who is likely to bounce off-site. Instead of leaving them hanging, make sure that you provide the next step they should take. If appropriate, use a call to action. Alternatively, direct them to other content on the site.

Images

Humans are visual creatures. That's why video is such a popular format on the internet. However, when looking at the UX big picture, don't forget the power of imagery.

Unlike video, images have the power to encapsulate a mood, describe a brand, and entice a user — all with one glance. That's why it's important to select the right images for your site, ones that will stand out from your competition and make your web presence memorable.

---

[39] *https://dmakproductions.com/blog/what-is-the-ideal-length-for-web-video-production/*

When it comes to using images on your site, here are a few things to remember:

- If possible, make image selection a part of the initial design or redesign phase of your site. There are two reasons for this:
  - First, images (unlike videos) are visual cues. They grab a user's eye and tell them where to look next. This means that all images on a page need to be designed with this flow and cohesion in mind. One misplaced image can interrupt that flow, causing lower average time on site and increasing bounce rates.
  - Second, the use of too many visual elements — different videos, image formats, and font types — can bog down your site's load time which, as we will discuss shortly, can be a deal breaker for ranking when it comes to Google.
- There's no magic number when it comes to images. Every site is different. Every audience is different. How many images you use, what they are, and where they'll be on the page, is dependent on your firm's brand, message, and outlook. Just remember to vet every image you use for effectiveness, appropriateness, and overall look. Overly compressed images or images that are too bright, too dark, or too small will negatively impact your site's UX.

Text

Just as they do with video and images, your users want text that is clear, understandable, and easily digestible. While we've emphasized the importance of imagery and video, the written word still contains considerable power. Every effective website creator knows this and uses copy and content that engages, informs, and convinces the user to take action. Your website should be no different.

When considering text, here are a few things to consider:

- Google wants more in-depth content and many experts say 1,600 words or more is what works both for SEO and even for social shares.
- Avoid long, monolithic blocks of content. As we've discussed, the attention span of the average user is short. This means that if you don't get to the point quickly, your user will never get to the point at all. Make sure that you use short, informative sentences and keep your paragraph lengths to no more than four to six sentences. Breaking up your text this way makes it seem shorter and allows the user to absorb it in smaller portions. This keeps them engaged, on site, and moving forward.

- Use structured text elements. In reading this content, you'll notice that much of the information, such as the current section you're reading, is in bullet point format. There is a reason for this. Lists and bullet points are another way to break up information for ease of use. The easier that you make it for a user to take in what you have to say, the better their UX will be.

Technical Considerations

In addition to the content- and design-related items discussed above, there are also some technical tweaks that you can make to improve your site's UX. These include:

- Using HTTPS. HTTP stands for hypertext transfer protocol. It's used to allow two systems to transfer information, most commonly from a server to a web browser. The problem with HTTP is that it isn't secure. Anyone with the right knowledge or tools can intercept any of the information being transferred. HTTPS adds the word "secure" to the formula. Using an SSL certificate, a HTTPS site protects the information, making any information transfer safer. This obviously means a lot to your users. It also means a lot to Google, which gives a boost in search rankings to sites that use HTTPS. In fact, upwards of *70% of the sites on the first page of any Google search are using HTTPS.*[40] HTTPS is good for your UX and your rankings. If you're not using it, you should be.
- Increasing site speed. Google loves good UX. That's why site speed and load time are a part of Google's algorithm. Faster sites may get ranking boosts, while slower sites get penalized. It makes sense. With an average 8-second attention span, no user will patiently wait for your site to load. It's either there the instant they click or they're gone. You can test your site's load speed using tools like *GTmetrix,*[41] *Pingdom*[42] or *Google Developers Page Speed Insights.*[43]

UX is one of the most important aspects of any law firm's online marketing strategy. You have a web presence because that's where your potential clients search for legal representation. It's imperative that you make those potential clients' experience on

---

40 *https://searchengineland.com/moz-report-50-page-one-search-results-are-https-273659*

41 *https://gtmetrix.com/*

42 *https://tools.pingdom.com/*

43 *https://developers.google.com/speed/pagespeed/insights/*

your site as positive as possible. When you do, you significantly increase the chances of converting prospects into clients.

Now it's time to learn another critical tactic which is often talked about but rarely executed well, and that is getting quality links pointing at your site.

6. Law Firm SEO Link Building

When it comes to SEO, link building is an effective strategy that helps you improve the authority of your site.

Link building is the process you take to generate links from other websites back to your own. However, there are good and bad techniques for acquiring links. An effective link-building strategy allows users to navigate between different pages of content on the internet relevant to their needs. When crawling your website, search engines also look at the links present on each page.

In this section, we look at the importance of high-quality links, how to acquire them, and what to do if you start generating bad links.

What to do before you start link building

Before you start building links to your website, you need to make sure you have great content that other websites will actually want to link to.

The issue is this: If you get links from sites that aren't relevant to yours, people might click on the link and immediately leave your website when they realize it offers no value to them.

When this happens, your ranking is affected negatively. In an ideal world, if you want to see SEO success from link building, you want to build relevant, valuable links from trustworthy sites.

When it comes to the type of law firm content people want to link to, it falls largely under the category of "usefulness." This could include anything from checklists, tip sheets, and other resources or lead magnets people to want to share with their own audience.

Evaluating current links

When it comes to looking for opportunities for link building, there are a number of different strategies you can implement to generate links. However, you first need to check the value of a link.

Search engines are very clear when it comes to link building: They want it to happen naturally and organically. Therefore, it's critical that you check just how valuable your links are, not just for Google's sake, but because you don't want to spend unnecessary time building links for your law firm site when they are useless.

Start by checking who currently links to you and whether or not those links are bad, or even worse, harmful to your own SEO ranking. You can use a number of tools like *SEMrush*[44] or *Ahrefs*[45] to check which sites are currently linking to your own website's content.

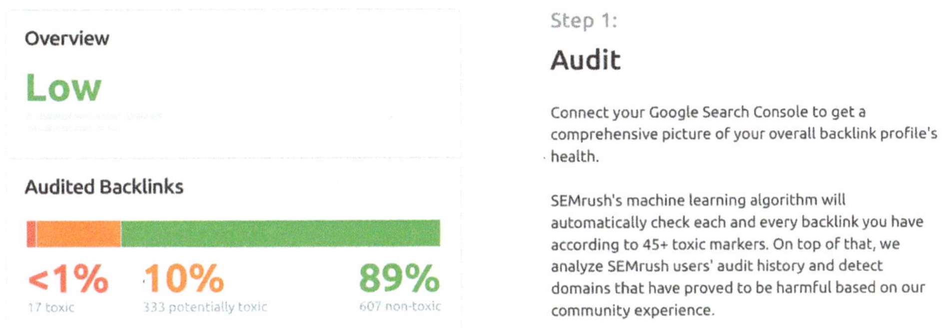

The great thing about these tools is that they show you whether or not the links will hinder your SEO efforts. The SEMrush backlink audit tool will also give you a rough indication of which backlinks you currently have that you should consider removing.

What to do if you find bad links

If you use these tools and see that there are a number of harmful, toxic websites linking to yours, it's time to do something about it. For the most part, Google is quite clever about identifying which links are toxic and ignoring them.

---

44 *https://www.semrush.com/analytics/backlinks/overview/http%3A%2F%2Fwww.legalmarketingreview.com%2F:root_domain*

45 *https://ahrefs.com/dashboard/metrics*

However, sometimes that isn't the case, and you may find your rankings increase if you remove these low-quality links. But remember these are other people's websites linking to yours. You don't have access to their websites, so just how do you remove the link?

The first step is to find the website owner and reach out to them via phone or email to see if they'll remove the link. Often, this doesn't work, which is where Google's bad link disavow tool comes into play. Disavow links is a feature of Google Search Console that helps you reduce any harm from unwanted links pointing to your site. You can access the tool by searching for Google disavow tool or by logging into Google Search Console.

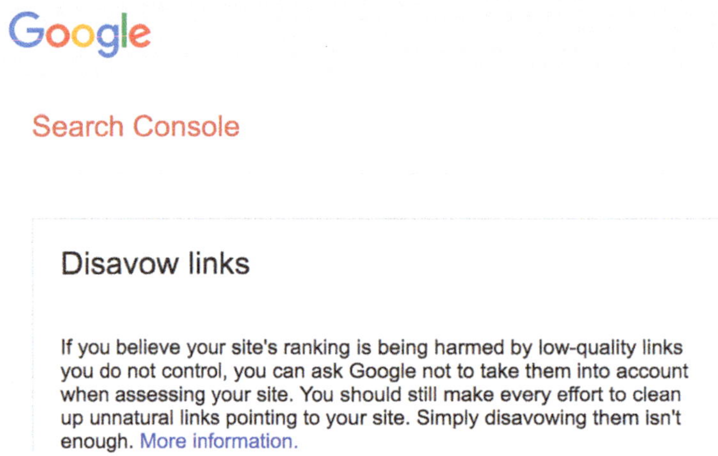

Please note that Google does offer a warning with the disavow tool. They explicitly say that it's an advanced feature that should only be used if you have a considerable amount of "spammy" or low-quality links to your site *and* you know they're causing issues. If you have only a few spammy links, you can likely ignore the tool, as Google is clever enough to understand and assess which links to trust.

If you're unsure whether your bad backlinks are harming your SEO ranking efforts, consult with a specialist before you use the disavow tool.

Initially, you want to use the tools listed above to find all the backlinks linking to your website. You then want to list each of these sites and where it links to.

It can be helpful to use a spreadsheet to organize all your data. I like to use Ahrefs and export the information into Excel, then sort it by Domain Rating high to low and investigate the lowest quality links.

When you have a list of all the URLs linking to your site, visit each site and decide whether you should keep the domain linking to you or add it to your disavow file.

When it comes to evaluating each domain, ask:

- Does this link have anything to do with the legal content I put on my website?
- Would I be worried if someone from Google saw this link?
- Was this link created with SEO in mind and not the user?

For example, if your law firm website has a baby toys website linked to it and there's absolutely no relevance, it will harm your SEO.

Once you have created a list of all the sites you want to disavow, put together a disavow file. List the disavowed websites in this format: domain:website.com. For example:

Domain:spammedbacklink.com
Domain:unethicallinking.com

Save this list as a .txt file to upload in Google Search Console. Remember, if you're struggling with this, or unsure at any point, reach out to an expert.

You should see immediate results from your disavow efforts after you file your document. Google will now consider those as "no follow" links, which pass no positive or negative ranking energy to your website.

Google Penguin

You may or may not know that Google continually releases different updates that can affect your law firm website's SEO.

One such important update is *Google Penguin*.[46] The update helps Google find websites that are trying to generate links in an unethical way to increase their search engine rankings.

When Penguin was launched in 2012, all kinds of problems arose for search engines. People even started the "SEO is dead" debate. Eventually Google provided the disavow tool to help website owners sort out problems from bad links, and today you likely just have to do some routine maintenance.

---

46 *https://en.wikipedia.org/wiki/Google_Penguin*

On the other hand, if you see a warning in Google Search Console, you need to address it immediately. The same is true if you have a large number of low-quality sites pointing to your site.

Be diligent in deleting bad links, but also make sure to look at sites before you delete them as some that get flagged as "bad" by tools may actually be good and some that are not flagged may be bad. So it's part art and part science.

Types of links

By now, you understand that, before you start building links, you need to have solid content and you should evaluate your current links. Before you start implementing a strategy to generate links, it's useful to know what type of links exist.

There are two core types of links:

1 Dofollow

2 Nofollow

Naturally, when you insert a link to your website, the default will be a **dofollow link.**

<a href="https://www.lawfirmwebsite.com/">Law firm</a>

The dofollow link tells search engines that the site you've linked to is valuable and should be given credit for it. This will increase your search rankings.

A nofollow link looks like the one below:

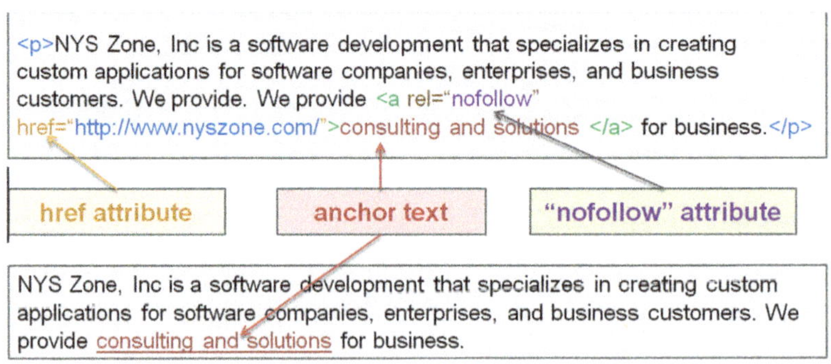

[47]

---

47 *http://www.nyszone.com/seo-nofollow-link-attribute.com*

A nofollow link tells search engines the website in question doesn't want any "link juice" to be carried over to the linked site and to ignore it.

Google is very strict about how you generate and give out links, so if you have experienced any of the following, it's good practice to make the link nofollow.

1. If you were paid to provide the link
2. If you received a product for adding the link
3. If the link will earn you affiliate revenue

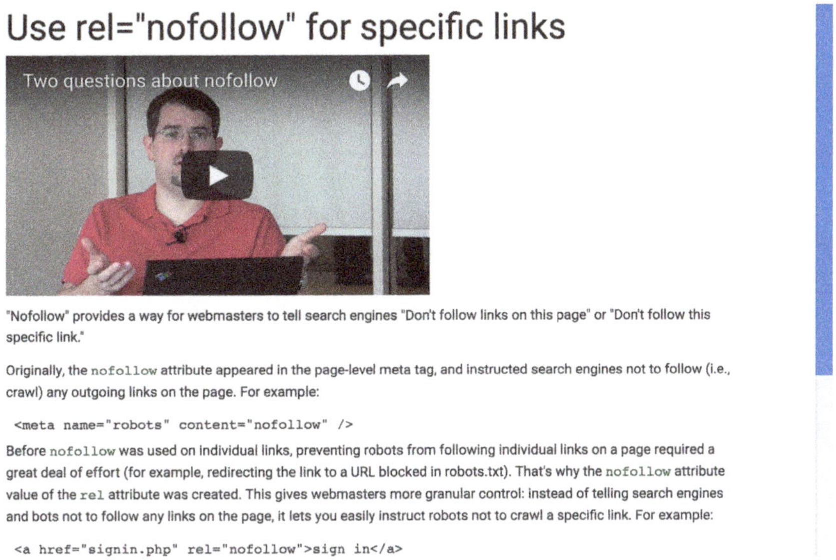

Use rel="nofollow" for specific links

"Nofollow" provides a way for webmasters to tell search engines "Don't follow links on this page" or "Don't follow this specific link."

Originally, the `nofollow` attribute appeared in the page-level meta tag, and instructed search engines not to follow (i.e., crawl) any outgoing links on the page. For example:

```
<meta name="robots" content="nofollow" />
```

Before `nofollow` was used on individual links, preventing robots from following individual links on a page required a great deal of effort (for example, redirecting the link to a URL blocked in robots.txt). That's why the `nofollow` attribute value of the `rel` attribute was created. This gives webmasters more granular control: instead of telling search engines and bots not to follow any links on the page, it lets you easily instruct robots not to crawl a specific link. For example:

```
<a href="signin.php" rel="nofollow">sign in</a>
```

In September of 2019, Google implemented two new link attributes, in addition to the "nofollow" attribute. Combined with "nofollow", these are the 3 link attributes now:

1. rel="nofollow" – for general use in linking out to untrusted links
2. rel="ugc" – for links from "User Generated Content" such as blog comments and forum posts
3. rel="sponsored" – for paid links, such as ads

Check out the McDougall Interactive blog for some important things to know about the new rules and link attributes,[48] in terms of how they might affect you and your site:

---

48 *https://www.mcdougallinteractive.com/blog/seo/googles-new-nofollow-link-attributes/*

And, if at any point you're still unsure, use *Google's support guides*,[49] which will walk you through when you should and should not use the nofollow or default follow link.

Outreach to find missed linking opportunities

Often, there will be an opportunity to link to your site that you have missed. In these situations, search for instances where your website has been mentioned but a link hasn't been used.

Buzzsumo.com is a great tool to help you identify when your brand name has been used without a link.

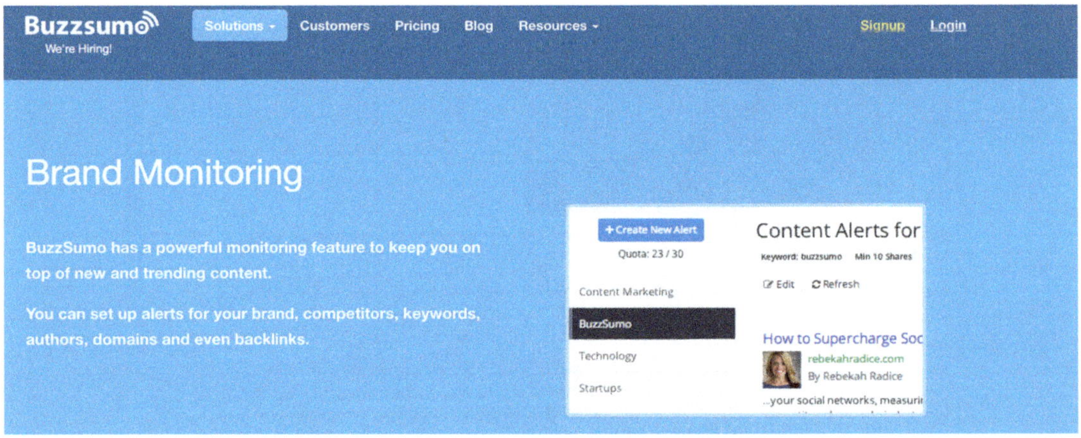

Using *Buzzsumo.com* sets up an alert for your brand name, and you'll receive a notification every time your brand name is mentioned online without a link. You'll also see the domain authority of the site, so you know whether it's worth pursuing the link or not.

If you determine the link is worthy of finding out more, then find the owner of the website using a tool like *hunter.io* and email them to let them know you're pleased they mentioned your brand and ask whether they'd mind linking to your website. If there's a specific (relevant) page you'd like them to link to, make it easy for them to do so by providing them with the link.

We'll turn next to a number of different strategies you can use to start generating valuable links to your law firm's website.

---

49 *https://support.google.com/webmasters/answer/96569?hl=en*

Building links with guest blogging

One of the best ways to generate links from authoritative sites is through guest blogging. When you guest blog, you offer valuable content to other people's sites. Because you're writing the content for their site, you are usually allowed to include a link back to your own website.

More important is that you are getting in front of a larger audience and building a following that leads to other natural links. So even a basic author profile link or nofollow link is okay if you build brand buzz.

When you reach out about guest blogging opportunities. make sure:

1. The site is one that allows guest blogs from law firms like yours,
2. You can pitch a good idea that will benefit their audience, and
3. Your idea follows the theme of the content your law firm currently produces.

I constantly find big sites like Forbes and a variety of other blogs ranking for keywords our legal marketing clients want to rank for. When you can't beat 'em, join 'em. Well, let's rephrase that as get on these sites so you get in front of a larger audience while also ranking and building your own audience.

Building links with social sharing

Another method you can use to build links to your law firm's website is through social shares. Although social shares don't directly affect your ranking, they indirectly help you widen the reach of your content.

The more people who decide to share your content on social media, the more people will see it. And if people are seeing your content, it's likely they will also link to your content, too. If you analyze your current content, you'll see that the content with the most social shares usually has the most links.

If you run your law firm website on Wordpress, you can add social sharing plugins to encourage others to share your content if they find it valuable.

Industry Surveys

Orbit Media did a blog survey of 1,000 bloggers and it made them famous in the content marketing community. If you do that type of survey and actually email hundreds or thousands of people and get them to fill out a survey form, you can create stunning blog content, a downloadable guide, and an infographic. All of this content will make it much more likely that you will get featured by journalists and that people will link to your website.

Did you know that you can use Google consumer surveys and for as little as $500 ask a question to some hundreds of people that relates to your topic? If you think surveys are out of your reach, you might consider this tactic. Given how hard it is to get attention for your content, doing something more dramatic like an industry survey can be a game changer, especially if you do it yearly.

Takeaways

Although building links to your law firm website is a great way to increase search rankings, you should do it with caution. Make sure you don't buy or sell links, offer excessive link exchanges, or generate links from irrelevant sites. Doing this will hinder, rather than help, your search rankings.

However, as we've outlined above, there are many ways to monitor your links and generate new ones if you want to become successful.

See page 219 in the section on link bait to learn more ways to get links.

7. Law Firm Social Signals for SEO

While getting links is critical for SEO, it is hard to do without the use of social media, which plays a part in the complete digital package. If you're not already active on social media, before we get into the finer details, you should be aware that social media is critical for protecting your referrals.

If you search for your brand name or your personal name, you may find your social media profiles popping up in the search engine results. You do not want any of your social media profiles to look like a ghost town or you will turn high-quality referrals away.

As it intersects with SEO, social media doesn't necessarily cause your rankings to go up. But, as we have mentioned in our link building discussion, social media shares usually attract organic backlinks.

Here's what the search engines say about this issue.

Bing said they do use social signals as a ranking factor: *We do look at the social authority of a user. We look at how many people you follow, how many follow you, and this can add a little weight to a listing in regular search results.*

Matt Cutts, the former head of Google's webspam team, at one point early in the debate confirmed that Google used links from Facebook and Twitter as ranking signals, and later put out a video where he said they don't.

In 2016, Gary Illyes, a Google webmaster trends analyst, was asked if Google takes social media into account for SEO. He then retweeted Cutts' video that said, *"Google treats Facebook and Twitter pages like any other web page for search, but not as a ranking factor."* He then said: *"The short version is, no, we don't."*

Yet according to Searchmetrics (one of the top ranking factor analytics firms) in their 2016 Rebooting Ranking Factors white paper: *"The correlation between social signals and ranking position is extremely high, and the number of social signals per landing page has remained constant when compared with the values from last year's whitepaper... The top-ranked websites in Google's rankings displays vastly more social signals than all other pages... This is primarily due to the overlap between brand websites performing strongly in social networks and being allocated top positions by Google."*

So while there is a big debate about the finer details of social media being a direct ranking factor in advanced SEO circles, for the purposes of this guide we won't worry too much about proving causation versus helpful correlation. Social media builds authority and helps you share your content, and *that* is what you should be focused on.

Let's look at a few different social platforms and how you can use of each these to increase the number of social signals your site generates.

What are social signals?

Social signals are in part various links and shares from people's social networking profiles to your law firm's website.

If you're looking at an infographic on a website, and you notice there is an option to "give it a like," you will be providing that website with a social signal.

How do social signals affect your SEO?

Social signals have a positive effect on SEO in a really interesting way. The first thing to remember is that Google favors page time or what they refer to in patents they have filed as "dwell time." That is, how long do people spend on your website consuming content?

If you stumble across a blog post on a law firm website that has been shared over 4,000 times, you're likely to infer that the content is good and worth reading. Adding these social indicators helps other people ascertain the value of the content they're about to read.

Secondly, think about it this way. The more social signals you can generate for each piece of content means that more people have visited your site in the first place.

All of these factors help Google understand that the content on your website is useful and valuable for the target audience. This will go a long way to increase your brand and search engine results page rankings over time.

Use social signals to learn what your customers are saying

Social signals are not only great for encouraging people to actively engage with and share your content, but they help you understand what your customers are saying about you and your niche.

Take each platform one by one and see if people are talking about you. Simply use each platform's search feature and type in the name of your law firm to see what comes up. If you can find out what people are already saying about you, it gives you a good opportunity to control and navigate the conversation.

You might find that no one is talking about your law firm. This could be due to a number of reasons that you have yet to figure out. It could be because your law firm hasn't done anything significant.

The next step is to take a step back from your own law firm and find out where people go online to discuss the questions and topics you care about. For example, if you're a family law firm, you might research where people talk about divorce or child custody.

To begin this process, put together (if you don't already have one) a list of keywords that reflect your own law firm's business. It will be helpful to phrase these keywords in the same way your customers might. The same way you searched through each relevant social media platform to find instances of your own law firm, find when and where people are discussing your search terms. What this tells you is where you need to put your focus to reap the most rewards.

Each social platform has different marketing strategies

Before you begin to put together your social signals strategy, note that you need a foundation of top (valuable) content. The whole idea of social signals is that people use their own social networks to share your content. This way, it reaches new audiences and grows your brand. However, if you don't have content worthy of sharing, you won't succeed.

It's also important to note that no two social networks are the same and each requires a different approach in order to have the most effective results.

Some of the types of content you might consider include:

- Industry surveys and research
- Infographics using research data
- Videos
- Press releases
- White papers
- Blogs
- Company news
- Guest blog posts
- Customer case studies
- Webinars

Below are just a few initial ways you can send good signals from social media and build your brand. We'll take a closer look at LinkedIn, Facebook, Twitter, and YouTube.

LinkedIn

LinkedIn is primarily a business-oriented social network used by professionals in businesses small and large to share content they find useful, source job opportunities, and connect with people from the same or similar industries.

In 2018 LinkedIn had 590 million total users, 260 million of them deemed active. A smaller number than Facebook for sure, but it's a business network and especially helpful for any law firm's social media and content marketing.

Almost 50% of LinkedIn users have a college or postgraduate degree, two-thirds are over 29 years old, and 45% have an average household income of $75,000 or more. Not to mention you can use LinkedIn ads to target people by job title, industry, and fine-tuned demographics.

If you are using LinkedIn, start by making sure your own personal profile is up to date, along with a customer-centric headline and description. You should also be asking a handful of people to give you references that will get posted in your profile. Then create a LinkedIn company page for your law firm and connect your team members to it. This lays the foundation you must have in place before publishing content on LinkedIn.

If we conduct a search on the LinkedIn platform for the phrase "divorce law," we get articles about how millennials are causing the US divorce rate to plummet.

Millennials are causing the U.S. divorce rate to plummet. Ben Steverman has terrible news for matrimonial lawyers.

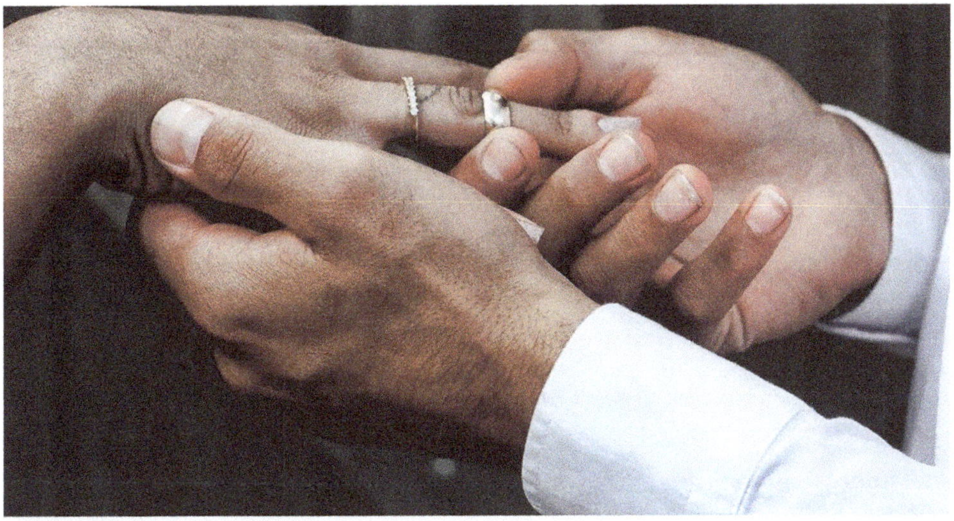

Millennials Are Causing the U.S. Divorce Rate to Plummet
bloomberg.com

202 Likes · 159 Comments

We can see that people interact heavily with shared content from top publications. In the example above, there were 202 likes on the post and 159 comments.

That's a lot of engagement.

If you can create stellar content using LinkedIn publishing and encourage people to share it across LinkedIn, you'll not only increase the number of people who organically find and read your content, but you'll get more people potentially clicking through to other pages on your website to find out more.

When you log in to LinkedIn, right at the top of your wall, you can add a little social blurb update or click "publish an article."

While making a reasonable number of basic updates to your profile is good to keep In front of your connections, publishing an article is even better for your thought leadership. And we know for a fact that Google respects authorities.

Just in case search engines later decide they want to consider something you publish on LinkedIn as duplicate content, we recommend taking half of the content from the blog posts that are on your website and re-posting them as articles on LinkedIn. Then you can put a link back to your blog where visitors can read more.

Getting extra LinkedIn eyeballs to come see the content you've already written is one of the basics that requires a small effort but offers significant rewards.

Facebook

Facebook had 2.41 billion monthly active users as of June 2019, which is an impressive feat. That said, they certainly have had their share of privacy-related controversies and it will be interesting to see how that affects them in the future.

If you want to use Facebook as part of your law firm's social strategy, the first thing you need to do is to create a Facebook business page, which is entirely separate from your personal information and posts.

Even if you post on your Facebook business page just once a month and grow to 500 "likes," you will look far more "alive" than if you are not there at all. You shouldn't buy likes on sites like Fiverr, but you can use Facebook ads to do "like" campaigns and jumpstart your activity very quickly.

In order to stay profitable, Facebook has greatly diminished the amount of organic reach your content will get, so using Facebook boosts or paid ads is far better than just doing it organically.

Studies from Conductor and BrightEdge show that only 2% to 5% of traffic comes from social media to websites, so in order to increase your chances of it actually producing leads, you should set up even a small Facebook advertising budget. Pay a minimum of $10 to boost every piece of content on your blog; ideally, invest $100-plus. Again, an easy thing to do that gets more eyeballs with little extra effort, if you stick to a system.

Another effective technique is to get reviews on Facebook, which helps build trust in your law firm. While you might be more inclined to focus only on Google reviews, what happens if you are targeting a group of people who prefer Facebook as their main place to hang out online? Don't let your own preferences block you from reaching your target audience.

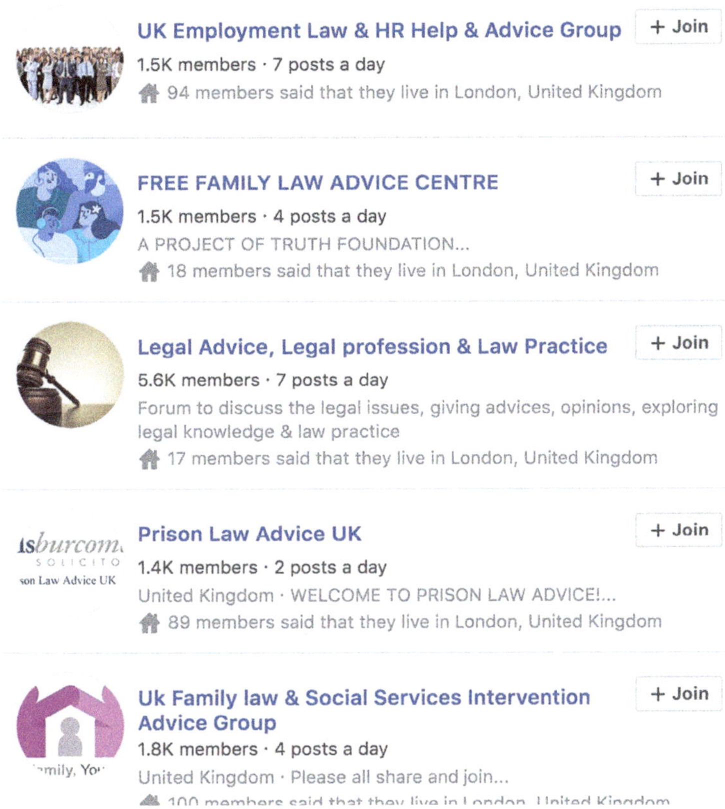

On Facebook in general, people only interact with and "friend" people they know. Therefore, the content tends to be personal. People like to share updates about their lives and look into the lives of the people within their network. As many Facebook profiles are private, it can be hard to infiltrate their profiles to know what they're talking about.

That said, there is a huge community of Facebook users who use the platform for business. There is a large number of Facebook groups dedicated to offering insights about legal issues.

These are often location-specific, so conduct a search to see if there's one in your area. If there are no Facebook groups, consider whether your firm could create one. That way you can help people with the law, as well as offer value by sharing your content.

Facebook is also fantastic for sharing your brand's personality and getting people to like you more. As the old saying goes, people buy from those that they know, like, and trust, and Google certainly appreciates a trusted brand.

Twitter

If you're looking to improve your social signal strategy, Twitter is an effective platform, particularly if you want to connect with journalists and get featured in the media.

Like it or not, even though being on Twitter isn't necessarily a requirement to be interviewed, journalists have stated over and over again that they greatly appreciate seeing that someone they are about to interview is a thought leader on Twitter.

The ability to "retweet" content you like means that even if you share your own content it can reach a wide network of people - simply by others sharing what they believe to be valuable. If you add topic-specific hashtags and @mention other people, your visibility on Twitter will go up even more.

Twitter is all about sharing great content and having great conversations. Because of this, people often use the platform to find recommendations.

In the example above, the Twitter user has asked in their network if anyone can recommend a good charity lawyer. Now, an approach you could take here (beyond recommending yourself) would be to provide a resource or some content that helps people decide how to choose an attorney, as in the next example.

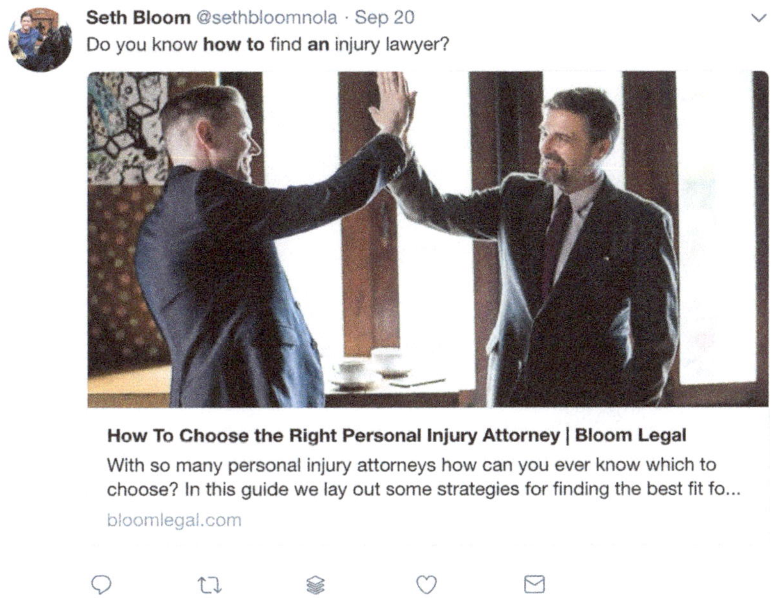

YouTube

YouTube is not only the second-largest search engine in the world, but it appears to be passing Facebook as the most popular social media platform.

A Pew Research Center survey from March 2018 revealed that the number of American adults using YouTube had climbed to 73% — more than Facebook, which came in at 68 percent.

And if that's not enough, by 2021, video will make up 80% of global internet traffic, according to Cisco. So you would be remiss to leave video out of your law firm's digital marketing strategy. For people who prefer audio and visual content, YouTube is just the platform.

Video should be professional, but even iPhones used with a tripod can give you a reasonably good-quality video that you can edit with iMovie.

Short videos (30 seconds to two minutes), especially FAQ-style videos, are a great way to build your brand on YouTube.

We have had legal clients tell us that not only do people call them and reference their YouTube videos, but attorneys have been interviewed by journalists because of the YouTube strategies we have recommended for them.

One of the four times Google flew us to their headquarters for our Google advertising partnership, one of their executives complimented us on how we not only focus on having attorneys give helpful content instead of sales pitches, but that we also include the transcript of the video's content for disabled visitors. The transcripts can help with your organic search rankings because of the in-depth content, which is much better than just having the video on the page alone.

Videos often pop up in the search results, and Google gives preference to its own video platform YouTube.

You can embed YouTube videos right into your practice area website pages, but you should also add them to a blog post with the transcript. Add the transcript into both the blog post and in closed captioning directly in YouTube. YouTube will auto-translate your video into text for the closed captions, but the results are often incorrectly rendered, so don't leave that job up to robots. Instead, be sure a human from your law firm reviews and corrects transcripts as needed.

In the example below, you can see that a lawyer is providing the audience with advice on divorce.

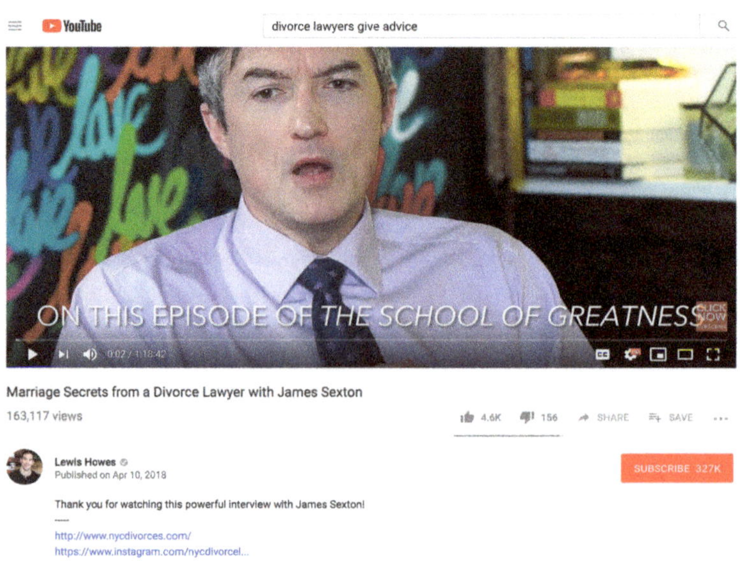

They've also included two relevant links back to their site.

As with all these platforms, the more people who share your content, the more people who will inevitably end up visiting your site.

In numerous studies about what content generates the most backlinks, videos come up in the top three. So, if you want your social media to impact your organic SEO, don't just put your helpful videos on YouTube but also add them in a shareable and linkable way to your website.

Other social media networks

Beyond the major social media platforms discussed above, there are many more available. From Snapchat to Pinterest and Instagram, there are lots of other social media networks that you could use. Outside of having a basic presence on the major channels mentioned here to protect referrals and send strong brand liking signals, the key is to focus on the platforms where you think your customers are spending the most time.

Social Media Content

Social media requires content. At the very least, you need to write little blurbs when you make a status update. Even better is to develop eye-catching graphics and links to the valuable content you have posted on your website. A big part of social media is engaging customers and interacting with them, but the content will make that easier in terms of having something consistent to offer that isn't just fluff.

For example, if you create an infographic, you can take little pieces of it and make smaller graphics that you can then share daily or weekly on your social media channels to promote that deeper piece of content.

If you have an industry survey, you can take quotes from the survey and make graphics out of them to share on a regular basis.

You get more bang for your buck when, instead of focusing mostly on creating content, you repurpose content and spend more time promoting it with a smart strategy.

Set goals

When it comes to social signals, make sure you set goals. These goals will help you understand which social channels will be best for your law firm to target and will help keep you accountable.

You can use your goals to measure how effective your social signals campaign is, and whether or not you need to make any additional changes to take you from where you are now to where you want to be.

Use Google Analytics to track the number of leads you get from social media, but don't be discouraged if it's not a large number. When you factor in social media as being a critical part of protecting referrals and promoting your content, the return on investment is clear.

Takeaways

One major advantage you have as a forward-thinking law firm is that there aren't too many lawyers or law firms really taking advantage of their social media, especially when it comes to social signals.

If you take the necessary efforts to ensure you are encouraging people to provide you with social signals for your website, you're doing better than most other lawyers.

Here's a quick recap of some of the reasons social media is more important than it appears on the surface.

- Protects your referrals
- Generates potential for attracting links
- Helps you build an audience
- Increases branded searches
- Helps with content promotion
- Videos, photos, and personal content increase conversions
- Social media profiles rank in search engines
- Social media channels are search engines too, and the number of searches in social channels is growing all the time

You might not be a social butterfly and it might just feel like there are one too many social media platforms to tackle, but if you start with these basics (and remember that you don't have to use every social media platform), it will pay off in spades.

At this point, you're starting to see how the pieces all come together for SEO to work properly from on-page edits to social media.

In the next section you will see how, even for local rankings in an organic search, Google looks at a variety of factors. So you can't just check a list of boxes in each tactic; instead you need to build overall authority from search and content to social and public relations.

Additional SEO Considerations: Local SEO for Law Firms

In addition to the most important ranking factors we just reviewed, you also need to consider local SEO for your law firm.

When you travel or visit a new city, how many times have you googled a phrase like "good Thai restaurant near me"? How frustrated would you be if you were in New York and Google showed you Thai restaurants in Florida? Pretty annoyed, I guess.

The idea of searching for results only in a specific geographic location is known as local SEO and it's super-important for law firms.

Law firm local SEO is a little bit different from traditional SEO and something you want to get right for your business if you want to generate high-quality leads.

For many legal practice areas, your prospective clients want to work with someone local. Sure, with powerful legal marketing you can get customers from all over the country, especially as you build your authority in niche areas, but it's important to rank extremely well locally first.

Here's a look at the different ways you can implement law firm local SEO on your website to improve your local rankings and increase the number of relevant targeted leads that come to you.

Benefits of local SEO for your law firm

Let's consider how the majority of people begin their search for a law firm. It either involves asking a friend or colleague who they'd recommend or heading to the internet to do preliminary research.

Directory listings, articles, reviews, and websites are all commonly used by people to find an attorney, and they often make use of these resources after getting a referral.

If a potential client searches for "law firm in [your area]" and you don't show up on the first results page(s), what will they conclude? That you don't exist or are not very good, even if they found out about you from a colleague or friend.

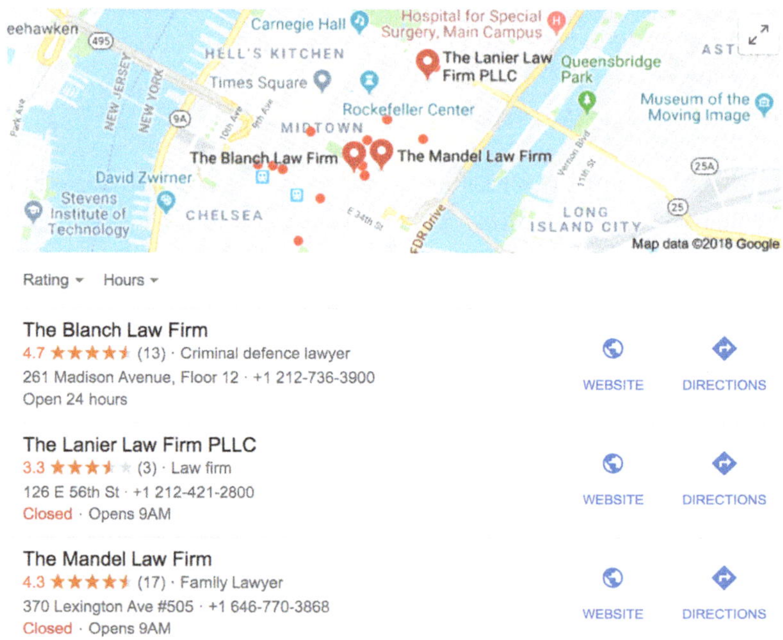

These were my results for "law firm in New York." If you run a law firm in New York, you really need to take specific measures to ensure your website shows up on Google for these specific search terms relevant to your location.

When you think about the type of traffic that comes through local search, it's super-targeted and quite a warm lead. If someone is searching for law firms, there are a range of things they could mean by that. They might be looking for a job, they might be looking to learn more about the legal industry, or they might just be like me, writing about law firm marketing.

However, when someone is looking for a law firm in a specific area, you can assume a certain level of intent and/or need. You're unlikely to search for law firms in New York if you have no interest in hiring a law firm in New York.

So, from a marketing standpoint, dominating local SEO gives you a great opportunity to convert free traffic into paying clients. What's more, the intensity of the competition is somewhat lower. Ranking in the top position for a search term like "law firm" will be a difficult task for most companies. There is just simply too much competition. But the more specific you get with your location, the less competition, and therefore, the easier it will be to rank more highly.

Keyword research for local SEO

One of the first steps you should take to optimize your site for local SEO is to think about what keywords you're using. The benefit of local SEO is that it's pretty obvious which keywords you should be targeting based on your location.

Ideally, you want to let Google know that each page of your website is for a local business. True, you might use your blog or resources page to create content that speaks to a wider group of people beyond your immediate geographic location. But your home page, services page, contact page, and about page should all highlight your location.

If you focus on family law in New York, key phrases you might want to use could include:

"Family law firm in New York"
"Family law attorney New York"

If you scroll down to the bottom of any results page on Google, you'll see a range of similar searches that show you just how detailed you can go.

Instead of just using "New York," you should also go further by specifying which area of New York you're based in, like Queens or Manhattan.

When it comes to enhancing your law firm's keywords with local SEO in mind, consider updating the following spots. However, be careful not to "keyword stuff." If every other word on a page is your location, not only will it not be an enjoyable experience for readers but Google won't like it either.

With local SEO you're going to do many of the same things you learned to do for on-page optimization, but this time make sure you include your geographic location.

Optimizing your home and contact pages along with practice area pages for geographic keywords will help the other parts of local SEO to kick in. The way to get started is to focus on basics like title tags, H1 tags, body content, meta descriptions, and alt text.

Title tag

Your title tag for your website should indicate the city or region you operate in, as well as your main keyword, e.g., "Family Law Firm Brooklyn NY."

H1 tag

You should find at least one opportunity to include your location plus a keyword in one of your H1 tags. Your H1 tags are there to split the content up and provide a hierarchy for the content on each page. In essence, it looks like this:

H1

H2

H3

H4

The contact page is often a great place to input your location and keyword into an H1 tag. When visitors have reached your contact page, it seems reasonable that they'd like a quick reminder of who you are and where you're based, and it won't come off as spammy.

Just remember that headlines with a benefit and unique selling position — and not just a keyword — will get you more leads every time.

Body content

Throughout the body of your web page content, wherever it feels natural, try to include the location of your law firm as well as the keyword. The body content is often where law firms should use variations of the core keyword phrase. For example, instead of just writing "family law firm New York," you might have a sentence that looks like this:

"We're passionate about helping you, the people of New York, solve issues regarding family law. Families are complicated, your law support shouldn't have to be."

Meta description

The meta description, even though in recent years it provides less footing for SEO click-throughs, is useful for people who want to check that the link they're about to click is relevant for them. In this example, you can see that Mandel is a law firm specializing in family law and they're based in New York. If this was something you were looking for, you'd likely click through to visit this law firm's website.

iFLG | International Family Law Group |
https://www.iflg.uk.com/ ▾
The International **Family** Law Group LLP look after the interests of **families** ... Our team includes specialist accredited English **lawyers**, **family** and civil mediators,

Compare that to this law firm where, other than the .uk in their domain, it's unclear where they're based.

Family Law Attorneys in NY | Divorce Lawyer New York City
https://www.mandellawfirm.com/ ▾
Mandel **Law Firm family** law attorneys in **NY** are well experienced in the field of divorce, child support, child custody, domestic violence & LGBTQ **family** law.

Alt text

If you use images on your law firm's website (and you should), the alt text is a great way to indicate to Google where your main practice is based and what services you offer. Images are indexed by Google, so having images like these show up on search results is a powerful benefit.

All of these images showed up on Google for a search of "family law firm New York." Each of the pictures clicks through to various different New York-based law firms. Don't ignore your images when it comes to local SEO, and make sure to take pictures at your office and at local events. You can then use those images on Google My Business and on social media.

Mobile-first local SEO

A vast majority of searches are happening on people's mobile phones, more so than on desktop computers. This is largely due to people wanting access to information exactly when they want it. Google has updated their own algorithm to support this. If your website isn't ready for local SEO on mobile, you're leaving potential clients behind.

When I type "family law firm," Google understands I might be looking for a local law firm and the first suggestion is "near me." Now, when you click this, Google will provide a number of recommendations for you, located near where you are right now. It's a no-brainer, then, that you should optimize your site to support such searches.

In order for your law firm SEO website to rank well for mobile searches, you need to make sure it's fully optimized with a responsive theme. You should also make sure you have included important information such as accurate contact details, addresses and team member names. Adding this data will give your website more authority within the search results.

Legal directories

With the dominance of the internet, people are using print directories like the Yellow Pages less often, but this doesn't mean directories aren't still used online. In fact, online legal directories are a great way to improve your local SEO ranking as well as improve the domain authority for your site. Just don't go overboard on this, because it could hurt your traditional search engine ranking if you start getting dozens or hundreds of low-level directory links.

If you want to increase your domain ranking further, you need people from authoritative sites to link to yours. This isn't an easy task and usually involves guest-blogging on a high level and the best legal-related sites. This is a time-consuming task and is more a long-term strategy, but it is more powerful than the basic directory listings that are used in local search.

It's very revealing to search Google for your main keywords and see what directories come up.

Gloucester Lawyers - Compare Top Attorneys in Gloucester ...
https://www.justia.com › lawyers › massachusetts › gloucester ▾
Compare 680 attorneys serving Gloucester, Massachusetts on Justia. Comprehensive **lawyer** profiles including fees, education, jurisdictions, awards, ...

THE BEST 10 Lawyers near Gloucester, MA 01930 - Last ...
https://www.yelp.com › Gloucester, MA › Professional Services › Lawyers ▾
Best **Lawyers** in Gloucester, MA 01930 - Egan Law Offices, Cunningham ... **Lawyers**. (978) 283-8101. 1 Western Ave. they represented me for an auto accident. i ...

Gloucester Lawyers - Find Your Gloucester, MA Attorney or ...
https://lawyers.findlaw.com › lawyer › statepractice › massachusetts › glou... ▾
Use the largest online **lawyers** directory to find detailed profiles of qualified Gloucester, MA attorneys and ... Find a Gloucester, Massachusetts **Lawyer** Near You.

Find the best lawyer in Gloucester, MA - Avvo
https://www.avvo.com › Find a lawyer › Massachusetts ▾
FREE detailed reports on 213 Attorneys in Gloucester, Massachusetts including disciplinary sanctions, peer endorsements, and reviews.

If Google is ranking certain directories well, they might be worth getting listed in. But if they have no visibility and have stupid names like "lawyer-link-directory-SEO.com," then you want to run in the other direction.

Updating "data providers" with your correct name, address, and phone number can also be a good idea. Infogroup, Acxiom, Factual, and Neustar/Localeze are the four major providers that push information across hundreds of websites online.

Be sure to update individual listings on sites like the following

- Google
- Facebook
- Bing local
- Yelp
- YP.com
- Avvo.com
- Findlaw.com
- Lawyers.com
- Superlawyers.com
- Your local Chamber of Commerce
- Your local Better Business Bureau

Even making sure a small number of the best listings have your accurate information can go a long way.

NAP citations

NAP citations are important for your local SEO. NAP stands for "name, address, phone number." If you want to increase your local SEO rankings, be sure to include your firm's name, address, and phone number on your website. But more importantly, the way you address these details should be consistent. For example, if you use "road" in your address in one instance, don't then use the abbreviation "Rd." in another instance. Remember to periodically monitor your listings, especially if your firm's address changes.

Google My Business

Although it's important to make sure your website is optimized for local SEO results, you also need to make full use of your Google My Business account.

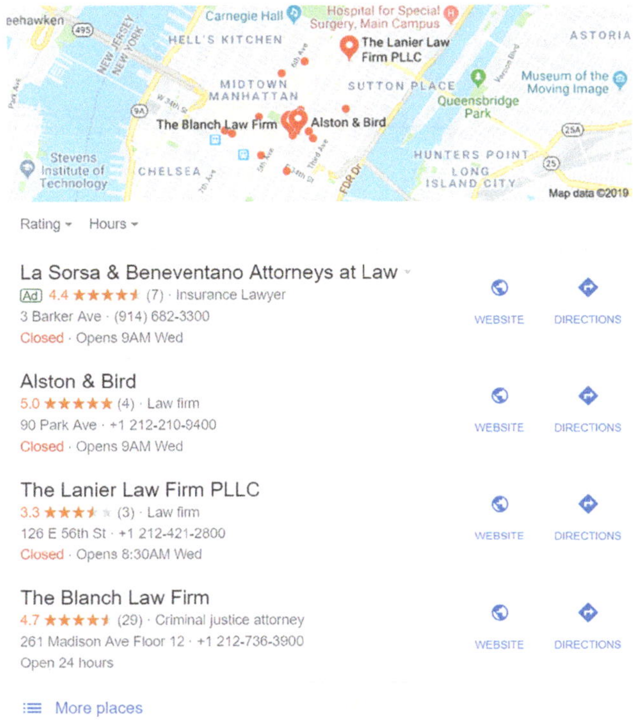

You'll notice Google shows you not only the companies' names but their reviews, contact details, opening times, links to their websites, and directions to the firms.

To get started, search for Google My Business and set up a basic account.

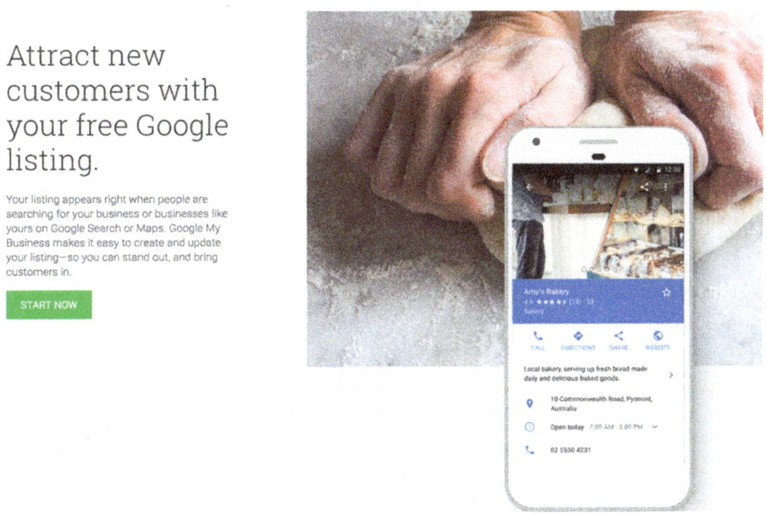

You'll then have the opportunity to input your details. Be as comprehensive as possible.

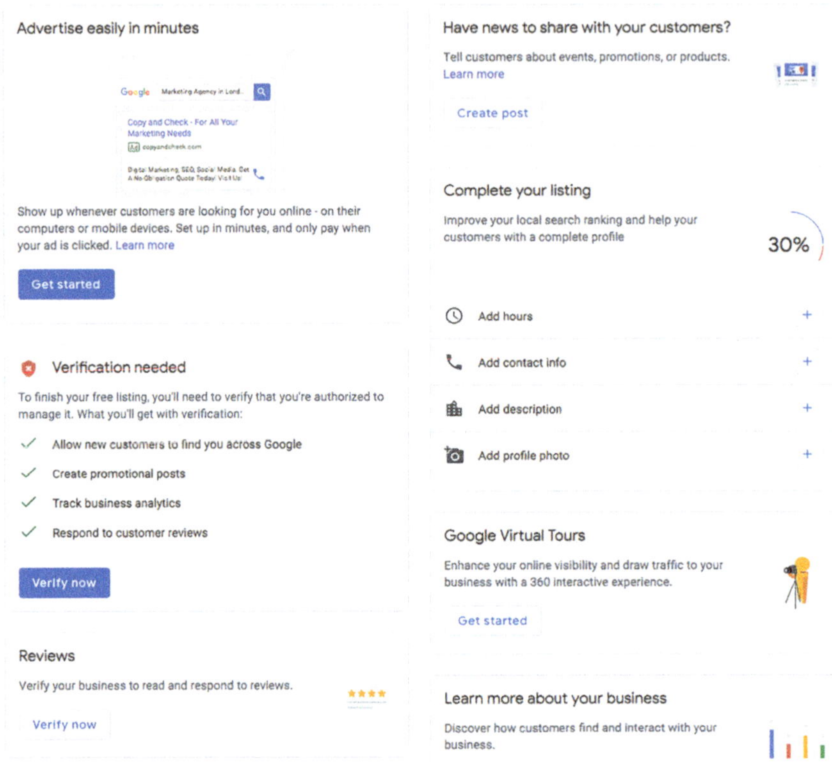

When adding your law firm's details, it's important that the information you provide is consistent with what you show on your website. Make sure that if you're providing phone numbers, you use local area codes to indicate to Google that you are actually a local firm. You should also make a Bing local page.

Reviews

It should come as no surprise that Google favors companies that use its tools, and one specific tool relevant to local SEO is Google reviews. When you generate reviews on Google, you can increase your search rankings. Google reviews directly impact a local business' ranking within the search results.

Positive reviews are not only good for local SEO, but they can help establish your law firm as an industry leader.

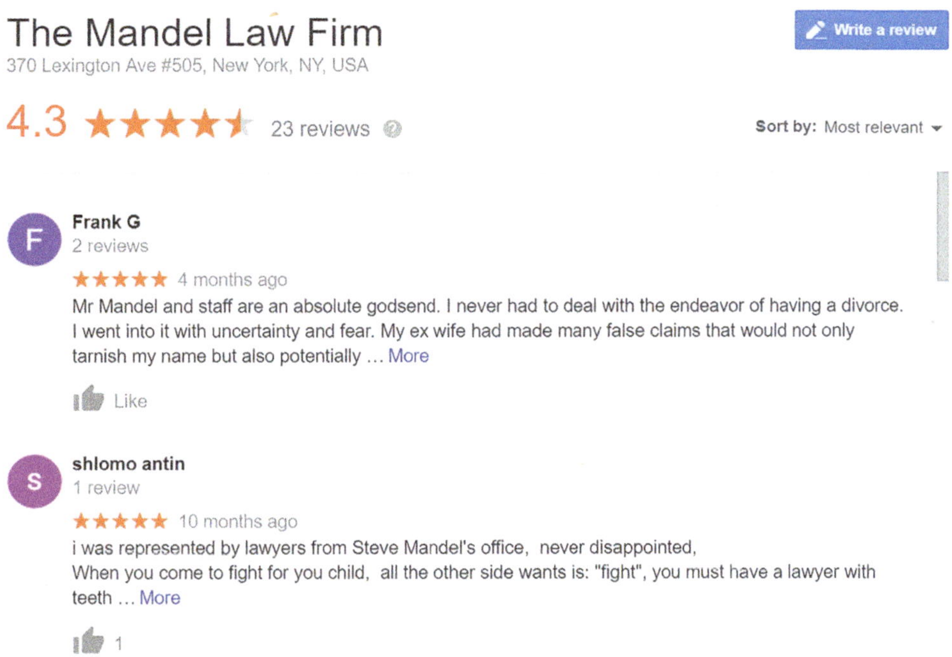

Making use of Google reviews and reaching out to your top clients to request a review is a great way to increase your rankings and protect referrals.

Make note of how many reviews your competitors have, because that will partially determine what you need to do to impress potential customers and satisfy Google.

Whatever you do, don't get fake reviews or pay for them. It's far better to email your customers or send them a postcard with instructions on how to post an online review. You might say something like, "Please avoid using words such as 'best' or 'guarantee' and simply explain what you liked about working with us."

Send them something like this:

Shortened URL to your Google My Business page
facebook.com/attorneyprofile
avvo.com/attorneyprofile

In addition to Google My Business, you should also ask for clients to post reviews on Facebook and AVVO. Yelp and Citysearch are other places where you can get reviews. Set up a Google alert or brand-mention tracking tool and respond to any negative reviews.

The future of local SEO

So, now you know that you need to optimize your website's pages for local search, create a Google My Business page, get into some high-quality online directories using a consistent name, address, and phone number, and ask for some reviews from your clients.

What if I told you that doing these things wasn't enough? You'd probably be mad at me, but I have to tell you it's true. Search engine optimization firms have been doing most of these things for years, so Google has to get way out ahead of it and find ways to prevent only the companies that get good at these tactics from ranking high in searches.

Add to that the fact that there are plenty of unscrupulous lawyers and attorney SEO agencies that are willing to create and post fake reviews and fake profiles in order to game the system. Not only are such efforts bound to fail, but they can pose an ethics violation problem (not good for a law firm!).

Currently, local search comprises about one-third engagement, one-third local data, and one-third traditional SEO like the on-page keyword plus geographic targeting and backlinks.

Get more engagement with a few of these tactics

Add these items to your local SEO checklist:

- Check your Google My Business timeline to see if people are asking questions of your business. You might not be getting notified and you will look like you are missing in action if you don't respond.
- Review your knowledge panel, which is the little box that comes up to the right when people search for your company name. It's your responsibility to keep that updated. If it's out of date, people won't engage with the brand they can't find.
- Google can see if people are opening your emails in Gmail, so do a good job engaging instead of selling customers, just in case Google uses this in the algorithm for the local map listings.
- Work on your social media engagement metrics, even though we are not 100% positive whether Google will use these directly as a ranking factor.

- Set up your major search terms in Zapier for anyone who mentions your keywords in your location, and if there is a way to engage them online, provide helpful information. Make it clear that people can send texts to your business.
- Provide clear travel directions to your firm, so people can visit and meet with you easily.

Takeaways

A local SEO campaign is a great way to increase your overall organic search rankings and make the most of the hyper-targeted traffic you can gain from good local SEO rankings.

Steer clear of gaming the system and prepare for a day when engagement metrics are used even more for local map listings than merely filling out a business profile, managing directory listings, and getting reviews.

There aren't too many law firms that are making serious efforts to get their local SEO right, giving *you* the opportunity to become the industry leader.

For the best results, follow the steps we've listed above and watch your rankings increase.

SEO is powerful, but have you heard that some bloggers have paid little attention to it and yet still manage to have famous blogs? That is because they do advanced and unique content marketing.

Many of these same bloggers have also admitted that they missed a few SEO steps. This resulted in them missing the even better results that the blogs offering valuable content with smart link and SEO strategies were able to get.

If you can stay the course and follow through on the content marketing tips in the next section and use what you have learned about SEO, you will be well on your way to dominating your niche and getting consistent leads.

PART 3
Content Marketing

Overview: How to Do Content Marketing for Your Law Firm

Content — whether it's read, listened to or watched on video — is how you attract your clients, prove your authority, and start to build trust. Content should be the center of your marketing efforts. It is how you reach out and touch your audience, letting them know that you have the ability to solve the problem they're facing.

You've probably heard the phrase "content is king." Yet how do you know if your content is worthy of wearing the crown? And can it break through and be noticed in the very "noisy" online world?

Well, it's not as hard as it seems. In general, good content is enjoyable to consume and its consumers feel it is worthy of sharing with their friends, family, and colleagues. Good content informs, educates, and solves problems.

However, in the end, if it doesn't satisfy Google, it may not be seen much and unseen content might as well have never been created.

While Google continues to be the final arbiter of quality in terms of search engine rankings, when it comes to content, satisfying their requirements isn't difficult if your content is actually good to begin with. Google wants the information that people find on the internet to be relevant and engaging. Therefore, its algorithm rewards what is deemed to be relevant and engaging content with higher rankings in the search results.

Content with higher ranking gets more traffic. More traffic means more visitors to your website and a better chance of converting those visitors into clients. It's that simple.

In the end the cream will rise to the top. So, if you start by producing engaging, interesting, and relevant content to begin with, Google will notice. It's almost a circular formula — good content ranks higher, higher-ranking content tends to be good.

Just remember that the content tactics of five or ten years ago, such as keyword stuffing, "spun" articles that were essentially plagiarized, and short, badly-written blog posts, simply won't cut it today.

So, how does this affect your law firm marketing strategy? Well, when you consider that 50 to 75% of any business' website traffic comes from organic searches, and when you further consider that there are over 3.5 billion searches performed each and every day, you quickly see how important it is to not only get your website ranking highly, but keep it there at the top.

What are the best ways to use content to improve your website's Google ranking while also increasing your law firm's reach? Here are a few guidelines to follow.

The Importance of Relevance

Google is increasingly relying on relevance when it comes to ranking. So much so, that relevance — how important a particular topic is to an intended audience — is becoming much more important than the use of keywords in the body of the content.

This is not to say that keywords have no importance; they are still something of a prerequisite when it comes to ranking. And, while you can technically still rank without them, why wouldn't you want to continue to intelligently use keywords to boost your posts? In the end, topical authority will continue to trump keywords. This is especially true as Google's AI algorithm continues to improve.

So while keywords haven't been totally thrown out of the equation, you'll see more results from content that contains phrases that flow naturally within the context, rather than a set number of occurrences of a specific keyword or keywords.

Here's an example: Let's say you're writing an article about the types of personal injuries that are likely to occur in an auto accident. Used to be, you'd perform keyword research on which terms are most searched each month and then add them as 2% of the article, whether they fit naturally into the context or not.

Today, you'd write a deeply informative article that offers the reader all the information they're looking for in one place. Will highly searched keywords be a part of that article? Yes! That's one of the biggest benefits of offering authentic, organic content — the correct keyword phrases partially occur naturally in the article context.

If you still want to make sure you're hitting the proper keyword phrases within your content, it's easy. By researching your latent semantic indexing (LSI) keywords, you'll find many phrases to use naturally within the context of your content. You can utilize a tool such as *LSI Graph*[44] by entering in a main keyword — "common auto accident injuries" from our example above — and you'll find myriad phrases that can be placed organically within your copy without negatively affecting the flow or readability of the article.

While you definitely want to use the right terms and phrases in your content, don't overthink this. A well-written article designed to convey a deep level of information to your potential client will, by design, incorporate what Google is looking for.

If results are weak even with what you consider great content, you can look at advanced tools to use even better combinations of related keywords.

Deep Content

We've briefly mentioned "deep" content a few times already. Let's define it: Deep content is content which is dense with information. It is an article that contains everything the reader wants or needs to know about a given topic. By its very nature, deep content will tend to be longer than the typical 500-word blog posts of the past.

The importance of deep content can be seen simply by looking at the type of content that shows up in the SERP results. The content in the top ten of a Google search tends to be longer — 1,600+ words on a desktop search, slightly fewer words on a mobile device. It also tends to be more informative, authoritative, and simply more useful.

---

44 *https://lsigraph.com/*

Still not convinced? Take a look at this example.

I know of a 2,000-word article on "best employee termination practices" written in 2010 that had its most successful month in terms of page views in 2017. The monthly views for that article went from 1,000 in 2014, to 2,500 in 2015, to 5,000 in 2017. This article is eight years old, but because it was "deep" before its time, it's now seeing a huge spike in organic traffic. Why? Because Google wants deep content.

Consider being in the shoes of one of your potential clients — what are they searching for and why do they need the information? The best way to get them to make a consultation appointment is to give them all the information they need in one place. If you can answer their questions and address their concerns, they'll see you as the authority on the type of legal representation they need, and the choice to contact you will be a natural one.

Deep content should be a part of your overall website plan for practice, resource, and about pages, and for more informationally dense blog posts as well.

Engage or Suffer the Consequences

Even in a specific practice area, let's say personal injury law, you'll have several different sub-niches within that area. For example, personal injury law could include car accidents, truck accidents, boat accidents, slip-and-fall accidents, and medical malpractice. And within each of those sub-niches, there are several different types of injuries commonly sustained, and possibly common ways to approach the resultant cases.

You should consider what each of these specific potential clients is looking for when they arrive at your website. When you create content, keep the needs of each of these potential clients in mind and write for them. The victim of a slip-and-fall accident at a convenience store will have different needs and will require a different approach than the victim who was hit from behind in traffic by a semi. By tailoring your content to each individual prospect, you will engage with them on a much deeper level.

This is why it's imperative that you know your audience before you set out to produce your content. When you know who you're addressing and why, you can ensure that the information you are giving them is right on target with what that individual's needs. And when you provide that kind of highly targeted information, you'll see the results in your Google ranking.

The reason for this is that Google currently employs the use of RankBrain, an artificial intelligence program that helps Google process search queries. RankBrain allows Google to check metrics such as click-through rate (the number of people who click on your site link in their search results) and dwell rate (how long an individual stays on your site once they click through to it). When you are receiving lots of click-throughs, and people are spending significant time on your site, Google knows that you've engaged your target audience and your site will rank higher.

There are a couple of tactics you can use to increase engagement that are often overlooked even if people have heard about them — developing personas and the "buyer's journey."

Developing personas

Create a document that clearly outlines who you are targeting. It's a great idea to even put a picture into each of the different persona groupings. Have a picture of business owner "Bob" with his likes and interests and where he consumes information. Do the same for marketing "Mary" and other key people that you want to target. Having this information will help you create more engaging content.

The buyer's journey

Customers don't just come to your website once and then buy from you. They are on a journey of doing research in the awareness stage, comparing your firm to another firm in the consideration phase, and finally being ready to contact you in the decision phase.

Your content marketing will benefit greatly if you use a spreadsheet to track your content topics and keywords broken out into stages of the buyer's journey. Google is deepening the level at which they can judge the intent of what someone really wants when they search for a keyword, so you want to make sure you are really clear when developing content on what a customer might be using that page or information for.

To learn more about putting together documented plans for personas and buyers journey mapping, take a look at our worksheets and checklists at *legalmarketingreview.com/downloads*

Resource sections: How to pull it all together

You might be thinking, "So do I really need to create so many kinds of content and with such depth?" Yes, if you want to rank for search terms that cost $100 or even in the future $1,000 per single click as a Google ad.

If you want to scale content marketing, you need lots of it. If you make lots of it, you will end up having lots of content formats, from blog posts and white papers to videos and infographics.

When you have lots of anything on a website, it needs to be presented in a way that users can find and navigate easily for a good user experience. Otherwise, users will bounce off your website and the content will have driven people to you but then lost them.

Our clients do really well when they make a link in the main navigation of their websites labeled "resources" or "learning zone."

When you hover over that link, it should look something like this:

Resources

- Blog
- Articles and FAQs
- Videos
- Podcasts
- E-books and white papers
- Infographics

You can add more to this as you grow and consider using a technique called mega drop-down menus. This lets you add bold category headings to the menu, and even pictures or calls to action.

In the above, by "articles" I mean text pages on the site, not blog posts. They may be more or less the same thing, but sometimes it is useful for content that is a long-term resource to be reachable through an easy-to-navigate section of the website. FAQs are great for voice search SEO and people may want an easy way to get back to them.

Sure, you could add all that in your blog but even with blog categories, it's harder to zip right back to.

Overview: Types of Content for Digital Marketing

In this section, we discuss the main types of content covered in this guide:

1. Main website pages
2. Blogs
3. Guest blogging
4. Video
5. Podcasts
6. Infographics
7. books and white papers
8. Press releases
9. Webinars
10. FAQ pages
11. Topic clusters
12. Link bait
13. Case studies

These should get you started, and you can certainly experiment with many other types of content marketing as appropriate. Here's a quick introduction to each of these types of content. A more detailed exploration of each follows later here in Part 3.

Main website pages

Your website must allow people to easily navigate to find more about what you do and why they should hire you. While the design of the website is important so that you look professional, it's really the content on the site that will do the most in terms of generating leads.

Your home page has to have various trust factors, search engine-friendly text as well as clear links to the most important practice areas.

People often overlook how important it is to work on your "about us" page and to improve the pages for each individual practice area.

If you don't make your website a great resource that is highly optimized, then the rest of your content marketing will be significantly less effective, if not an outright fail.

Blogs

Of course, you have better things to do than attempt to become a professional blogger. But that doesn't mean you can't think like one when you produce the content that'll be responsible for bringing clients in the door.

A successful blogger thinks like a publisher. Your aim is to publish something good — not something mediocre just to satisfy an arbitrary timeline. While you should be putting out content consistently, how often you do so is up to you. With the move toward deeper content, blog posts and articles are taking longer to create — around 3 hours and 16 minutes on average according to OrbitMedia. A lawyer's busy schedule dictates that content taking this long to create simply won't be published as frequently as less-deep content. But quality will win over quantity every time.

It's important to mix it up on your site. Write long, in-depth articles, alternated with slightly shorter blog posts. Sometimes, what you have to say can succinctly be conveyed in a few hundred words. Other times, if you're tackling a deeply complicated legal subject, you'll need to put in more time, effort, and of course, more words. Remember, a well-written 1,000-word post will always trump a 2,000-word post larded with irrelevance and fluff.

With that said, content with 1,600 to 1,800 words or more is what ranks best on average. So think hard about how you can add leads through depth, not fluff.

Guest blogging

Your blog is likely to have a small number of visitors when you first begin. If you can share your content or blog on larger sites like the National Law Review or Forbes, you will get your valuable content in front of a much larger audience. Keep in mind, it's not easy to get onto the highest-profile sites without some serious thought leader credibility.

Guest blogging was abused by search engine optimization firms because they did it just to get links on crappy websites.

Done right, however, guest blogging is a lot like other public relations techniques and requires careful outreach to journalists or the owners of blogs. You'll need to pitch yourself and the content your propose to share by sending them an email that explains why you are a valuable resource for their readers and offer them a "teaser" blurb or two about ideas that would be relevant and useful to their audience. Just keep in mind that demonstrating the level of thought leadership that gets you onto Forbes doesn't happen overnight and is not a one-off effort.

Many of the famous bloggers in the world in general were initially more focused on this tactic and then pulled the audience over into their own blogs.

Video

Law firms are finally realizing that video is one way to bridge the trust gap and get SEO rankings at the same time. By viewing a video, a potential client can get a feel for the personality of an attorney before making that all-important first call to schedule an appointment.

Law firms can utilize video to "humanize" their firm and make them more approachable. Videos are also more likely to keep a potential client on your website, and that can help increase your Google ranking as well. Not only is YouTube the world's second-largest search engine, but it is also shaping up to be the most popular social network.

Podcasts

Podcasts are audio interviews that let you share your thought leadership easily in your own unique voice. Podcasts are becoming more popular as people want to just click and listen while they drive or watch while they work out.

Podcasts get you up on iTunes and give you something of substance to share on social media, but they also boost your SEO, especially if you add the transcripts (or at the very least, a solid description subtly sprinkled with keywords).

Infographics

Infographics are a superb way to convey information in an engaging manner. Statistics and graphics relevant to your law practice that your potential clients would find interesting can be turned into eye candy. For example, imagine that you are trying to explain to one of your prospects the many stages of securing a trademark. Visual representation of this can go a long way in helping people understand what is involved and how it would be wise to hire an attorney to help them through the complex process.

In fact, infographics are one of the top three to five ways that search engine optimization firms get links to their client's websites, so don't overlook this tactic.

E-books and white papers

Most people aren't ready to buy from you when they pop onto your website after a quick Google search. They are researching and if you offer them something for free, like a downloadable e-book in exchange for their contact information (often just a name and an email address), you are much more likely to reach the 95% of people who are not yet ready to fill out the contact form on your website or call you directly.

If you are already blogging, then it's a shame not to repurpose that material and turn that content into something that people can download.

Press releases

Writing and submitting a press release online is a great way to announce important events and changes at your law firm. Don't issue press releases for minor things, but when you have something substantive and specific dates or milestones to share, sending out a press release (and posting it on your own website, perhaps on a "news and events" page) can get you in front of new websites in a matter of hours.

Paid options include Business Wire, PR Newswire, and similar reputable services. They are not cheap but they can be helpful in getting your press release in front of the right audiences. In addition to putting a press release on your own site, send it to selected local media outlets and share it on social media platforms where you and your firm are active.

Occasionally your press releases will get mentioned on larger news sites. If this happens, you can feature a link to that site on your homepage to show credibility.

Press releases that you submit online to a site like BusinessWire also show up in the search engine results and can drive calls from customers or journalists directly.

Webinars

A webinar is just a seminar that you offer over the internet instead of in person. GoToWebinar is a great tool and reasonably easy to set up. You'll need to put together a PowerPoint presentation and then deliver it online while managing some technical elements of GoToWebinar software.

If you are accustomed to presenting seminars in front of in-person groups, it may seem strange to give a seminar online and not be able to see the looks on people's faces as you share your exciting information.

The software for webinars usually has a feature that allows webinar attendees to ask questions or comment by typing text, allowing some degree of interaction, but it is not exactly the same as doing an in-person seminar because you can't get a feel for body language, etc.

Webinars give you a great opportunity to capture prospects' contact information by enticing them with a free event. Webinars are good, and co-branded webinars are even better. You can find an industry association or other organization in your niche and offer to provide a jointly presented webinar to their audience. The trust that you get from doing this and the fact that you get in front of an audience you wouldn't otherwise have had access to makes this tactic very powerful.

FAQ pages and voice search optimization

Many clients ask us how they can do better at showing up in voice search results. Whether people are asking a question on a mobile phone or querying their Google Home or Amazon Alexa devices, if you want to be these robots' favorite, there are some very specific things you need to do.

One of the best ways to have an organized strategy for voice search is to have frequently asked questions (FAQ) pages where you pose common questions and answer them succinctly.

Beyond that, you need some technical elements like schema markup (which we will get into later in this guide). Google will not rank your Q&A section if your website does not have topical and link authority, and it all starts with quality FAQ pages. This type of content can help not only attract visitors but also keep people on your website longer.

Topic clusters

Topic clusters are one of the most effective current search engine optimization strategies I know of. Writing a bunch of blog posts is not nearly as effective as writing a comprehensive page about a topic and then writing clusters of blog, video, and podcast content that interlink, forming a guide that is much more powerful when all the individual pieces are collected together.

Wikipedia is a good example of this. They rank highly in search results because they have long, detailed pages on critical topics and then interlink to all the relevant subtopics.

For your law firm, you need a pillar page, which is a long general page about the topic with one paragraph each for a dozen items, which you then link to shorter content about the subtopics.

Link bait

Sometimes you just need to step outside the box of the basic content you are creating on your blog. You need to create something that really stands out and makes people want to share and link to it. We call that "link bait."

Infographics and industry survey data make great link bait. A piece of content like the "ultimate guide to protecting your intellectual property" can be link bait. You might do this once a quarter or maybe even just once a year to build links.

Once you create the content, you must persuade people to link to it. Sending emails to people who link to similar content and buying social media ads to promote the content are just a couple of ways to make your link bait more visible. We have had entire marketing campaigns be transformed by a single piece of link bait that lifted the rankings not only of that page, but of the entire website.

Case studies

In the middle stage of the marketing funnel, people are comparing you to other firms. It's important to allow them to see the smiling faces of your customers and the stories of their success. It can be as simple as writing a paragraph that summarizes the background and the client's challenge, the strategy, and the results.

If you do it right, these case studies will pop up in Google searches and give you something to share on social media. You can use Facebook ads and/or LinkedIn ads to drive people to your case study content.

Conclusion

Focus on creating the highest-quality, most information-dense content at regular intervals, and you'll reap the rewards in your Google rankings —- and in the number of appointments you schedule with clients.

Think in terms of campaigns. Every major topic or practice area you want to promote should make use of the following content types:

1. A topic cluster – a series of blog posts interlinked from a pillar / general page on that topic
2. An e-book
3. Calls to action offering the e-book
4. A landing page for the e-book

5. A video
6. A podcast
7. An infographic
8. A deep piece of content worth linking to

If you want to go a step further, you should also create a quality "thank you" page that people hit after they fill out your forms. These thank-you pages will have links to more quality information and they also get set up in Google Analytics as the touch-point required to track a goal conversion. In addition, they can trigger email marketing automation "drip" campaigns using a tool like HubSpot.

These drip emails will send even more powerful content, such as a link to a relevant blog post, then a case study, then a request to talk. Such emails go out every three to five days automatically, so you are nurturing prospects as you sleep.

Content marketing is very sophisticated now and artificial intelligence is only making it deeper and more complex to organize.

Automated tools are great and information flows freely on how to do these things, but it all comes down to having an organized process and a team of people designated to handle specific tasks.

It may feel overwhelming, but once you get into the flow, it becomes more of a rinse-and-repeat process, where creativity and insight are more important than just the tactical factors.

If your firm has something to say, don't let law firms with less experience do all these things that I have outlined; they'll come up in search and social media ahead of your firm, and capture leads that just might be your ideal customers. Now let's turn to an in-depth look at how to organize your website's pages to create rich soil in which effective content will grow.

Types of Content for Digital Marketing and How to Use Them In Depth

1. Your Main Website Pages

Back in 1995 we had to convince people that websites were important. Today there are very few people left who don't understand that your website is at the heart of all of your marketing, yet websites are often left up to committees and people who don't study what will simultaneously be truly useful for customers, increase leads, and satisfy Google.

Here are some useful insights we've built up over almost 25 years of building and marketing websites.

Home page

Your home page should include your unique selling proposition (USP), thought leadership, a few testimonials, logos of media where you have been featured, trust badges (such as your AVVO rating and/or Superlawyers designations), and key practice areas to make it easy to navigate. You should also feature one or two practice areas where you really dig deep into content.

You should have a call-to-action strategy that includes not only your phone number and a free consultation form. Ideally, the top-of-the-funnel call to action (where 95% of visitors are in the funnel) should offer something like an e-book, along with more interactive elements like live chat.

Tools like UserTesting.com, HotJar heat mapping, and Google Optimize can help make sure you have a winning combination of elements on your home page

You will also want some text for search engine optimization. A good website designer can make all of these things work together and give you great search engine results and a streamlined user experience that helps you get more leads.

About us pages

About us pages are one of the most critical parts of your website. Ninety percent of the time, they are the second most-visited page after the home page, although for law firms, bio pages about individual lawyers jump just ahead of them. The about us page should share more "who you are" than just "what you do," because people buy from other people they know, like, and trust.

It's fine to include the number of years your firm has been in business and the highlights of your firm's accomplishments. Just don't make it all factual information; let people know what your mission is. If you have some quirky pictures of your team at a company outing or charity event, this is a great place to use them, to give the about us page some personality.

Bio pages

It's time to rethink the bios of team members on your website, especially if those bios are outdated and dry. People really do look at your team before hiring your firm, in most cases. Your bio should tell your story and show your part in the firm's overall brand and unique selling proposition.

You will make a much better impression upon potential new customers if your bio includes elements like a list of blog posts that you have written, a short video where people can see and hear your style, any books or e-books that you have published, and/or any speaking engagements, media features, or webinars that you are part of.

Be sure to include contact information and make it easy for people to connect with you on LinkedIn and/or highlight other social media platforms where you are active.

Your news and events page

Law firms and attorneys that are featured in the media have much more authority, and therefore garner more trust, than those that are not spotlighted.

If you like, you can add a page for press releases, a page for clips of (or links to) your media features, as well as a page for journalists looking to easily download your logo, short and long descriptions of the firm, and photos of attorneys.

A good designer can add it all on one page or make a nice sub-navigation to allow visitors to access all this information. However it is arranged, be sure it is easily accessible and shows that you and your team are currently considered thought leaders in key practice areas.

Resource pages

What's the difference between a resource page and a blog post? A resource page is an evergreen piece of content simply put on a regular website page instead of on the blog.

FAQ pages

FAQ content and some types of articles are useful to have on resource pages instead of in blog posts. Half of all searches will be voice searches by 2020, according to ComScore, so having FAQ pages where you answer common questions is essential. These then need to be easily accessible in a text resources section of your overall resources area.

Testimonials and case study pages

The secret behind marketing is giving clients the type of information that they need to make wise purchasing decisions. Client testimonials and case studies are crucial in encouraging new visitors to your website to believe and trust in your site. People hate being "sold to," or at least, they don't want to be sold to in the way they were in recent years.

Rather than expecting customers to "take your word" when they visit your website, client testimonials and customer reviews let prospective new customers hear the other side of the story from real customers. If your firm has any drawbacks, rest assured that some previous clients have talked about perceived flaws, but you can speak to how you overcame those, and glowing testimonials from satisfied clients can help win people over.

I personally think it's a good idea to have practice area-specific testimonials sprinkled on the pages they relate to. I also think it's a good idea to have a separate testimonials page that links to case studies / verdicts and settlements as well as client reviews.

Adding reviews to your law firm brand's strategy is something you need to consider if you are interested in improving your law firm's SEO and conversions. Customer reviews can help you understand, as an employer, who are the most effective lawyers in your firm. Customers will almost always talk about the experience they had when working with a specific lawyer in your firm.

According to a survey by *Zendesk*,[45] around 90% of respondents claimed that the sites that had positive testimonials influenced their buying decision, while 86% claimed that the negative reviews influenced their decision.

Contact pages

At the top of any contact pages, include a clickable link that allows prospects and clients to call you from a mobile phone, as well as your law firm's street address. Make sure it matches your NAP listings (name, address, and phone number).

Optimize this for your main key phrase (like "employment Law Firm in Brooklyn NY") in the title tag and the heading for the page.

You can also connect to a Google map and provide directions.

Add a contact form but also allow people to call or email you. Include a friendly heading on the form that invites visitors to interact. Try wording like: "Ask us any questions. We're here to help." You might also test using headings like "Free consultations" and "Request an appointment" to see what works best.

Thank-you pages that appear after filling out a form

Even though you can do tricks with coding to track form submissions without an actual thank-you page, we prefer to have real thank-you pages for the following reasons:

- Thank-you pages make it super-easy to track conversion goals in Google Analytics.
- These pages are a great place to add links to valuable content and your social media profiles, instead of just sending these highly engaged people off to other people's websites.
- These pages should be the starting point that triggers your marketing automation drip email "nurturing" campaigns.

---

45 *https://www.zendesk.com/resources/customer-service-and-lifetime-customer-value/*

Law firm optimized practice page areas

When putting your website together, how much thought went into your practice area pages? Did you rush them at the end? Or did you take time to make sure they outlined the key issues in your industry and positioned your firm in the best way?

Too often, these pages are haphazardly put together, not optimized for SEO, and thus don't provide any serious benefit for the firm.

Let's look at what makes a good practice area page and how you can optimize it for success.

Should your practices and industries be separate?

If your firm has a smaller focus, such as personal injury law for businesses, you're lucky in the sense that your practice areas and your industries are quite narrow. People coming to your website can quickly establish what you do and whether or not you're right for them.

But what if you operate within multiple industries and have a range of different practice areas? It can quickly become confusing for your audience to know what you do and whether or not you'd be able to help in their specific situation. That's why an optimized overview page and then specific pages for each practice area are so important. When people see powerful pages on subtopics they know you can meet their needs better than a firm with a weak 300-word page.

Here's an example for a firm that has several specialized practice areas. Here is how you would arrange to have a page for each practice area as well as sub-pages for the most important ones.

```
yourlawfirm.com
yourlawfirm.com/practices-areas
    yourlawfirm.com/mergers-acquisitions
    yourlawfirm.com/taxation
    yourlawfirm.com/employment-law
        /discrimination
        /wrongful-termination
        /unpaid-wages
```

You then link the sub-pages of employment law with the main employment law master page. You also interlink blog and resource content with these pages.

We used to always recommend you add the sub-folder into the URLs for SEO "silo" best practices: yourlawfirm.com/**employment-law**/discrimination. But with the advent of topic cluster strategy and given that short URLs rank better and get clicked more, we feel it is okay to just use yourlawfirm.com/discrimination.html or something similar.

As long as you do a good job of interlinking related content, Google will understand you have a lot of good content on that one topic and rank you properly.

By having a number of pages and resources on your website, you build topical authority and will more likely be able to compete with sites that are 100% about that one practice area.

Forget technical language

Instead of writing about a long list of practice areas in a way that your potential clients might not understand, try to writing using less technical language so they can decide for themselves whether or not you're right for them.

Make it easy to navigate

In the example below, this law firm uses icons to help users understand which industries they serve.

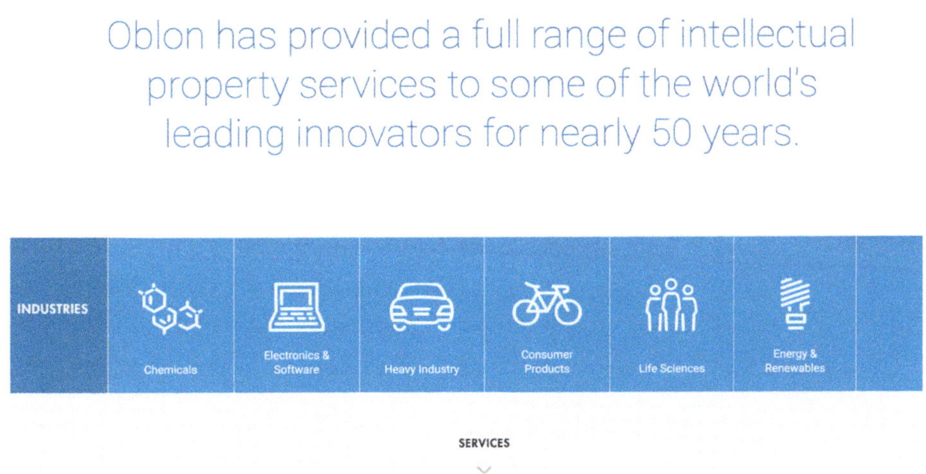

As a user of this site, all you need to do is click through to the industry you're in and you're presented with further information that's directly relevant to you.

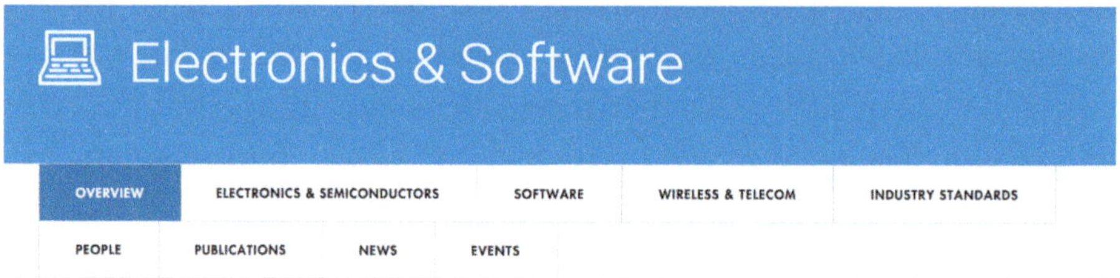

If people don't know what industries you work with, how do they know if you'll be able to help them?

Be careful about duplicate content

One of the crucial mistakes law firms make when putting together their separate industry and practice-area pages is using duplicate content. What usually happens is that someone will produce some great copy for an industry page and want to also use it on a practice area page, just in case the user doesn't read the first piece of content.

However, duplicate content can affect your SEO negatively and should be avoided. To combat this, use internal linking to link back to any relevant information your clients might need. This will improve your site architecture as well as increase the amount of time someone spends on your website.

Optimizing your practice areas

There is a wide range of steps you should take to optimize your practice area pages. One of the crucial things you need to think about is search engines.

If you are an estate planning lawyer in Delaware, then when someone searches for "estate planning lawyer Delaware" you want your website to show up. But more than just having the website show up in the search results, you want the page the user clicks on to contain enough relevant information that your visitor knows they made the right choice.

If they're in any way confused by the content on your website, they won't get in touch to find out more. Instead, they'll simply hit the "back" button and find a different firm to look at.

To come up in the top five search results, you have to look at the word count of the top pages and how many links the page and site have. If your site is not comparable, it won't likely rank well enough to bring leads to your firm.

If all of the top three to five ranking sites contain over 1,000 words of helpful content — including interlinking with supporting sub-pages and blog content — and you only have 300 to 500 words about how great you are, don't be the least bit shocked if you don't do well in Google.

Make a good first impression

When you've caught a prospective client's attention on search engines, you need to make your page attractive. Your practice area pages are there solely to attract attention of new clients. Use this as an opportunity to speak directly to your clients throughout your copy. Make sure you communicate what you do, how you do it, why you do it, and why someone should choose your firm over your competitors.

When deciding on the written copy you'll use, picture your ideal client in your mind. What might they be feeling when searching for a lawyer? If they're going through a messy divorce, they might be feeling frustrated or hurt. You need to use your practice area pages to let them know you empathize with them and understand the struggles they're going through.

At the end of all that, encourage them to reach out. Tell your prospective clients what to do next. Should they call you for a free consultation? Should they use the form on your website to enquire further? Whatever action you want them to take, let them know.

Answer all the burning questions

It's very likely that prospective clients will have a range of questions they need answered. They also might be looking at a number of different law firms and the practice area page is usually one of the first thing they use as a comparison point.

By the time the prospective client has viewed your practice or industry page they should know:

1. What issues you deal with
2. What the process of becoming your client involves

3 What would happen to them if they didn't take action

4 What benefit they'd have from choosing you over your competitor

A practice area done right is often what will compel a prospective client to reach out to you further. You understand the significance of these pages. But if your website doesn't include well-executed practice area pages, any potential client will be turned off and seek out your competitors.

Follow the tips above to make sure your practice and industry area pages are optimized and bringing you new leads.

Takeaways

It's the role of your law firm's website to explain to anyone who lands on it exactly what kind of law you practice and why someone should hire you.

Your firm's website also will make or break your SEO if it does not have enough quality pages or if it is hard to navigate.

By using your site's main pages to dive deeply into the content that's important to your prospects and clients and by using usertesting.com to get feedback, you can build a website that people love.

While your main website pages are critical, they will also rank much better when you add a blog to really amp up your authority for customers and Google. In the next section we explain how to write blog posts that aren't just for show.

2. Law Firm Blogging 101

As you know, the more people know about your law firm and the work you do, the better chance you have of them reaching out to you. But how do you expect them to reach out to you if they don't know you exist in the first place?

For many lawyers and law firms alike, getting that coveted reach among people looking for attorneys is difficult.

For starters, when you search for "law firm + your area" there are usually thousands of different options.

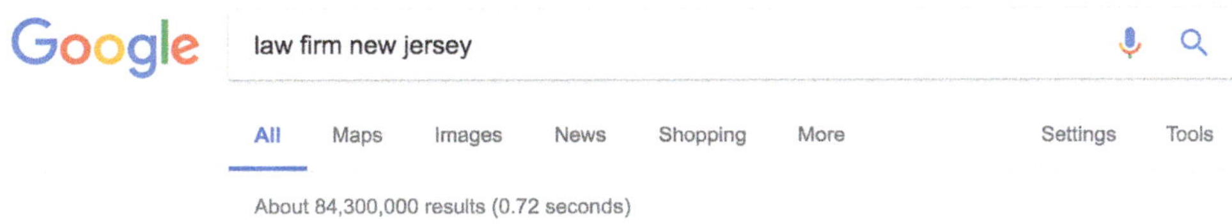

How do you expect to compete against all of these options and even appear on the first page of search results?

Well, you already know the secret to appearing on the first page of Google is to develop a strong SEO strategy, but we'll now discuss how (and why) blogging should be a crucial element of that strategy.

In this section, you'll find out why blogging is beneficial for showcasing your expertise as a law firm and why you should use it to help you appear on the first page of Google search results.

Before you start blogging

Before you start blogging, you need to understand a little bit about how it works in terms of driving traffic to your website. If you already have a sizable audience, you shouldn't have any difficulty when starting your blog. You simply write your blog post, push it out to your audience and wait for the traffic to roll in. But what if you don't yet have an audience?

Building an audience takes time and is often is the result of multiple factors. If you don't see any significant results after three months, don't stop. Keep going, because eventually, consistent blogging will reap rewards.

It can often take a couple years to generate any sort of significant traffic. Geraldine DeRuiter, wife of SEO platform MOZ's former CEO Rand Fishkin, spoke about how it took her two years to generate significant traffic to her blog.

Don't let this discourage you, however, as It can happen faster and one of the benefits of blogging is that the content is there forever. With paid ads, when you stop paying money, you stop generating traffic. With blogging, you can generate traffic forever.

Where should I put my law firm's blog?

I once wrote an article on The National Law Review website and Kevin from Lexblog chimed in and disagreed with one of the points. He said that putting a lawyer's blog on the firm's main website is a mistake because nobody cares to read a corporate blog as much as they like a niche blog.

In some ways I agree with this, but it's not always practical to have multiple websites and multiple budgets to optimize each.

We have driven tens of millions of dollars in leads with both strategies — having separate URLs (like a 500-page mesothelioma website we wrote and created) and alternatively, working successfully with plenty of law firms where their blog is part of their main website.

The advantage of having your blog on your main website is that your practice area pages and your local map rankings will get better because the main website has authority. The authority is driven by the links to the valuable and engaging blog content that you will create. That is priceless for proving that your main website deserves high search rankings.

The advantage of having your blog on a separate domain, like yourtrademarkblog.com or something along those lines, is that it is only on one topic. People researching that topic will find your site more engaging and interesting if it covers that topic completely and is more personal than some of the dull law firm blogs out there.

If you have it in the budget, you should do both. If there is no blog or interesting content on your law firm's primary website, you will miss out on leads for people searching for law firms and not just the pain points that a separate blog would address. That said, having an authority site on a niche topic can be extremely powerful, and if you go that route, put the best content there that you can.

Here are examples of some authority sites that aren't exactly just blogs, but they show the value of dominating a topical area.

Birth Injury Guide (*https://www.birthinjuryguide.org*) is a niche site that ranks for 54,288 keywords. If you had to buy those keywords as Google ads they would cost $990,000 a month.

Asbestos.com (*https://www.asbestos.com*) ranks for 62,000 keywords worth $6.3 million a month if you had to buy them as ads. Who has over $6 million a month in their paid search budget to compete using advertising instead of content marketing?

Findlaw.com (*https://www.findlaw.com*) has 3.4 million keywords ranking that are worth $29 million a month!

Here are examples of various types of legal blogs on and off-site (in terms of being part of a firm's main website or not).

Above the Law (*https://abovethelaw.com/*) ranks for 165,191 keywords worth $165,000 a month if paid for in Google ads.

China Law Blog (*https://www.chinalawblog.com/*) ranks for 15,303 keywords worth $6,300 a month if you had to buy those keywords as Google ads.

Hillary Bricken's Canna Law Blog (cannalawblog.com) ranks for 21,422 keywords worth $6,600 a month.

And did you know that Fox Rothschild has over 30 topical blogs!

Mintz.com ranks for 45,863 keywords worth $68,900 a month in ads. Here is an example of an article on their main websites insight center that ranks for 880 keywords: *https://www.mintz.com/insights-center/viewpoints/2226/2017-06-**intermittent-leave-under-fmla-basics***. And, it drives 2.48% of the site's traffic.

This one ranks for fewer keywords (780) but drives 18% of the website's traffic: *www.mintz.com/insights-center/viewpoints/2226/2017-06-**intermittent-leave-under-fmla-basics***.

Below are some of the keywords that have an extremely high cost per click in Google ads where Mintz is ranking organically in the top 100 results. In order to rank better for these keywords, they need to keep adding content and/or start niche blogs on other domain names, if it's in the budget.

Keyword	**CPC**
frcp 20	$195.79
white collar defense lawyer	$191.15
samuels law group	$171.73
health care medicare and medicaid	$170.53

california state tax attorney	$144.64
long term disability attorney nj	$132.20
tax attorneys los angeles ca	$109.42
finra suitability rule	$104.17
cab boston treatment center	$100.45
famous new york criminal lawyers	$96.75
anthem data breach litigation	$94.90
pro rata formula insurance	$91.37
young jenkins attorney dallas	$90.98
seattle tax lawyer	$89.77
lee bankruptcy law firm dallas tx	$89.57
best seattle divorce attorney	$89.27
erisa attorney san diego	$86.77
amex discovery card	$82.79
ford greene attorney	$78.98
attorney big al	$74.20
long term disability attorney florida	$74.17
sec whistleblower attorney	$74.03
doj antitrust	$73.76
tax attorney ct	$73.72

Considering the high cost per click, whether you want your main website to rank or have the ultimate engagement with an off-site blog, the return on investment will be there if you stick it out long enough to rank in the top ten, where almost all of the clicks are.

A website called *Blog Metrics* has some interesting rankings of legal blogs that you might peruse for inspiration.[46]

So, in the end, where you put the blog depends on your goals. Whichever way you do it, the most important thing is the quality of the content.

46 *https://www.blogmetrics.org/law*

What should you blog about?

When it comes to what you should blog about, you have a number of options. You might choose to blog about your law firm itself, the types of cases you've been working on, and the plans you have for the future. This can help attract new lawyers to your firm and also give your potential clients a good understanding of what you're all about.

Second, you might decide to blog about legal topics to demonstrate your expertise. The benefit of doing this is that if your content performs well, there's a good chance you'll show up when people have topical questions.

If you're blogging to generate interest from potential clients, then the most crucial thing you need to think about is what type of questions your prospects need answered, what searches they might conduct, and what keeps them up at night.

For example, a potential client might ask "How much does a divorce attorney cost?" or "What should I wear to court?" These are search queries that people who need a lawyer might make, but if your site is just optimized for the search term "law firm + your city," you'll never show up in these search results.

The key with these sorts of searches is for your audience to take the following path:

> They search for an answer to a question they have.
>> They come across a blog post on your website that helps them answer their question.
>>> They value your firm as a useful source of information.
>>>> They bookmark your site for when they're ready to work with an attorney.

Here is a list of blog topic ideas from Tim Baran of Rocket Matter to keep you thinking.

1. Current court decisions
2. Legal technology
3. Practice area news, information, and resources
4. Legal marketing
5. Process and productivity
6. Legal writing and research tips
7. The business of law
8. Current trends and issues

9. Attorney wellness
10. Topical newsletters
11. Curation of content from other sources

Who should write your blogs?

When it comes to actually writing your blog posts, you have a number of options. You can write them all in-house, you can outsource the writing, or you can opt for a combination of the first two. Here are some of the benefits (and considerations) of each tactic.

In-house

If you decide to write your blog content in-house, you have a unique advantage as you already have a wealth of knowledge. You practice law every day, so putting accurate content on the page should come easily to you. However, you are probably very busy. As such, do you really have time to write blog posts? Beyond that, while you possess industry knowledge and legal expertise, do you understand how to write in a way that informs, delights, and entertains your readers? If you don't have this capability, you'll struggle to retain your readers.

Outsource

Another option is to outsource the blog writing and blog management work to someone outside your firm. This can be a great way to build your blog content, especially if you have the budget to hire a good writer. Be sure to do your due diligence and check that the writer in question either has a background in law or enough experience writing in the legal space to create the type of content you want.

The worst thing you could do would be to hire a writer who produces factually incorrect content that actually ***harms*** your SEO efforts and your law firm's reputation.

Mixture

The third option and the one chosen by many companies is to use a mixture of in-house and outsourced content. In many cases, the split is that the lawyer chooses the topics and themes of the content (and sometimes provides rough drafts or bullet points), and the hired writer does the actual writing. If the lawyer chooses the topics, be sure they have been well researched by your SEO and competitive analysis team.

This is a good solution, as it means you get to impart your wisdom via a blog, but you can focus on your important legal work while your writer produces the content.

Another way to create blog content is to offer videos and podcasts that also include the transcripts of what was said. Potentially more importantly, this content can then be repurposed by your writer(s) into in-depth articles and blog posts.

Here are the basics of lawyer blogging and legal SEO best practices

1. Tie your blog topic ideas into your business goals.
2. Create a list of content styles that you will use, such as how to, trends, or evergreen content. HubSpot has mastered this and has a great deal of variety on their blog because they present content in many styles.
3. Make sure you know who you are targeting by developing personas.
4. Do keyword research and select a primary keyword phrase to put in the title tag. Also document LSI or related keywords for the writers to sprinkle in.
5. In your keyword research, specify what stage of the buyer's journey each keyword relates to, such as awareness, consideration, and decision.
6. Add the keyword phrase and a unique selling position for the post into the meta-description to increase the click-through rate.
7. Use the keyword phrase in the headline of the post, but most importantly make it engaging. Write 10 to 15 headlines and pick the best one.
8. Use H1 tags for headlines.
9. Repeat the main keyword phrase early in the blog post, ideally in the first sentence.
10. Put other related keywords in H2 tags but do not repeat the main keyword phrase in these.

11 Start your blog posts in an engaging way, with a story and a summary of what readers will learn. Empathy is the key.

12 Consider using the inverted pyramid format, where you include the key information at the beginning of the post.

13 Make sure your content is the appropriate length for the topic. Keep in mind that 1600 to 2000+ words is a good target length, instead of the basic 500- to 1000-word posts.

14 Make your blog post scan- and skim-friendly by using short sentences, paragraphs of two to five sentences, and bulleted and numbered lists.

15 Link out to other influential websites to show Google that you're connected to other experts.

16 Send an email to the experts you quoted, letting them know they are included in your blog post.

17 Link to other pages on your site.

18 If you use WordPress, select a primary keyword phrase in the Yoast SEO plugin.

19 Use Alt tags to describe images.

20 When you publish a post, do not publish using "admin" as the author. Instead, use a specific attorney's name (even if the post was ghostwritten).

21 Identify the author of the post using schema markup, which can be done with a WordPress plugin.

22 Encourage people to share and link to your content using social media "share" buttons.

23 After every blog post goes live, share it on social media and boost it with paid social advertising.

24 Send emails to your list and to influencers that like this type of content.

25 Add a call to action at the end, in the middle and/or in the right-hand column, directing visitors to a page where they can download an e-book or white paper, which helps you get more subscribers and leads.

26 Use marketing automation to drip emails to those who signed up to have your firm send them more related blog posts, downloads, case studies, and requests to chat.

27 Use MeetEdgar.com or Hootsuite to reshare your posts so you share them more than once.

Takeaways

You might have questions about who should produce your content and what content you should write about. This section has offered you some food for thought about the best approach to take.

However, if you're questioning whether or not a blog strategy is right for your firm, the answer is always YES if you want your law firm's search engine optimization to work and be positioned as an authority.

Start blogging today and over time you can cut back on paid ads.

Now, suppose that your website and blog are great, but your traffic levels are low. Here's how to add some "Miracle Gro" to your web presence —- use guest blogging to get in front of larger audiences.

3. Guest Blogging Opportunities for Law Firms

As a new or established law firm, it's not enough to have just a website and/or social channels. The reason is that your reach can only go so far. When you launch your new website, or you want to gain more exposure for an existing website, it can be hard to find that initial traction and encourage people to visit you. What's more, if they don't know who you are, why should they give you the time of day?

One solution you might try is paid advertisements, either on social media sites like Facebook, Twitter, or LinkedIn, or through search engines like Google. The issue, though, is you'll be competing with a range of other law firms similar to yours, in an arena where the costs per click (CPC) are among the *highest for any industry.*[47]

The solution?

If you want to increase your organic reach, set yourself up as an authority in your area of practice or geographic location, and try guest blogging as a solution. Read on to learn exactly what guest blogging is, why it's useful, and which sites may be happy to take submissions from law firms like yours.

---

[47] *https://searchenginewatch.com/2016/05/31/the-most-expensive-100-google-adwords-keywords-in-the-us/*

What is guest blogging?

Guest blogging is a method used by bloggers and websites to increase traffic to their own site. This can also work in the same way if you allow other people to post content on your blog.

It works well for small and large businesses alike. To start, create a list of potential sites to which you want to submit your content ideas. (Skip ahead if you already know what guest blogging is and just want to see the list of potentially useful sites for legal guest blogging.) Then you reach out to each individual site (including online publications) and submit your ideas. If your pitch gets a "yes," you'll need to write the blog post.

When you do submit your guest post, avoid being "salesy." Keep it informative and useful. You may be allowed to link back to your site within the post, or you might just have a byline (a line or two of text at the end of the post with your name and a brief professional bio). However, if your post is full of sentences like: "Click here for the best personal injury law firm in New York," people will be turned off by that and will ignore your content (if your overly promotional post is even allowed).

Ensure you're adding value for the audience of the publication or website you're pitching to and they're likely to click through to your website to see what else you have to say.

Why is it important for your law firm?

There are two main reasons to consider guest blogging.

The first is authority. When you develop content for a site other than your own, it helps expose your website, blog, and business to a whole new audience. It also helps establish you as a thought leader in your industry. When you provide value, as explained above, you have the opportunity to say something new to a whole new community, some of whom are then more likely to want to build a relationship with you or subscribe to your firm's content.

Even though you've posted the content on an external site, it doesn't mean you shouldn't think about promotion too. Once it's been published, share the blog post on your own social networks.

The second reason is backlinks. Guest blogging is a great way to increase your domain authority by having a number of high-profile websites linking back to your site.

Should you buy links or pay for guest blogging?

If you're hoping to use guest blogging as a way to boost your SEO and generate backlinks, one thing you should definitely refrain from doing is buying backlinks. Google is especially against people generating backlinks by paying or gaming the system with "fake" or made-up networks of cheap blogs.

If Google does assume you're paying for guest blogging, you'll be penalized and all your efforts will be for nothing.

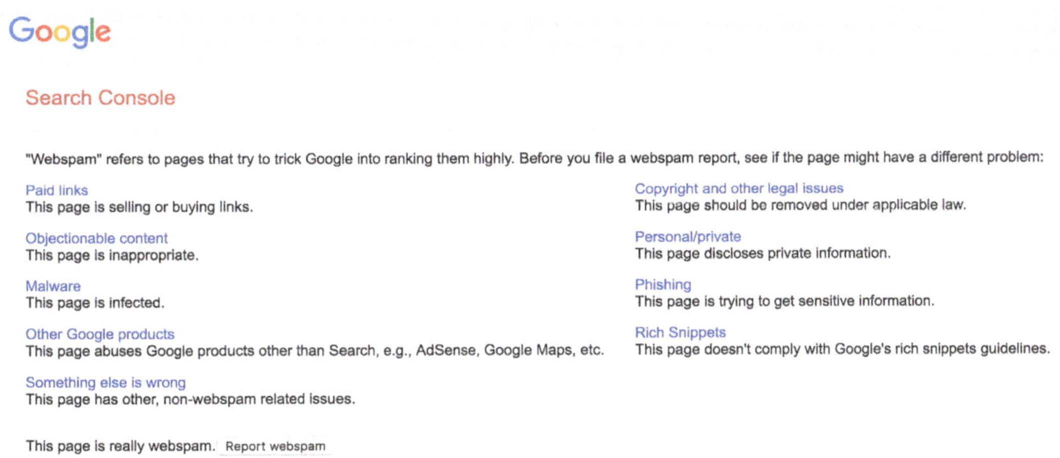

As you can see, Google has a feature on its site where people can submit complaints about sites. So if you're using a guest blogging strategy for the wrong reasons, you might find that someone reports your site for malpractice.

The best way to avoid this is to ensure that you only guest blog on sites where you truly believe you can add value. Even if you don't get a backlink from the post, you can still generate traffic. Google is now better able to give you credit for people mentioning you, even if they do not link. If people think your post is valuable, they're likely to do their own research as to who you are and how they can get in touch, regardless of whether there's a direct link to your site.

Should you guest blog everywhere and anywhere?

It's not useful to guest blog about your law firm on a blog that only talks about dogs. Although you might generate a backlink, the content and audience won't be relevant, and the exercise is a waste of your time.

Think carefully about what sites you approach as a potential guest blogger. You might want to boost the professional reputation of one particular lawyer and so you'll use them as the lead author for all your guest blogs. Or perhaps you want to boost the reputation of your law firm in general; in this case you might designate your law firm (as a whole) as the author of all your guest posts.

How to find guest blogging opportunities

When it comes to guest blogging, you need to think about how much of an influence the site in question has and whether the site in question is relevant to you.

1. First, search for the keywords you want to rank for, and see what top sites come up. If they are major media sites like Forbes or The National Law Review, you should eventually be published there.

   You will need to reach out to editors and very briefly email them explaining your level of thought leadership in a niche and offer several topic ideas in the form of interesting headlines (and a short descriptive paragraph of what your post would cover).

2. You can also use PRLeads.com and HelpaReporter.com to see what journalists are writing about and who might even need full articles. Answer based on what they request, such as providing a short list of tips.

   As you build relationships and show you are helpful, these journalists might have other opportunities for you as they sometimes write for multiple publications.

3. Brian Dean of Backlinko has a cool technique: Google Reverse Image Search. He describes it this way: *"First, find someone in your niche that writes a lot of guest posts. For example, Noah Kagan tends to contribute to a lot of blogs in the marketing space. Second, grab the URL of the headshot they use in their author bio.*

   Finally, pop that into Google Reverse Image Search. Boom! You get a list of places they've guest posted… presented to you on a silver platter."

4. I love using the Ahrefs common backlink tool. Enter the websites of several of your competitors and you can see which other sites they are most commonly linked to. Look through those linking sites for ideas for magazines and blogs where you could also be a guest blogger.
5. You can also find sites that actively seek authors, but be careful of the quality.

   Below is a list of sites that accept guest posts from lawyers. These are the types of sites that come up when you are searching broadly for legal guest post opportunities. Work your way down the list to see if any of them are relevant to you and your firm, and of a high enough quality level.

   a. *https://1stcounsel.com/write-for-us/*
   b. *https://abaforlawstudents.com/2015/11/01/before-the-bar-blog-guidelines/*
   c. *https://abovethelaw.com/2014/01/interested-in-writing-for-above-the-law-heres-how-to-apply/*
   d. *https://www.attorneyatwork.com/writing-guidelines/*
   e. *https://www.enjuris.com/resources-for-attorneys/blogging-help.html*
   f. *http://www.findattorneys.org/guest-post/*
   g. *http://www.finduslawyers.org/guest-post-guidelines/*
   h. *https://www.fizzlaw.com/packages/*
   i. *https://www.halt.org/write-for-us/*
   j. *https://www.youblawg.com/guest-law-blogging*
   k. *https://lawyerist.com/guest-blogging-lawyers/*
   l. *https://www.brycelegal.com/post-submission/*
   m. *https://www.legalserviceslink.com/guest-blog*

This is only a small sample of sites that accept guest blogging. You can do more of this research yourself by searching "law firm guest blogging" or "legal sites that accept guest posts." If you want to widen your search even more, you can search for legal blogs and reach out to them (using the email template below) to see if they'd consider a guest blog from you or someone in your firm.

How to land guest blog opportunities for your law firm

You'll find you have more success as a guest blogger if you understand the correct approach to asking people if they'd like you to write a guest blog post on their site. Think about it — if you received an email from a random stranger asking to write content on your blog, would you accept? Probably not. So, if you do want to write a guest blog for someone's site, first check to see whether they have guidelines for guest posters. Some sites have very specific guidelines about post topics, length, and how you should send a submission. Here's an example from Above The Law of what such guidelines might look like:

> Here are the general columnist guidelines:
>
> - We are looking for columnists to write once a week, on a mutually agreed upon day of the week. We have some contributors who write for us on a case-by-case basis, but we've found that lawyers work best with deadlines.
> - You can write under a pseudonym or your real name. We prefer that writers use their real names — it's easier to do reporting or interview people when you're not working behind a pseudonym — but we recognize that sometimes pseudonyms are necessary.
> - You should write about a particular subject matter or area — e.g., the in-house world, small firms, legal technology — or from a particular perspective. We aren't looking for columnists to offer their random thoughts about the legal world at large.

If you can't find any guidelines, then send a personalized email to the specific site you'd like to write for. Here's one email template to use:

```
To [NAME],

As an [XYZ] attorney, I'm a big fan of your work on [ABC]. I
noticed on your site that you're open to accepting guest blogs.

I'd love to write some content for your site.

Here are some posts I've previously written:
Example 1
Example 2
Example 3
```

```
I think your audience might appreciate a post on [XYZ], as we
noticed you haven't covered this topic yet [or recently].

If this is something you'd be interested in, please let me know
and I would be happy to send you a first draft on the topic of
your choice.

Thank you,

[your name and contact information]
```

The reason this sort of email works well is that you show the recipient that you understand the type of content they already publish and you demonstrate that you already have some experience writing such content.

Who writes guest posts?

As we mentioned in the previous section on blogging, you have a number of options for who should write your guest blogs. You might write them in-house, you might outsource the work, or you might do a combination of the two.

Your guest blog posts should be of the highest quality. The worst thing would be for you to spend time producing your guest post, only for the other site to reject your offer due to poor-quality content.

Use your guest posts as an opportunity to share your best content with new audiences. This could very well be the first time your content gets in front of these people, so you want to make sure you're presenting the best possible image of your firm.

Takeaways

You now have a good starter list of where to find guest blogging opportunities, as well as an idea of how to approach the sites you'd like to write for. Make a short list of the sites you'd like to write for and draft your personalized and relevant pitches.

After your main blogging activity and your guest blogging are both in order, it's time to consider adding videos to your law firm's website to increase engagement.

4. Law Firm Video Marketing and YouTube SEO

According to Cisco, by 2021, video will make up 80% of global web traffic. It just so happens that videos are one of the top three to five ways you can get links to your law firm website.

Videos humanize your firm. We have even heard website test users in our conversion optimization studies state that a law firm suddenly felt "nice" and "approachable," as soon as they heard an attorney speaking in a video. That's a contrast to what the test users said before watching the video; they said things like "this firm's website seems okay but kind of dull." Once they saw the video, however, one of the test users said the attorneys sounded approachable and they could picture working with them, and the test user's tone of voice shifted from bored to stimulated.

Businesses (especially law firms) are slowly starting to see the many benefits of producing videos.

In this section, we look in further detail at the benefits of producing videos for your law firm, and discuss the types of videos your firm can create.

We also provide a mix of free and paid tools to help you get started, along with some basics on optimizing your YouTube videos.

Why law firms have been slow to use videos

The more you talk to law firms, the more you realize a lot of them seem to echo the same sentiments. Sure, they've given video marketing a go, but few have actually seen a good return on investment for the effort they've put in. Does this mean you stop reading here and disregard video entirely? Absolutely not. Done in the right way, video can provide positive results for your law firm.

The issue other law firms face is they don't know how to create an effective video. So before you grab your camera, it's important to know how to craft a video that converts well enough to give you a positive return on investment.

Quality is important but not everything

How annoying is it when you watch a video on YouTube and the maximum resolution is so low the entire image is blurred? Although (initially) you don't need to buy all the latest and greatest video equipment and software, you do want to make sure you follow some level of consistency when it comes to quality.

If you film indoors, make sure there is enough natural light — that way you won't have to buy extra lights. If you want to use your mobile phone to record your videos, use something as a camera rest or tripod to ensure you don't record shaky footage.

Don't limit videos to sales pitches

Yes, your clients are interested in what you do. But they don't want to spend their time watching your videos if they ultimately turn out to be poorly disguised sales pitches. What your clients (and potential clients) care about is what your firm does and how it can improve their lives.

If you're a divorce lawyer, you don't just provide them with a legal service, you help better your clients' lives by helping them exit potentially toxic relationships they're stuck in.

When you tailor your content to focus on the benefits your firm provides, rather than the sales-specific details, people are much more likely to pay attention and want to learn more.

Where to host your videos

When it comes to video hosting, you have a number of options. You might host the videos on your own website. This is a great idea if you want to keep all your content together. However, be aware that hosting many videos on your website takes up a lot of space and could slow it down as it loads. Remember, a slow website will deter users from your site. So unless you have super-fast hosting, try to limit the number of videos you have on your site.

You could use a video hosting platform like Vimeo. This platform is good because they understand the need for high-quality videos. However, keep in mind that your audience might not be on Vimeo.

Or you could use YouTube, a platform with videos about everything and anything. What's more, YouTube videos show up in Google's search results. So if you get your video SEO right, there's a chance your video could rank on Google and generate thousands of views.

Finally, if you've ever thought about streaming, you could present your videos live. This way there's no need to edit. You simply turn your camera on, talk to your audience (who are able to interact with you) and at the end, you have a working video that can be saved and watched again by other potential clients.

How to optimize YouTube videos for SEO

In July 2014, Google changed their Rich Snippets algorithm, which greatly reduced the number of video snippets that are showing in the "universal search results." Videos are now much more likely to come up in search if they are YouTube videos (Google owns YouTube, so this is not surprising).

If you're trying to build thought leadership for your firm, you really need to use YouTube as part of your overall marketing and SEO. Here's how to do that.

1. Find keywords that people search for on YouTube: Use YouTube's autocomplete feature to find top searches as you type your key phrase ideas into the YouTube search box. A YouTube keyword tool like *keywordtool.io/youtube* generates tag lists, video ideas and more for free.
2. Create an account: You must create a channel on YouTube before you can upload a video.
3. Upload your video to YouTube.
4. Use keywords in the title but don't go overboard.
5. Add relevant tags.
6. Add a YouTube "SEO description": Write a summary of what the video is. Use the full HTTP:// URL of your site so that people can click through to it if they are interested, and position it early in the description so it is visible.
7. Upload a transcript of what's being said in the video to the closed captions. Otherwise the robot-generated text version of the video is likely to be half gibberish. Go into your creator studio on your YouTube channel, click "Edit" on your video, then click "Subtitles and CC," which stands for closed captions.

8. Post the video on a practice area page or blog post for basic sharing of the content in addition to what you get from YouTube visitors directly. Do not have the video start to autoplay with the sound on.
9. Add the video in a blog post and include the transcript because that will add helpful text for search engines. That's not duplicate content, because closed captions are in a totally different format than the text on your website, and they serve a completely different purpose.

YouTube Optimization Summary

The takeaway here is that YouTube is the number two search engine in the world and potentially even more popular than Facebook! Video humanizes you in the eyes of potential clients. It's also the first step to local and national TV stations considering you for interviews.

It's harder than ever now, because of some changes that Google made, to get listed in Google search with third-party hosted videos, making YouTube just more important than ever.

At minimum, you should create one video a month where you address customer questions. Keep it short, one to two minutes maximum.

Repurpose your content

As with every piece of content you create, you should actively look for ways to repurpose your video content. For example, you might have content that works well as an infographic but could also work well in video format. Likewise, you might have powerful video content that could be repurposed into a blog post, infographic, or social media posts.

What results do you want?

When it comes to thinking about the results you want from your video, it's helpful to first think about your audience. Who are you trying to target? What do you want to do with the video?

Once you know this, you'll have a clearer idea of the sorts of topics that will drive the results you want and keep your target audience informed, engaged, and/or entertained.

Regardless of the aim of your video, you need to find ways to make it unique. Your law firm is unique and your videos should reflect that.

The goal of your videos doesn't have to be to generate leads. You might decide to film an office tour, including the key members of the firm, to help potential clients familiarize themselves with you and your team.

You could also provide general tips for a larger audience. For example, if your firm has just handled a case involving a human resources dispute, you might make a video that explains the next steps someone should take in such a situation. Be sure a number of your videos contain this sort of timeless content that will be "evergreen" in that it has a long shelf life.

Takeaways

Videos are a great marketing asset, but many lawyers and law firms struggle to get them right. As a result, they end up spending more money and time to create them than it's worth. Use the tactics listed above to ensure that your video marketing is effective.

If you're not a fan of appearing in a video and or want an easy way to get content done quickly, try podcasting.

5. Podcast Marketing for Law Firms

With the rise of the internet, potential clients, other lawyers, and industry experts have full control over how they consume their information. Some like to read blog posts, some prefer to watch videos, but a growing group of people prefer to consume their content in the form of a podcast.

A podcast is a great way to humanize your law firm as listeners get to hear you speak. They can hear the varied emotions, but most of all, they can hear the passion you have for your chosen topic. It's this sort of passion that can greatly benefit your firm by positioning you and your team as industry experts, as well as helping generate new leads.

In this section, we explain how podcast marketing can help your firm and how to get started.

Benefits of podcasting

Although some law firms might be able to generate new business based solely on their reputation, most have to use external marketing activities to drum up new potential leads. Podcasting is an extremely effective way to do just that. Podcasts give you an opportunity to expand your reach. If you attend networking meetings to generate new business, you're limited by the number of people in the room. Podcasting, however, gives you a regional or even global audience.

It allows you to share your authenticity as well as your experience — in your own voice — with an audience larger than your own. What's more, you might find that some people come across your podcast before they've even come in contact with your firm.

Because of the low barrier to entry, podcasts are an affordable marketing tactic for small to medium-sized law firms. You can get started with just your computer, a microphone, and some simple sound editing software. However, although the technology barrier is low, creating a podcast is not as simple as it sounds. You need to create the sort of podcast that represents your firm in the best way and enables you to achieve your marketing goals.

It's well worth the effort since this content can also create a roadmap to guide content writers on exactly what you have to say on certain topics, providing them with information and perspectives that it would be hard for them to gain without your deep expert input.

How to choose a topic

Podcasting can help your SEO and content-generating efforts even if it does not become popular. Before you choose your topic, think about your audience. For example, you could choose to market your podcast to other lawyers within your industry. This is good because it helps you establish yourself and your firm as industry experts within your own professional community.

However, if you're hoping to use your podcast as a way to generate new business, it's in your best interest to market it to people who have a legal problem and may need an attorney's services in the future.

If you just want a strong batch of podcasts to keep your blog active and help with SEO, you do not have to be as broad and can dig right into niche topics. If you want a wildly popular podcast and will be doing extensive outreach to get reviews and fans, then think about a more broad topic for the name of the entire "show."

Whatever topic you choose to focus on, be sure there are enough subtopics to create multiple podcast episodes about it. If you decide to concentrate on a narrow niche and, for example, produce a podcast about drone injuries at weddings, you could find that you soon run out of things to talk about.

You could have the best topics in the world, but if your law firm's podcast doesn't seem to be authentic, it won't resonate with listeners. The ideal speaker to feature in your podcasts should be someone who is articulate and able to talk about the chosen topics with confidence and passion.

How often to podcast

How often you choose to release a podcast is completely up to you. If you want to do it once in a while for the purpose of adding audio and text to your website that benefits clients, improves your SEO, and gives you more to share on social media, then it's fine to create podcasts infrequently. I have seen some of our small business clients get solid increases in organic SEO / search traffic by doing only podcasts with transcripts. Ideally, use them as part of your overall digital marketing mix.

In short, deciding how often you should podcast involves looking at your resources. If you're having your top lawyers talk in the podcast, do they have time in their schedules to commit to podcasting once a day or even once a week?

When it comes to how often you should publish your podcast, there are a range of different answers. The "right" answer for your firm will be unique to you and your audience. Research other similar podcasts in your industry to see how often they post. This will give you a good idea of the frequency you should choose.

When you begin podcasting, listen to your audience. Ask them directly if they'd like to hear more from you or less from you. Keep in mind that if they say they'd like to hear less from you, it doesn't necessarily mean your podcast is bad, it just means they might not have time to consume your content at the rate you're putting it out.

Whatever frequency you choose, the key is consistency. If you choose once a month, then stick to that. Likewise if you choose weekly, stick to that too.

It could also be helpful to pre-record a number of podcasts before you launch. This way you save yourself having to rush to get something released if other business tasks take over and you run out of time to create a new one as scheduled.

Examples of podcasts

Law Firm Marketing
Cindy Speaker

Law Firm Excellence
Michael Bell, Founde...

The Law Firm Leadership Podcas...
Chris Batz and The Li...

The Enchanting Lawyer Podcast |...
Jacob Sapochnick

Murthy Immigration Podcast
Murthy Law Firm

ABA Journal: Modern Law Library

Features top legal authors and discussions of interesting legal theories and historical events.

Finnegan IP Law Podcast Series

Covers the latest developments in patent, trademark, copyright, and trade secret law, including counseling, prosecution, licensing, and litigation.

Bloomberg Law Podcast

Prominent attorneys and legal scholars analyze major legal issues and cases in the news.

I Am the Law

Interviews law school graduates to convey what the practice of law is really like.

The Lawyerist Podcast

A weekly podcast about lawyering and law practice.

Legal Talk Network

Legal Talk Network is an online media network for legal professionals.

TED Talks – Law

A collection of TED Talks related to the topic of law.

Use a podcast to connect with industry experts

You might have one main speaker who "anchors" your podcast but that doesn't mean you can't have guests. You might decide to ask industry experts to join you on your podcast. This is effective if you want your podcast to be shared further. Guests have their own audience and will be likely to share your podcast with them.

If your podcast is targeted towards your own clients, you could invite a client or past client to appear on the podcast. They could ask you questions and you could answer them directly on the podcast. Just make sure to get a signed form giving you permission to use the content and make sure there are no ethical constraints. This is great because if one client has questions about a particular topic, it's likely your other clients (or prospects) do, too.

Repurpose your podcast content

One of the benefits of podcasting is that it's good for those users who want to consume your content in an audible way, on the go. However, there may well be other people who prefer written content. The key thing to remember here is, you don't need to separate your podcast content from your other content. You could repurpose your content into a blog post, infographic, video, or social media bites and include a link to the full podcast if anyone wants to listen further.

This way, a wide range of prospects get the value you're offering, through a medium of their choice.

We like to have our clients do six 10-20 minute podcasts and six 1-2 minute videos in an afternoon. We do the FAQ videos right after the podcast and cover the same topics, but focus the video on the biggest takeaway or question from the podcast.

We find this helps people to get into a productive, comfortable workflow. It also lets clients efficiently create a video and podcast per month, for six months, for their website!

How to start a podcast: The basics

What equipment do you need for podcasting?

You can use Blogtalk Radio and do it 100% online, use your iPhone, or buy a collection of gear like what we started with below.

- Mackie ProFX 8 Mixer $229.99
- Shure SM7B $349.00
- Roland R-05 $199.00
- Heil PL2T Broadcast Boom $120.00
- Sony MDR-7506 Headphones $99.99
- Cloudlifter CL-1 Mic Activator $149.00
- Kopul Studio Elite 4000 6' Mic Cable $17.99
- Kopul Studio Elite 4000 3' Mic Cable $15.99
- Two six-foot 1/4" to 1/8" cables $20.00
- 3 ft, 3.5mm Right-Angle to RCA Cable $10.00
- Logitech USB Audio Adapter $29.99
- TOTAL $1,240.95

Once you've done the recording, what then?

- Edit the file
  - Audacity (PC or Mac) is free
  - Trim the beginning and end
  - Fix any mistakes
- Transcribe the content
- Post the transcript to your blog or website
- Include the MP3 audio file in a player

Hosting

Knowing where to host your podcast is also important. You can of course use Spotify or iTunes to host your audio content, but there are a range of other platforms you should try out. Some tailor themselves to those with small audiences. However, there are others that are more suited to those with a large audience.

When choosing your hosting platform, think about how your audience will find you and pick a platform that works best for you.

Media hosting basics

If you just want to post to your blog on SoundCloud (soundcloud.com):

- Similar to YouTube, but for audio
- Has a good embeddable player

If your podcast will go on iTunes:

- LibSyn (libsyn.com)
- Blubrry (blubrry.com)

To post your podcast to iTunes:

- Upload MP3 files to Libsyn / Blubrry

- Copy URL of media file
- Paste to PowerPress plugin in WordPress

Resources

- Podcast Answer Man
  - *http://www.learnhowtopodcast.com*
  - *http://podcastanswerman.com/equipment/*
- PowerPress Plugin for WordPress
  - *https://wordpress.org/plugins/powerpress/*
- iTunes
  - *https://www.apple.com/itunes/podcasts/*
- Stitcher
  - *http://www.stitcher.com/content-providers*

Think strategically

Make sure to think strategically when structuring and promoting with keywords, SEO, ads, hashtags, and think about creating trust. Find keywords using SEMrush or a similar tool to make sure your podcasts cover topics that will help you rank well in Google searches.

You should also use hashtags when you post your podcast episodes on social media to get more visibility.

Facebook and LinkedIn ads are a great way to boost your visibility now that organic social media has limited reach.

Post the podcast on a practice area page on your website or on your blog page for basic sharing of the content in addition to what you get from SoundCloud and iTunes visitors directly.

Add the podcast in a blog post and include the transcript because that will add helpful text for search engines.

Takeaways

Google Hummingbird likes FAQs and Q&A content. So if you want your law firm to come up when people are searching via voice, you need to ask and answer questions. That is exactly what podcasting does.

Content that solves problems and answers customer questions helps people to feel comfortable with your firm and positions you as a thought leader.

Podcasting is also far less competitive than other types of content. According to PodcastInsights.com, there are about 660,000 active podcasts worldwide, which is far less than people blogging or using YouTube to promote themselves.

By comparison, Cisco says, "It would take an individual more than 5 million years to watch the amount of video that will cross global IP networks each month in 2021."

Podcasting connects you directly to your listeners in a personal, intimate way. No makeup needed!

You can also use podcasts to generate e-book and book content — or at least create "starter" material for a writer to use as a springboard — so you can kill two birds with one stone.

Podcasts are a great way to get to know your audience better in a truly authentic way. Not only that, it's a great way to showcase your firm's expertise.

Why not give podcasting a go and add it to your marketing arsenal?

6. Infographics and Images

It's said that a picture is worth a thousand words. That is why your content needs to include images in addition to text, audio and video. Infographics are an effective way to take images to the next level, and this section will help you get started and avoid potentially time-wasting mistakes.

If you're looking for an easy, shareable way to present complex content, an infographic might be a good choice. You already know that content is a valuable asset for your legal marketing strategy, but did you know that if you want to stand out among your competitors, you need to vary the type of content you create?

Many law firm websites neglect to include a range of visual content because they believe that their prospects and clients prefer written content. This simply isn't the case, though. To stop your website visitors from losing interest in your content, add variety to your blog posts. This will also help you generate more quality backlinks for your legal SEO.

In this section, we look specifically at using infographics as part of your law firm's wider marketing strategy and provide you with a framework to create appealing infographics that your audience will be excited to share.

What are infographics?

An infographic is, as its name suggests, a graphical way to present information. Law firms can use infographics to present complex ideas or information, or to break down monotonous text. Infographics allow you to present a wealth of content and data in an easy-to-understand way. For example, Keating Law Offices uses infographics to explain the 3-foot rule when it comes to cyclists in Illinois.

You can use infographics to present a range of different content. For example, you can offer step-by-step guides that show someone the exact process of getting from A to B. For many people, looking at statistics or data in list format is difficult, but they find the information easier to grasp when you add context through images and illustrations.

How to make an infographic

When you've decided you want to start using infographics in your content marketing, you have two main options when it comes to creation.

You can outsource the work to a graphic designer who can work from a creative brief. In most cases, you'll produce the copy (words and data that should be featured on the infographic) and the designer will put it together with the requisite artistic flair. (At my agency, we do all of that for you.)

Or, you may choose to create the infographic yourself in-house. If you have a designer on your marketing team, this shouldn't be a problem, but if you don't have anyone who can help you design, there are a number of free (and paid) tools you can use to create infographics. *Canva* (shown in the example) is a popular free design tool that is simple to use even for those without much design experience.

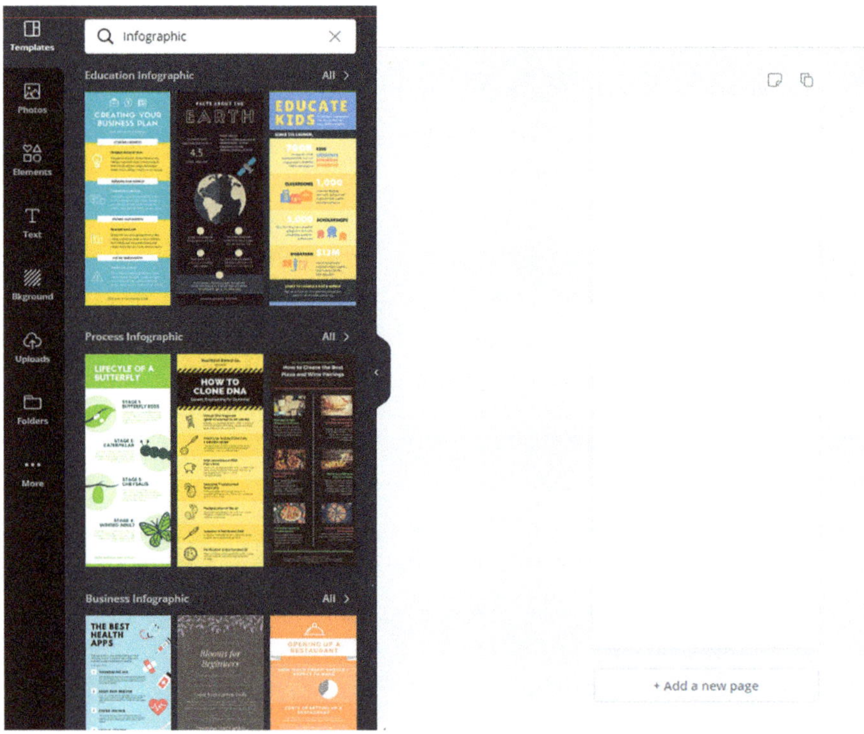

Canva includes a range of free templates, fonts, and illustration assets to choose from. However, you can also make use of the specialized paid assets if you wish.

Piktochart[48] and *Infogram*[49] are other useful tools for creating infographics.

---

48 *https://piktochart.com/*

49 *https://infogram.com/*

Assembling infographic content

Whether you are creating the infographic yourself, or outsourcing the work to a designer, you need to put together the content that will be featured on it. Data is meaningless without an element of context. This means there is no point creating an infographic with just a numbered list of facts or statistics; without an explanation of why the information is important, the infographic will not mean anything to your audience.

To provide your audience with a clear idea of the context, decide on the purpose of your infographic. You might be creating an infographic to simplify complex information. You might be creating an infographic to show the *difference between a private attorney and a public defender*,[50] or perhaps you are presenting a step-by-step guide to a legal process.

The purpose of your infographic will affect which data and information you choose show. Don't get bogged down with trying to include every piece of data or statistic you can find. Focus on the narrative. What do you want the infographic to say, and which data best supports your argument? Tell a story. As you produce more and more infographics, this will become easier.

If you're writing endless paragraphs, you're not doing it right. You can of course have very short paragraph explainers at the beginning of each infographic section, but ideally you're looking for short "bites" of actionable information that your audience can digest quickly and efficiently.

Infographic best practices

You need to make sure your infographic makes sense and tells a story, especially when it comes to infographics for legal content marketing. Remember, people only share what they find useful or interesting. The best way to work out what this could be is to look at some of the core problems your audience faces. You could send out a questionnaire to your audience, or alternatively, look at the comments on previous blog posts to see what people's major concerns are. When you have this information, you can decide how to create infographics that help your clients and prospects solve a problem.

---

50 *https://www.legalmarketingreview.com/content-marketing/how-attorneys-can-use-infographics-for-legal-marketing/*

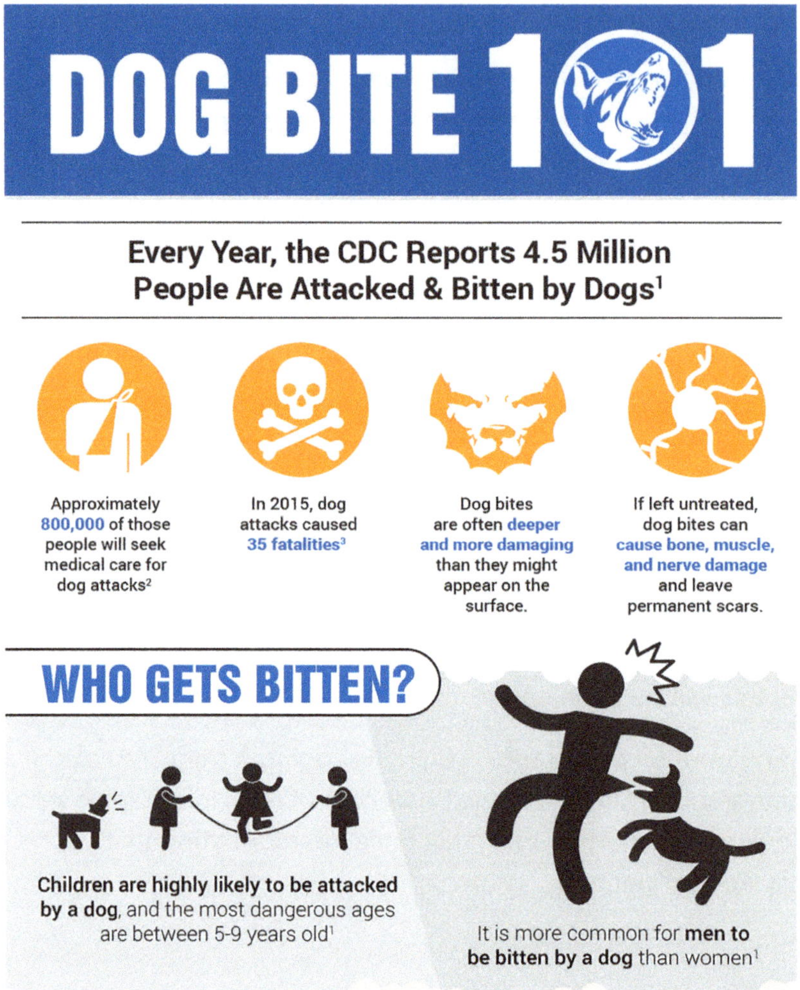

Helping Injured[51] has a useful infographic that walks readers through the ins and outs of dog bites, who is likely to get bitten, and what illnesses and problems occur as a result.

Especially important in the legal industry, take the time to check your facts. You don't want any inaccuracies that will diminish your reputation in the eyes of potential clients. Include citations and references for each statistic you use.

Having a beginning, middle, and end is important in stories and infographics. If your infographic is about the rise in corporate tax evasion, then you should include data

---

51 *http://www.helpinginjured.com/severe-injury/dog-bite-attorney/*

on past and present tax evasion, and some predictions for the future of corporate tax evasion. This way you have covered how it used to be, how it is now, and how you anticipate the trends will run in the future. For example, Paul Norris Law created this infographic to explain four simple rules for giving good testimony. Readers can quickly and easily digest the information the law firm has presented.

Don't forget SEO

This wouldn't be a guide to law firm marketing without some mention of SEO. You should be aware that if you just post your infographic to your site without some key components, it won't get seen by Google or readily linked to by other sites.

First, the infographic needs an introduction and a conclusion. You can house your infographic in a blog post, or as a standalone page on your website, but you must add an element of text description to allow Google "crawlers" to understand what they're looking at.

Second, you need alt text. Alt text is a standard field to use when adding images to your blog post or website, and an infographic is no different than any other image.

When you've added these elements, you might find that using infographics increases your search engine reach. When you include a keyword-rich file name, as well as a caption and alt text, it helps the image to be found through the search tool Google Images.

People will also share your infographic on social channels, so make that easy to do by providing "share" buttons that link to the social media platforms most popular with your readership.

Takeaways on infographics

Did you know that 93% of all human communication is visual? Creating infographics is a great way to add some variation to your legal content marketing and is an engaging way to educate your current and potential clients. Infographics allow you to provide user-friendly information and data that takes seconds to read and digest, a bonus in today's fast-paced world.

Infographics are a great way to make your content stand out from your competitors' content and to grab the attention of your time-strapped readers.

If you really want to get the most mileage out of all this great content you are creating, it's time to start making e-books. The next section explains how they can work for your law firm and fit into the overall content marketing mix.

7. The Benefits of Creating E-books for Your Law Firm

Did you know that most people searching the web or visiting your site are not ready to hire you when they land on your website? In terms of where they fit in your sales funnel, they're generally right at the top, still researching various options. This means you need to use your website as a tool to acquire their contact information so that you can continue your marketing efforts so that when they are ready to hire a law firm, yours is the first one they think about.

But most people are cautious about what data they give to whom. They don't want to be hounded by emails or receive calls from you three times a week. If you want to persuade your prospective clients to give you their data, you need to give them something of value in return. An e-book is a fantastic way to do this.

In this section, we explain why you should be creating legal e-books and how they work to set you up as a firm with expertise and provide you with real leads that could turn into customers.

Demonstrate your thought leadership

If you're not already using e-books as part of your marketing portfolio, you should be if you want a viable way to demonstrate your knowledge and provide your audience with useful information they can access as and when they please.

You might not think you have enough content for a book. Or, the idea of creating an e-book seems well beyond anything you'd be capable of or have time for.

But when you think about it, as lawyers, you and your team members write every day. You know your industry well, and an e-book is a great way to showcase your expertise.

One way to easily create enough content to fill an e-book is to use interviews. You are an expert in your field of law, so talking for an hour at a time about a specific topic you think your audience might find interesting and having it transcribed is a relatively painless way to create the base of your book content.

Brian Tannebaum,[52] a criminal law attorney from Florida, created an *e-book*[53] that helped prospective clients understand what factors to consider when hiring a criminal defense lawyer. It's a great tool because anyone who's read the e-book and subsequently contacts Brian has already been educated on what they should or shouldn't do when hiring a defense lawyer.

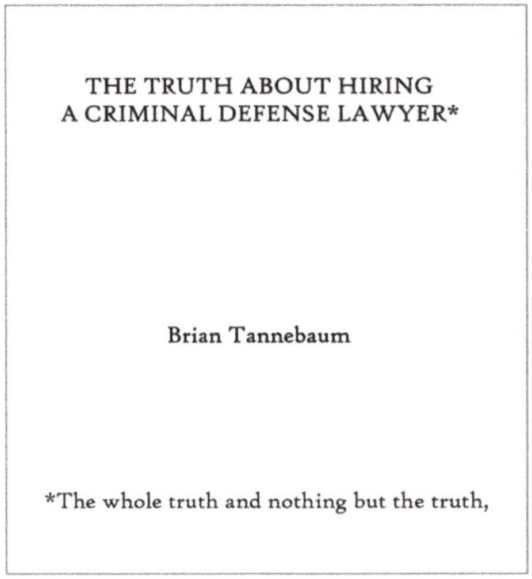
THE TRUTH ABOUT HIRING
A CRIMINAL DEFENSE LAWYER*

Brian Tannebaum

*The whole truth and nothing but the truth,

Not the snazziest cover design, but at least he got it done — and it can always be improved later.

Remember, you don't have to reinvent the wheel, as you likely have enough content on your blog or through other resources like podcasts, videos, or email newsletters that you can pull together in an e-book.

How long should my e-book be?

Your e-book should be as long or as short as it needs to be, although this perhaps might not seem like helpful advice. The rules of thumb are:

1. Only say what you need to. If you can convey the same point in 10 words as in 100, use 10 words.

---

52 *http://www.criminaldefenseblog.blogspot.com/*

53 *http://d.scribd.com/docs/nanslgq2ymtlgsp4x2a.pdf*

2. Only cover the topic outlined. Your audience is time-conscious and if they want to read an e-book about Florida criminal law changes, then that's exactly what they want to read about.
3. In the same way, however, you don't want to rush through the points so quickly or superficially that the reader doesn't get any value from reading your book.

That said, legal e-books can range in length from five to ten "pages" all the way to 40 pages and beyond.

You can even make a one-page checklist-style PDF that is a bit like an e-book and will help you get subscribers but is easier to create.

If you're struggling to think of ideas for your legal e-book, we've come up with seven topics to spark your thinking.

1. How to Protect Your Intellectual Property: A Quick-start Guide
2. The Guide to Divorce Law In New Orleans
3. How a Car Accident in Georgia Will Change Your Life
4. Immigration Information You Need to Know in Michigan
5. Disability Benefits Ultimate Guide
6. What You Must Know about Boating Accidents in Oregon
7. Your Family's Guide to Understanding the Basics of Wills and Trusts

The best e-book topics are those that you are an expert on and/or those that represent the practice areas your law firm specializes in.

Design

Your cover design should be carefully thought out to compel people to click "download" and provide you with their contact details. If they don't believe they'll get any value out of your e-book, they won't click. You could outsource the design of your cover, or you can do it in-house, perhaps finding an e-book template online to produce the cover yourself. If you're cash-strapped or don't have any graphic designers in your network, this is an option to consider.

HubSpot offers 13 free e-book templates you can use.

Click to Tweet:

Get your copy! > 13 Free Customisable Ebook Templates by @HubSpot

http://bit.ly/1xNH3Qx

Ideally, you'd want to hire an expert graphic designer who can give your e-book cover design a "wow factor." Our e-book cover designer, for example, doesn't do any other work for us beyond design, which is just one example of using highly specialized team members.

Lead generation tool

We mentioned earlier that most website visitors are not yet ready to hire you and so creating and distributing e-books that are hidden behind a data capture wall is a great way to feed prospects into your sales funnel, thus giving you a chance to further engage and persuade them through your *marketing automation techniques*.[54]

The way to do this is to create a landing page for each e-book, where a user must give you their email address in exchange for downloading the book. Their contact information (name and email) are then fed into a "drip" workflow campaign that is intended to take them further down the sales funnel until they're ready to hire you.

---

54 *http://www.legalmarketingreview.com/news/avvos-mark-britton-on-how-avvo-can-help-take-your-law-firm-marketing-to-the-next-level/*

When you create your call to action (CTA), you need to make it compelling. "Free quote" or "buy now" is not convincing enough, nor relevant. Instead, try a CTA like "read now" or "download."

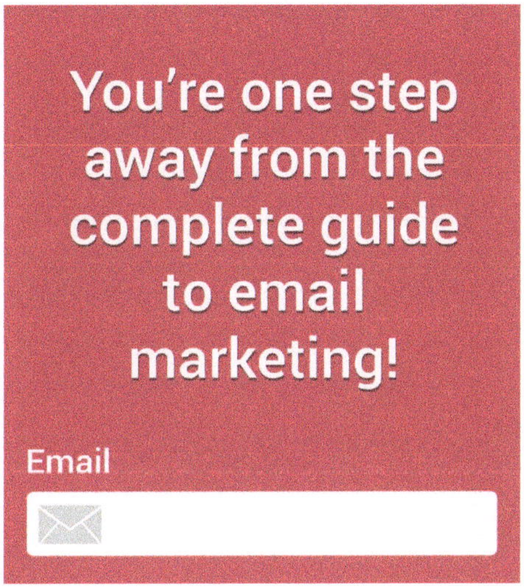

[55]

Distributing your e-book

When it comes to distribution, you have two options. The first is to put the content behind a wall, whereby prospects have to give you their email address and name to access it. This is a good method if you want to use the e-book as a lead generation tool as explained above. If this is the option you choose, consider using HubSpot, MailChimp PRO, or iContact Pro to put together your email campaign. The second option is to give it away freely, as added value to the site, but not make people give up their contact details to download it.

Takeaways

Legal e-books are a great "bribe to subscribe." They are top-of-the-funnel content pieces that help you increase your leads and position yourself as an authority. However, don't forget to tie your content and landing page into your overall marketing strategy.

---

[55] *http://contentmarketinginstitute.com/2015/02/key-elements-ebook-marketing/*

You should write your e-book with your target keywords in mind. And when you do, you'll start to see a number of benefits, like being able to explore specific legal topics in much greater depth as well as length.

Your clients will be able to access easy-to-understand, state-specific information on the legal issues they care about most. You'll set yourself apart from other law firms as you'll consistently be offering a valuable resource for those in need.

A series of shorter e-books can also be combined to make a longer printed book, which is an even bigger step forward to becoming the "big dog" in your practice area.

Once you have created an e-book or a print book, you are just the type of thought leader that journalists want to hear from. In the next section, we explain how to use press releases to get journalists to help get your public relations efforts off the ground.

8. Law Firm Press Releases

Press releases are a great way to spread the message about your law firm, whether it's new cases you've won or new partnerships you've built. They do not replace full-scale PR outreach to journalists but can get your story out quickly.

In this section, we explain how to best use press releases to market your law firm.

What should your press release be about?

Journalists tend to ignore and delete press releases that do not specifically offer something that they consider newsworthy and/or of interest to their readers, and that fail to include the who, what, where, when, and why in the first paragraph.

A press release is not an article or an ad, and it's a common rookie mistake to write one that is an overt sales pitch.

The purpose of a press release is generally to help you make an announcement to the world. Because of this, the topic you choose should be unique and also timely. For example, if your firm gained a new partner three years ago, it's not a good idea to send out a press release about this now, as the information is old news.

8 basic ideas for press releases

1. Milestones such as 10, 25, 50, 100 years in business or number of cases
2. Announcing a speaking engagement
3. Forging new partnerships
4. Opening a new office
5. Winning an award or receiving recognition
6. Hiring new team members
7. Winning a significant case (perhaps one that was being closely followed)
8. Offering a new service or a new practice area

A securities law firm that we work with has seen very good results from writing press releases about breaking news related to pending litigation involving wrongdoing by large companies. This is known as crafting your press release to have a "news hook," and leads come pouring in when people search for that company name and that legal situation and find our client's press release in the search results.

Always be sure to follow proper ethics guidelines when commenting on specific cases, and get consent if you are including client information in a press release.

Focus on the headline

After you've chosen what to write your press release about, spend some time thinking about the headline, since that is what will drive people to click through to your website to read it.

If you don't get your attention-grabbing headline right, people are unlikely to want to read on. You don't just need the meat of the story, you need the sizzle.

You can add a key phrase into the headline to help with SEO efforts even for other sites it goes onto, but the headline should be short, strong, and engaging.

For example, take a look at this sample law firm press release.

> **NEW PARTNER ONBOARD: GSK STOCKMANN REINFORCES INDUSTRY-COMPLIANCE GROUP WITH PARTNER HIRE FROM POHLM**
>
> December 2017. Press Releases by GSK Stockmann + Kollegen (view listing).
>
> **GSK Stockmann reinforces its compliance group with a lateral hire from Pohlmann & Company and continues its push to focus on specific industry sectors and internationalization. Eric Mayer (51) will join GSK Stockmann on December 1, 2017 as a partner and will play a key role in growing the compliance group at GSK.**
>
> Read more…

The headline lets the reader know the press release will be about a new partnership, and explains that one of the benefits of acquiring a new partner is growing the firm's compliance group.

The first paragraph

The first paragraph must contain the most important (or newsworthy) information, and readers should be able to find the who, what, where, when, and why at the top.

Most press releases that go out to the media should only contain three or four short paragraphs and fit on one page. You can always add extra information to the "evergreen" version that is posted on your own website or blog.

Add quotes and stats

A press release should include quotes from people involved, such as partners at your firm or others connected to the news topic.

You should also back up all your points with statistics and data as appropriate.

Multimedia

Your press release doesn't just have to be plain text. You can make it more exciting by adding elements like videos. Embedding videos in your press release gives you further opportunities to offer content people might find useful. Keep in mind it may cost more when you submit them to wire services if a video is included (see below).

Subtle calls to action

You can also add links to other pages of your law firm's site or blog that are relevant and support the story. This way you can direct people to further reading to learn more about your firm or to an attorney's bio page.

Remember, no sales pitches!

About your firm

At the end of the press release, add one short paragraph about your firm that is not an overt sales pitch but rather helps illustrate your firm's unique value.

Contact details

Make sure to include information that allows journalists to reach the key media contact in your firm, or include your PR agency's contact info.

Submitting your press release

Use reputable sites like BusinessWire, MarketWire, or PRWeb.com. Using these paid services should cost you under a thousand bucks for the basic local release, and sending it out nationally can cost significantly more.

One high-paying or long-term client brought in initially because of a press release could certainly pay for the whole venture. Not to mention that if you really do have a newsworthy story and it gets picked up, not just by distribution sites but by bloggers and journalists covering the topics, you will get some high-quality backlinks.

Going beyond press releases

HARO (Help a Reporter Out) and ProfNet are services that feed you leads about journalists who are looking for sources for their articles. Check them out as you develop a variety of PR skills.

Takeaways

Press releases are a great way to tell your law firm's story and possibly get you tapped as a source by media covering the news in your industry.

If you can figure out how to include the "steak" and some "sizzle" in your press releases to attract the attention of journalists, you just might find you start having fun being your own public relations expert.

Press releases and PR tactics in general may eventually get you television coverage, which can be very powerful to highlight on your website because you appear as a celebrity in your niche.

Follow our tips above to make sure your press releases get the best coverage and organic search visibility and generate new leads for your law firm.

9. Benefits of Webinar Marketing

Webinars are one of the most engaging and personal types of content, and they can help your firm get great leads and build your email list. Different from seminars, which usually happen face-to-face, webinars are conducted online. This means you are able to attract a regional or even global audience.

It doesn't matter if your law firm is based in Illinois or Nebraska, using webinars allows you to be location-neutral and connect with people from all over the world.

Think about what potential clients are looking for when reaching out to a law firm to do their initial research.

They want a forward-thinking firm that's happy to provide information and guidance. Some firms like to offer free consultations to discuss issues in a broad sense, but this costs your lawyers time. How much is their time worth? Moreover, if ten people contact you about the same issue, you need to have the same conversation ten times. This is more time that could be spent doing other (billable) things.

The benefit of using a webinar is that while you can offer it for and/or distribute it to those ten people, you only need to do the work once. The webinar allows you to connect directly with your target audience, and if they find value in it, they're likely to share it with their own network, again broadening your reach.

Webinars give you authority and competitive edge

Webinars help you establish yourself as an authority and give you and your law firm a professional competitive edge.

It's a much easier sell to encourage someone to attend an event online or watch your free replay than to get them to spend time and money to attend your seminar in person.

Doing webinars shows your audience you care about the level of service you want to provide. Many aspects of the law are confusing for those who aren't in the industry or have never studied it. Webinars are a great way to help them understand specific concepts. You can use webinars to become seen as an authority. If you specialize in corporate law, for example, you could update people once a month or once a quarter with any new changes they should know about.

Repurpose your current content

You probably already have a supply of content you can repurpose in a webinar format. If you already have blog posts or other content that generates buzz for your business, you could repurpose that content as a webinar. This way, you're not actually creating any new content, you're simply using the content you do have in a new format.

If you do use webinars as an occasion to produce new content, you can then create blog posts from the webinar material to boost your SEO. Normally, videos hosted on your page are unlikely to gain enough exposure or traction on search engines unless you create a page for each webinar that can attract links.

Before you launch your webinar

Before you launch your webinar, plan out the content you want to produce and when you plan to launch the webinar. Here is a basic webinar planning checklist to take you from idea to post-webinar.

1. Set up a kickoff meeting with your team (the speakers/tech person).
2. Set the event date.
3. Create an invitation email.
4. Find the right audience (such as start-ups).
5. Consider partnering with a larger company in your niche.
6. Create a PowerPoint deck and rehearse your webinar talk out loud at least three to five times.
7. Begin registration and track sign-ups.
8. Hold a dress rehearsal with your team.
9. Hold the live event and record it for future replays.
10. Review the relevant metrics.
11. Begin lead nurturing with the people who attended the webinar.

It's also useful to plan your webinar to make sure it provides enough value for your audience. If they find it boring, they can "leave" it at any time. Choose your topic with your audience in mind. You might choose to talk about a specific legal issue or one that seems topical and timely in the current climate.

Once you've decided on the topic, do some research to add to your existing expertise on that topic. You may find it's an added benefit to write a supporting blog post about your webinar topic — there's the SEO bonus of having the blog post drive traffic to your webinar sign-up page. Consider using paid ads on relevant media to get extra eyeballs.

When planning your webinar, remember that you won't be marketing it to "everyone." You might decide to market to other lawyers or to your prospective clients. Whomever you choose, make sure the content you put together is targeted for them.

Creating your webinar

When you've planned the content and topic of your webinar, it's time to put it together with one of the different webinar software options available.

One of the most popular is *gotowebinar*.[56] Pricing starts at $89 a month for 100 participants and $199 allows up to 500 participants. The cost goes up significantly to hundreds of dollars a month if you anticipate having a very large audience. However, the amount of business you will get if you have over 500 participants in a webinar will far surpass the cost. You can adjust your plan up or down depending on how many people actually register for the webinar, so you can start small and build.

If your webinars prove popular, you can scale up the efforts by making use of one of GoToWebinar's premium plans. You can also use the software to look at your analytics to see what you need to improve for the next webinar.

Creating your webinar presentation slide deck

PowerPoint or Apple's Keynote are tools you can use to create a visual presentation for your webinar. If you want to make your life easier when developing the content for the webinar deck, base it on a numbered list, like "top 10 myths about creating a business trust and how to properly protect your assets." Knowing that you will cover exactly 10 items helps you focus your efforts and get the project done much more quickly. Structuring your program around a numbered list means your webinar attendees will also have a better sense of where they are in the program while listening to you present.

As with any visual presentation, don't put too much information on each slide. Stick to one main point per slide, and make it easy for your audience to follow along.

Photos with a headline or a few small bullet points here and there can work well. Personally, I tend to use lots of slides to illustrate my points and keep me on track. Some people like Seth Godin and Malcolm Gladwell can speak with a couple slides or no slides at all, but I will leave that up to people with perfect memories and no ADD.

---

56 *https://www.gotomeeting.com/en-gb/webinar/lp/easy-webinars?c_name=Google_EMEA&c_date=Evergreen_Google&c_mark=EMEA_GB&c_prod=GTW&c_cell=NonBranded&c_kwd=webinar_software-Exact&c_cmp=sf-701000000005pR0&nst=0*

Some speaking experts will mock you if you have a slide a minute for a presentation. However, especially for a webinar, you will need to test having more information than normal because you will not have the back and forth that you would with an in-person audience, and it's important to keep things moving along quickly.

The goal is to leave people with a clear message. Keep bringing people home to one single key point that they just might remember forever.

Promoting your legal webinar

While you don't need to rent a venue to hold your webinar, you still need to come up with a promotion strategy. If you already have an email list, use that to notify subscribers of your upcoming webinar and include a link where they can register. Remember to also send a reminder email a day or two before for anyone who might have forgotten. GoToWebinar automates this, but having a webinar and sharing it is a great sales outreach tactic.

You can also make use of sites like *webinarbase.com*[57] or *webinara.com*[58] to help promote your event.

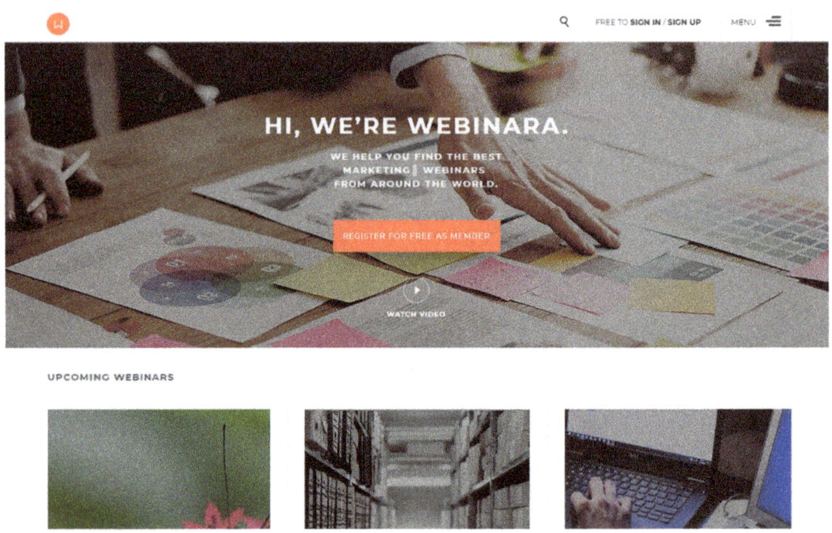

57 *https://webinarbase.com/*

58 *https://webinara.com/*

For example, the firm *Norton Rose Fulbright*[59] uses their webinar page on their website to let visitors know about upcoming webinars.

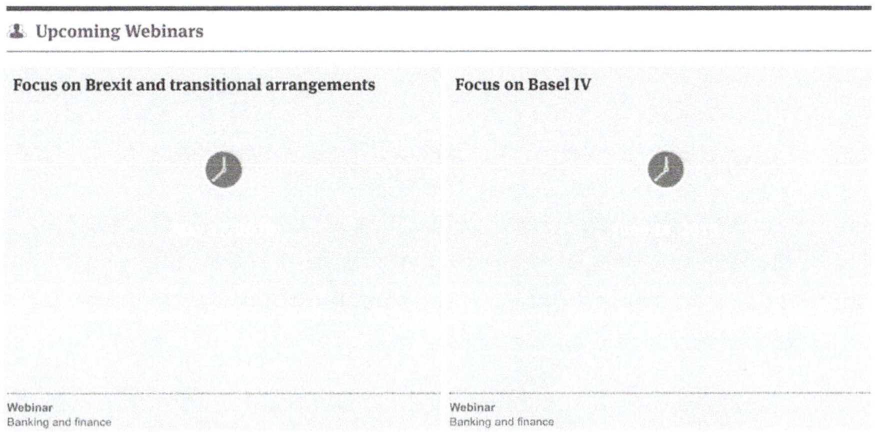

One of the easiest ways to get a lot of people attending your webinar is to promote it and present it with a partner organization that is larger than your firm. You may partner with a leading national magazine, another industry media outlet, or your local Chamber of Commerce.

When you get in front of someone else's audience in addition to your own, you will have an easier time getting enough people to make it worth running the webinar.

Takeaways

If you're looking for a way to stay memorable, you should definitely start planning your first webinar.

By creating a webinar, you're able to provide multiple people with immense value as they need it. You can position yourself as an authority within your own specialized legal niche and use your webinar to get referral clients.

The benefit of using a webinar as part of your law firm's marketing arsenal is that it's cost-effective and a better alternative to one-on-one consultations, which can often take up hours of your valuable time.

59 *http://www.nortonrosefulbright.com/knowledge/webinars/*

So why not create your first webinar to get yourself and your firm noticed and further establish yourself as an expert in your field? Better yet, partner with an association or influencer and offer the webinar together to get in front of their audience. You just might find that their email list starts to migrate into yours.

10. FAQ Pages and Voice Search Optimization for Law Firms

If you have been studying digital marketing, you might be sick of hearing the phrase "artificial intelligence" because everyone is trying to take advantage of it. In this section, we look at how you can get in front of voice search engines and robots like Amazon's Alexa using specific types of website content.

ComScore says that 50% of all searches will be done by voice search in 2020. That means that understanding this technology is no longer optional.

It's time to embrace the fact that we are moving towards a world where you can have a *Star Trek*-like computer that interacts with you and can tell you verbally about almost anything.

Technology is advancing at such a rate that people are now able to choose how they search for information they need. One such search method is voice search. Law firms can also make use of voice search to increase the number of ways they can be found online.

Voice search is different from a "normal" search on say, Google, because you're using your voice instead of a keyboard. However, is that the only difference? In the annual *FindLaw Consumer Legal Needs Survey*[60] (2017), it became apparent that 27% of people were already using voice search when hunting for an attorney. These people usually use a mobile device (the Siri app on an iPhone) or an at-home device (Amazon Alexa, Google Home) to conduct their searches. So it's important to get it right straight away.

In the next section, we provide a framework for optimizing your own law firm website so it is ready to attract prospects who are using voice search.

---

60 *https://wwaw.lawyermarketing.com/blog/things-know-legal-consumer-2017/*

How to optimize for voice search

Optimizing your law firm's website for voice search involves understanding how people actually voice search and what (small) incremental changes you can make to your website to have the greatest effect.

Think about the types of questions people might ask, based on what stage of the sales funnel they are in. You could have people who are at the beginning of their search, curious about general information. They might ask questions like "what does an estate planning lawyer do?" Next, you might have people farther down the funnel, who could ask "how much does an estate plan cost?" Beyond that, there will be people who are much farther down the funnel and will be looking for specific details about specific practices. They might ask, "Who is the best estate planning lawyer in Manhattan?"

As you can see from the examples above, there are a number of opportunities to target keywords. If you can optimize your website so that search engines can easily find answers to user questions on your site, they're likely to present prospects with your information.

One tactic to help you do this is to make sure your structured markup is in good working order. Structured markup is a type of code that tells Google what type of content is on each page. Google then uses that markup to decide what content they should display on the search results based on the specific query. To implement structured data, visit schema.org,[61] which has a semantic vocabulary of tags or microdata that you can add to your HTML code.

And try Google's schema helper tool.[62]

Here are some law firm website pages to add schema to (these are just examples):

- The home page. The home page can be marked up with organization schema, as well as "website" schema.
- The contact page. Detail comprehensive contact information as structured data.
- Practice area pages. Schema App makes it easy to mark this content up with what's called "article" schema.

---

61 *https://schema.org/Attorney*

62 *https://www.google.com/webmasters/markup-helper/u/0/*

- The law firm blog. There's a schema for blog posts called "blogposting" to use on all posts.
- Prominent staff. Create "person" markup for individual biography pages. If a lawyer earns a knowledge panel in search, it helps.

A simple example:

```
    <script type="application/ld+json">
{
"@context": "http://schema.org/",
  "@type": "Book",
  "name": "Super Book",
  "description": "Ultra interesting. Super impressive.",
  "aggregateRating": {
  "@type": "AggregateRating",
  "ratingValue": "88",
  "bestRating": "100",
  "ratingCount": "20"
  }
}
</script>
```

If this seems like Martian code to you, then the good news is that there is a WordPress SEO Structured Data Schema plugin. It gives website owners a super-easy way to add schema for the following:

Organizations
Local Businesses
News Articles
Blog Postings
Events
Products
Videos
Services
Reviews
Aggregate Ratings
Restaurants

You can find it on *wordpress.org*.[63]

Another way you can increase the chance of your law firm's website being used for voice search queries is to speed up the website. Remember that Google uses website page loading speed as a deciding factor as to which pages they show in the top search results. The same goes for voice search. If you can decrease your site's loading speed by just a few seconds, you can significantly improve your rankings.

Use natural language

To optimize your law firm's website for voice search, you need to include keyword-specific answers to the questions your target audience has. But how do you phrase these answers? Should you use industry jargon? Should you use language that your audience might use instead?

The answer brings us back to the differences between normal search and voice search. Normal search is much smarter than it used to be. Today, you could search "personal injury lawyer Miami" and get some useful results.

Compare that to the voice search, where the user is probably more likely to say something like: "Siri, tell me the best personal injury lawyers in Miami." See the slight differences in the two search questions?

With voice search, you need to use natural language, and the best way to do this is through trying to target long-tail keywords. Most people don't talk to their Amazon Alexa and just say "family lawyer New York." They're much more likely to be specific about the type of family lawyer they're looking for. So they might ask their device to "give me a list of child custody lawyers in New York" or "find me a list of divorce lawyers in New York for women."

If you can improve the ways you use natural language on your website, you will increase the likelihood of your content showing up in the results for a voice search query.

If you're concerned about having natural language (instead of industry jargon and buzzwords) on the core pages of your website, an FAQ page can be a wonderful way to ensure that you have a hub or area on your website that provides valuable information for users and is completely optimized for voice search.

---

63 *https://wordpress.org/plugins/wp-seo-structured-data-schema/*

FAQ pages as part of your resource section

In fact, one of the best ways to optimize for voice search is to create an FAQ page. Such pages are not only good for helping your law firm website rank well on the search engine results pages (SERPs), they're also useful for optimizing for voice search. This is because FAQs help to answer direct questions — the exact same type of questions people might be asking their helpful voice-activated robots.

When putting together your FAQ page with voice search in mind, be sure to think about the types of questions your target audience is likely to ask and how they might be phrased.

If you're unsure what questions they might ask, look through the historical data from your live chat or customer support to see which topics crop up repeatedly. If a number of people are asking the same questions, then it is probably wise to create direct copy on the website that helps address these questions.

You can also use a range of online tools to help you discover which are the most popular questions that people search for on Google. Answer the Public, for example, gives you a cluster of questions based on a specific keyword. In the example below, we can see a number of different questions people might ask when it comes to the subject of "family law."

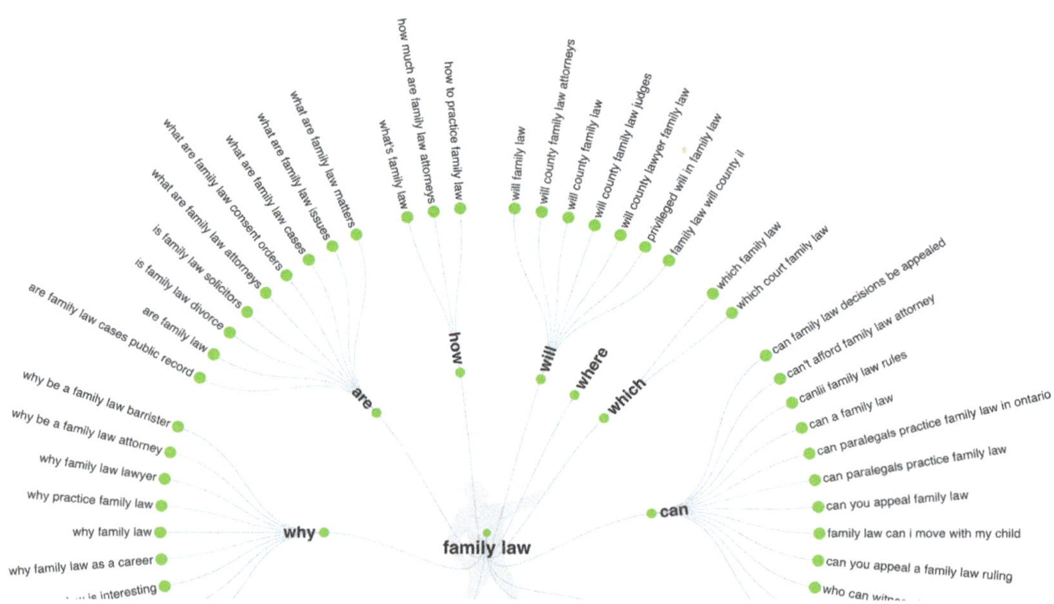

If you have ever used a voice search tool, think about the types of questions you might ask:

"How much does it cost to file a trademark?"
"What's the closest law firm to me?"
"What's the phone number for XYZ law firm?"

Organize your FAQ content in such a way that it directly answers the question your audience might have.

Think about how you write the copy for your FAQs. Don't be afraid to return to it to update it as needed, and don't use overly technical language.

Your audience may not be highly knowledgeable about legal phrases and, if they are in the early search stage of the sales funnel, you don't want to overwhelm them with content they just don't understand.

Make sure each answer for each FAQ question is provided in the first paragraph (if an answer has multiple paragraphs). If you don't organize your content on a paragraph level, the search engines will struggle to find the information they need to process your prospect's question and might not supply your page in the search results. Any supplementary information that's still important should be placed in the second paragraph and beyond.

This way you're optimized for voice search where the most important information is listed first. But also you're optimized for regular search. where people can choose to read more detailed information about a point if they wish.

You can even create an FAQ table of contents with links to each of your separate pages that answer questions in short and long form.

Know Queries and Know Simple Queries

In the 2015 Google Quality Rater's Guidelines & Handbook, they discuss how they analyze different types of queries.

According to Search Engine Land, "Know simple queries" tend to be the type of queries that often show a featured snippet or other type of knowledge boxes, and "Know Queries" are ones where the result couldn't be answered in a short list or one to two sentences.

If you do a Google voice search and check the word count of the paragraphs and pages that come up in the top three results, you will get the facts about the text depth that is chosen by Google to place at the top of the search results pages. You can then test using that text depth for writing your own short and long FAQ content.

Clean up your local SEO

We've spoken about optimizing your website for voice search for terms like "what does a divorce lawyer do?" However, people searching for answers to questions that are so general usually aren't close to becoming customers.

Your only (or main) aim may be to attract people further down the sales funnel — people searching for "phone number of the best criminal defense attorney New York." One of the easiest ways to optimize for this is to make sure your local SEO is in good working order.

Your local SEO is important if you want prospects in your geographic area to have a clear understanding of your business, where it's located, and the different methods people can use to contact you. You can also (if you haven't already) claim and update your Google My Business listing to help the search engines understand more about your business. Make sure the listing has your correct business name, phone number, address, and email. Make sure your social links are consistent with your website and any directories you might be featured on.

Takeaways

Simply having FAQs on your website is not enough. You need an authoritative law firm website in order for your questions to be considered for position zero (above the main search results) or position one on the search results pages.

If you can keep in mind the differences between the ways a spoken question is phrased and the ways a "normal" online search is conducted, you'll be well on your way to optimizing your website for voice search.

11. Topic Clusters For Advanced Law Firm SEO

With so much content on your site, now you need to make sure to organize it in a "modern" way. A topic cluster strategy will do just that.

Getting the coveted page-one spot on Google search results is becoming increasingly harder, especially for law firms. Every so often, Google releases a new algorithm update outlining the factors it takes into consideration for ranking opportunities. These often have animal names, like Penguin, Panda, and Hummingbird, to name a few. The reason Google does this is to ensure the right content is ranking. They adjust their algorithm with users in mind, to improve the way the search works.

It's important to keep track of these updates, as failing to do so will see you with an outdated SEO strategy and your law firm will struggle to rank well. One important new change to Google's algorithm is the introduction of topic clusters.

Let's look at what topic clusters are and how you can use them to ensure your website ranks as well as it should.

What are topic clusters?

One of the reasons for the constant updates to Google's algorithm is because the competition has increased. When SEO first became a thing, all a user had to do was fill their page with keywords and they'd have a high chance of ranking on the top of AOL and Yahoo!

This led to hundreds of spammy websites with no added value appearing on the first page of search engines. Obviously, this isn't good for Google, or the user. If a user searches for "law firms in Illinois," then they want to see law firms in Illinois in the search results.

These search algorithm changes and updates have led to what's known as a topic cluster model. It works by website owners creating a "pillar" page, which is the main hub of content for a particular topic. The pillar page should then link out to multiple other content pages all related to the overarching main topic.

Each individual page should also link back to the pillar page. Doing this tells Google that the pillar page is the ultimate authority on the topic and the other pages are supporting pages.

This way of organizing your website improves the site's architecture and tells the search engines you've carefully considered what a user is looking for and have helped them find the information they need along the way.

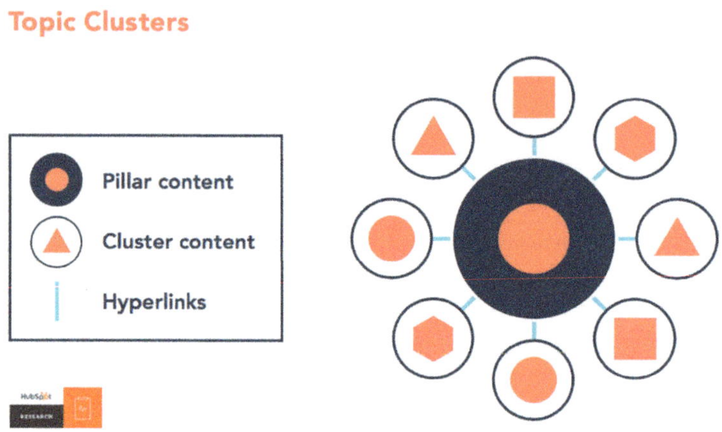

Why topic clusters are important

If you think about your law firm's website, it's quite likely that many of your pages cover similar topic areas. What this means is that when Google crawls through your website, it's met with a number of competing pages, all vying for the top positions.

What the search engine isn't always able to do is determine which page or pages are most important and where it should start. Hence, the need for topic clusters. When you interlink your content and organize it through *topical clusters*,[64] you are effectively telling Google which page should take priority, and then Google is able to organize into one cluster the rest of the pages related to the main topic.

Making topic clusters work for your law firm

For example, let's choose the topic of "family law" as your core topic cluster. Within that cluster, you might have topics such as divorce law, child custody law, and prenuptial agreements.

---

64 *https://research.hubspot.com/topic-clusters-seo*

So you create a pillar page (kind of a mother ship) for "family law" and this serves as the main hub. The topic cluster pillar page for family law should broadly cover the entire topic. It needs to be obvious and make sense for the cluster content to link to it.

Then, create cluster content / pages that are in-depth explorations of that topic. You then link to all the subcategories we just mentioned and on these pages, you must also link back to the pillar page.

The reason this approach works so well is that it forces you to think about topics you'd like to rank for, rather than just keywords.

If you think about the way you currently organize your content on your law firm's website (blog posts, practice area pages, videos, etc.), you likely have chosen a bunch of topics and just created them with little to no system for how these pages build up a logically organized repository over time.

How attorneys and law firm SEO can benefit from topic clusters

When you start re-organizing your content in topic clusters, you are effectively deepening and improving the way your content is interlinked on your own website. Studies have shown the more you interlink, the higher you appear in the search engine results pages (SERPs).

As an attorney, you're likely putting out content, either for yourself or on behalf of your firm. You will be producing content that answers your clients' questions. But search engines are recognizing the growing demand for users to receive the answers they want, when they want them. Hence the rising popularity of topic clusters.

Your clients are now in control and they get to decide how they want to engage with your content. For example, if you're an employment law firm, do your potential clients want to read a broad overview of the whole employment space, or do they want to know specifics about a certain topic? You need to provide both on your site.

How to find topics

You might be struggling to know which topics to choose for your pillar page(s). Remember your pillar topics should be broad enough that you can create clusters of content around that topic, but not so broad that it's meaningless to create content around it.

One way to do this to do analyze your competitor's content. You can use a tool like *Buzzsumo*[65] to do just this.

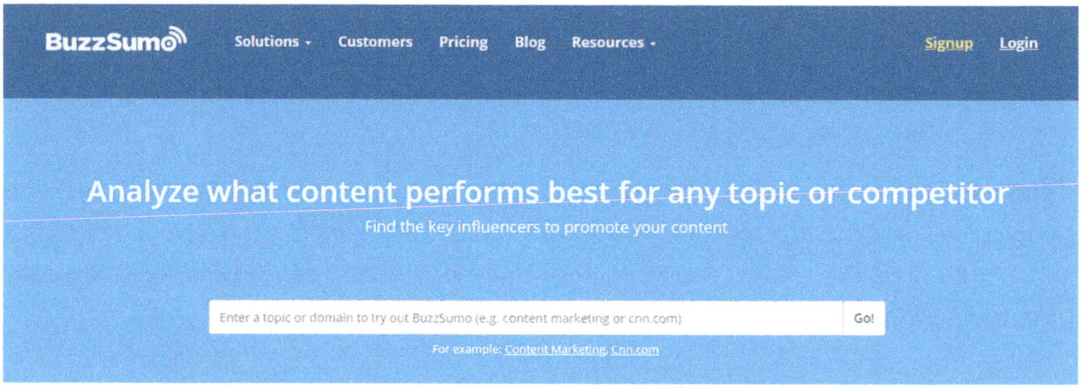

First, enter a competitor's URL and you'll be presented with a list of blog posts from their website that have been frequently shared online. This will give you a clear idea of the kind of content that resonates well with your audience.

You can also use SEMrush to look at the top pages on your competition's websites. These are often pillar pages or pages that rank for hundreds of keywords.

For example, FindLaw has a page on US constitutional amendments that ranks for 2,755 keywords, worth $260,000 a month if you had to buy them as Google pay per click ads! The page links to separate cluster pages on each of the amendments.

Keyword	Position	Search Volume	CPC
amendments	1	165000	2.33

---

65 *http://buzzsumo.com/*

Keyword	Position	Search Volume	CPC
constitutional amendments	1	60500	1.33
the amendments	1	18100	1.57
us constitution amendments	1	12100	1.55
what are the amendments to the constitution	1	3600	1.2
how many amendments are there	4	27100	2.25
what are the amendments	2	8100	1.25

If you want to rank for a keyword as broad as "constitutional amendments," good luck doing so with a 500-word single page when this pillar and topic cluster is out there for Google to gobble up like SEO candy.

Planning your pillar page SEO and keyword strategy

You'll recall that we began this discussion with Google's updates, and mentioned how search engines are getting smarter and website owners also need to become smarter about how they present their information for their audience.

In order for your pillar pages to be effective, you need to inject some SEO keyword strategy into them. Choosing which keywords to try to rank for largely comes down to the pillar topic you've chosen.

Use a tool like SEMrush,[66] ubersuggest.com,[67] or *keywordtool.io*[68] to come up with a list of related keywords about your topic.

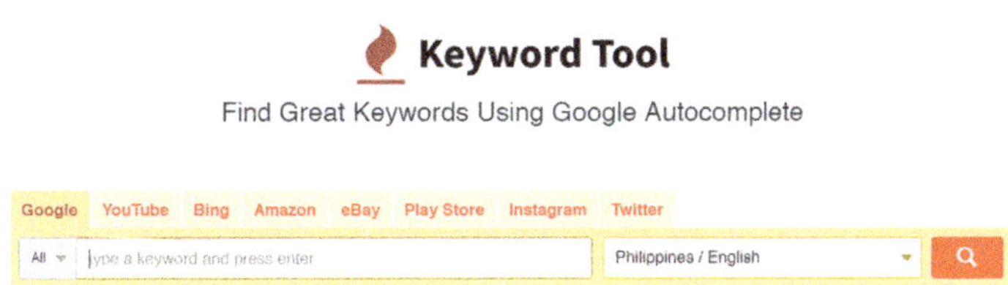

66 *https://www.semrush.com/*

67 *https://neilpatel.com/ubersuggest/*

68 *https://keywordtool.io/*

If we go back to our family law example, we can see these related keywords:

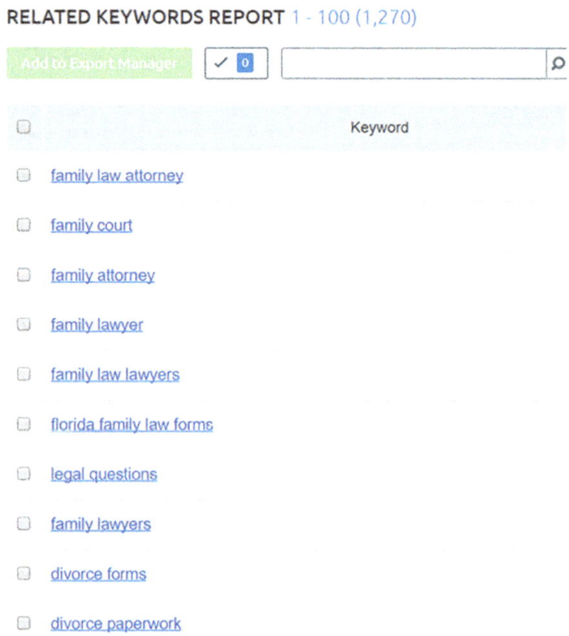

Armed with this information, you can now start making a note of any keywords that are relevant to you. You will need to cover things like "family court" and "divorce forms," not just jam into your practice area page the phrase "divorce attorney Boston MA." Google doesn't respect you at all if keyword placement is all you do.

It's important to keep note of these important phrases, since you'll have better quality pillar pages sprinkled organically with related / *LSI*[69] keywords and phrases.

Spending time coming up with these ideas will enable you to have more blog post options when it comes to working on your cluster content.

Advanced tools include the following

MarketMuse[70] analyzes how many pages your competitors have and what keywords they use so you can do even better at building topical authority.

---

69 *https://www.searchenginejournal.com/what-is-latent-semantic-indexing-seo-defined/21642/*

70 *https://www.marketmuse.com/*

Screaming Frog[71] web crawler can be used to download information about your site and competitors' sites into Excel. You sort all the URLs / pages by topic and list what pillar page they belong to.

SEO PowerSuite[72] gives you keyword ideas to boost your pages' relevance. It brings together the TF-IDF algorithm Google uses (short for "term frequency-inverse document frequency"), Hummingbird, and RankBrain. (I haven't tried it yet, but sounds cosmic, right?)

SEMrush[73] has a topic research tool that lets you select a topic for which it generates an amazing mind map of what relates to the topic and even gives sample headlines for cluster content.

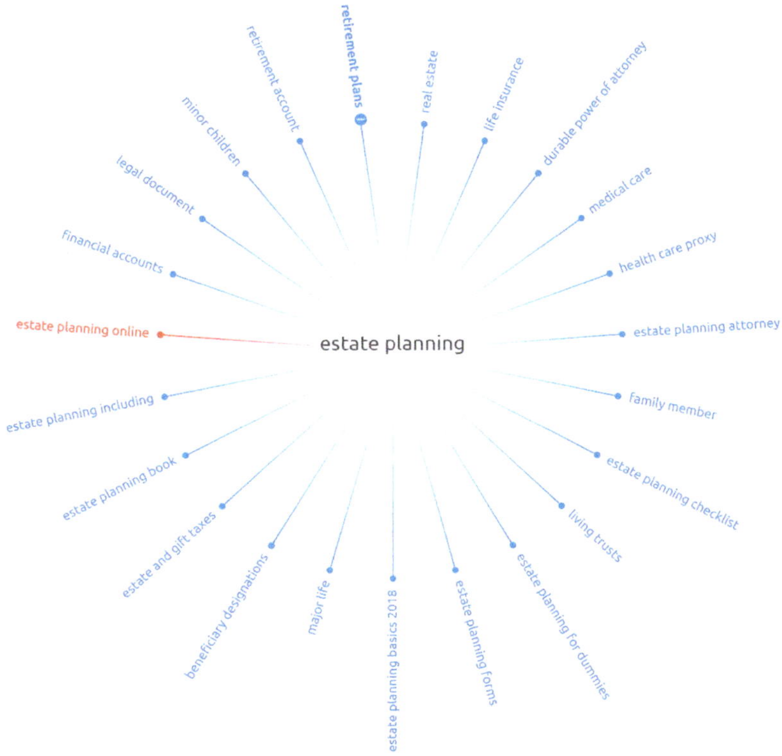

---

71 *https://www.screamingfrog.co.uk/seo-spider/*

72 *https://www.seopowersuite.com/*

73 *https://www.semrush.com/*

Then you get headlines that get the most backlinks, as well as the top questions people are asking.

Headlines:

- Retirement Accounts and Estate Planning
- How are Retirement Plans Handled in an Estate Plan?
- Estate Planning for Persons with Large Retirement Accounts
- Estate planning in retirement
- Don't Forget Retirement Accounts In Estate Planning
- How retirement accounts factor in to estate planning
- Retirement Accounts - Transfer on Death
- Planning with Retirement Benefits
- 6 Important Estate Planning Considerations – Part 5: Retirement Assets
- Estate Planning For Retirement Plan Assets

Questions:

All | What | How | Is | Why

— What are the best retirement investment plans?

— How to create an 'estate plan'?

— Do rich people bother with retirement plans?

— What does estate planning entail?

— What is your retirement plan?

— How should a 25 year old plan for retirement?

— What is a good estate planning checklist?

— What is the best way to save for retirement at the age of 40?

— What is the purpose of estate planning and insurance?

Searchmetrics Content Experience Topic Explorer[74] gives you general information about a topic and what potential competitors are saying on that topic.

---

74 *https://www.searchmetrics.com/content/discovery/*

- Understand user intent: information searches versus transactional searches, etc.
- Drive strategy by understanding when during the year a topic is most likely to drive revenue.
- Find the subjects that others have missed with a graphical view of topics and related keywords.

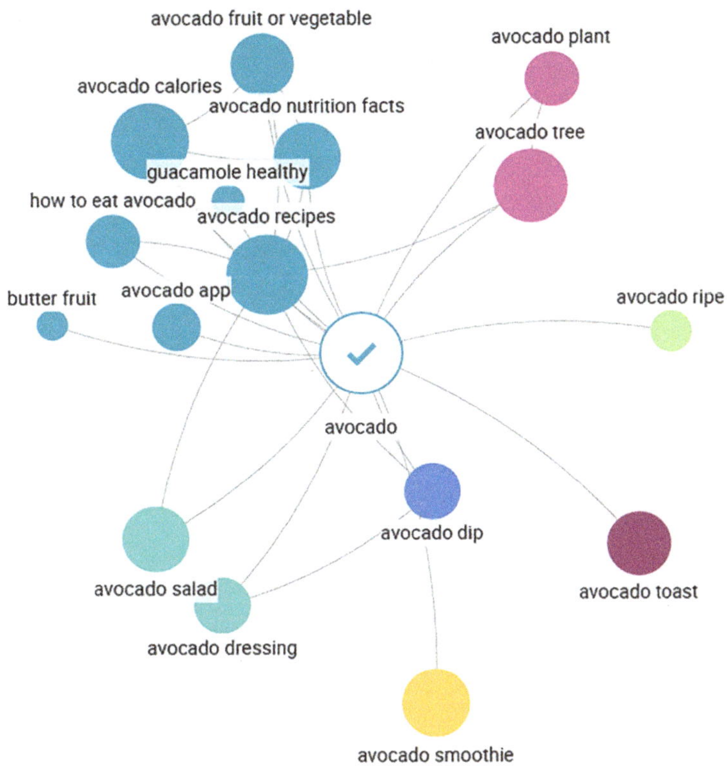

Writing your cluster content

When you have created your pillar page, it's time to start creating your cluster content. You might already have a lot of content on your law firm website that can be part of your clusters.

If this is the case, all you have to do is make sure each cluster blog post or piece of content links back to the main pillar page. Also make sure the pillar page has a link to the cluster content.

However, if you don't have much content on your website, it's time to start creating some. Because you've already created your pillar pages, it won't be too difficult to come up with ideas for cluster content. Ideally, you would preplan your pillar and clusters, but it's fine to simply go through your pillar pages and highlight any keywords, phrases, or topics that would be worth going into more detail about.

Remember, your cluster content is your opportunity to really show your expertise on a topic and let Google know that your site is a well-organized authority to speak on that specific legal topic.

Takeaways

With the increase in the amount of content being produced every single day, and marketers becoming smarter about how they approach SEO, it's getting harder to rank for specific keywords.

If you want to win at SEO, then your content strategy needs to include some element of topic clustering.

Using topic clusters helps you guide Google to your specific content and helps you reach your potential clients.

If you don't use topic clusters, you run the risk of only covering parts of an important subject. Your prospects and clients are looking for specific answers to their questions, and topic clustering allows you to provide an overall explanation of a topic and to dig deeper into the specifics of related subtopics.

12. Law Firm Link Bait

Given that Google admits that content, links, and RankBrain are the three main ranking considerations, getting links is not optional. Here's how to get links without giving in to black hat (unethical) tactics.

The great thing about high-quality link bait content is it builds links faster than waiting for them to happen naturally. You already know that driving relevant links from authoritative sites is an effective way to improve your SEO. In this section, we explore a number of different types of link bait content assets and explain how you can use these to boost your marketing arsenal.

Types of link bait

There are various different types of link bait. The ones most relevant to your law firm include:

- Research studies
- Original data
- Infographics
- Humorous or informative pages

This white paper from *kmjdconsulting.com*[75] shares 10 different knowledge strategies for law firms.

- **Top 10 Knowledge Strategies for Larger Law Firms**

  This 57-page white paper contains ten recommendations about knowledge strategy initiatives for larger law firms (100 to 1,000+ lawyers). It is principally authored by Jack Bostelman and was prepared for the Knowledge Strategy Interest Group, which he chairs, in the ABA's Law Practice Division.

  Click here for a summary of the ten knowledge strategy recommendations.

  Click here to learn more about the Knowledge Strategy Interest Group and to join it in order to receive a copy of the 57-page white paper.

The document is over 57 pages, so you know it's bound to have some sort of value.

This law firm infographic by *Robert Half Legal*[76] helps explain the four top trends that are transforming the legal profession.

---

75 *https://www.kmjdconsulting.com/white_papers*

76 *http://businessoflawblog.com/wp-content/uploads/2014/09/Trends-Shaping-the-Legal-Industry-large.jpg*

The material in the infographic could have been written as a blog post, but it wouldn't have that visual "wow" factor that the infographic does. What's more, if you don't have much time, consuming an infographic can be a much quicker task than reading through a blog post.

Benefits of link bait content

Link bait assets tend to build more links than blog posts or roundup posts simply because they go so much deeper than your average post. People enjoy the content and they consume more and more of it every day. However, too often content is produced that's nothing more than a rewrite of another post on the web.

When you make the extra effort to create link bait content, what you're really doing is making the extra effort to create impressive and relevant content for your law firm.

Your prospects and clients will love it.

Your peers will link to it.

Your business will grow.

How to plan

Before you plan your link bait content, ask yourself a few questions:

1. Do we already have content we can repurpose?
2. Do we know what topic we want to write about?
3. Who is the target audience for this content?

1. Do we already have content we can repurpose?

You already know that your link bait content needs to be better and more informative than any of your other blog posts on your website. However, that doesn't mean you can't use your current content to help put together your link bait assets.

Suppose you have a number of different blog posts about the changes in divorce law. You could consolidate this information and create an infographic to describe the changes and what they mean.

Or you could consolidate this same information and create a white paper or report on how divorce law has changed over the years. Since you already have most of this information in your existing content (a series of blog posts on this topic), half the battle is already won.

The benefit of using your current content is that you already know what's working. Look at your analytics to see which pieces of content are really resonating with your audience. When you find the content that gets the most attention, focus on tapping into this to create your link bait content, because you've already validated that people are interested in the topic.

If you go further and deeper into the topic, what do you think will happen? They'd love your content, of course. This is how you get links.

2. Do we know what topic we want to use?

If you're unsure what topic to choose for your link bait asset, then you can use techniques such as pulling content from infographics, or researching your competitors to see what's already ranking well and how you could improve it on it.

Research a number of topics relevant to your firm and decide on the type of asset you want to create.

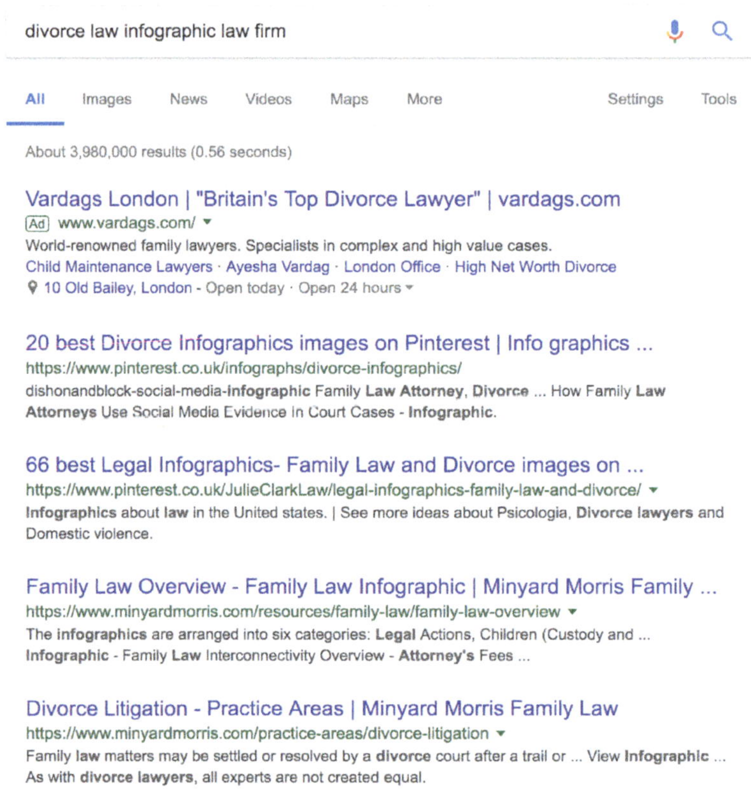

This should give you a good idea of what sort of content works well and can act as an inspiration before you begin to create your own link bait asset.

Because of its complexity and length, link bait content often takes much longer to produce than, say, a short blog post. It's important to be sure you've chosen a worthwhile topic before investing your time.

3. Who is the target audience for this content?

Lastly, it's important to understand who the target audience is for your content.

The aim is to get as many relevant eyes on the content as possible. Yes, you might be able to get 500,000 views of your new link bait asset, but if only five of those viewers are people in your industry or potential clients, there's no point in going for volume of views alone.

So, ask yourself the following questions:

1. Who do we want to read this content?
2. What benefit will they have if they do read it?
3. Who is most likely to share it?

When you have answers to these questions, you'll have a better idea of how to promote your content once it's been published.

How to create link bait content

You can create link bait content in a number of ways. Your choice will depend entirely on what type of link bait content you want to produce and the resources available within your law firm.

Your two main options are to either:

1. Outsource
2. Create in-house

If you want to outsource, you can find freelance graphic designers and writers who can help your vision come to life. You might want to hire a digital marketing agency to handle all the moving parts, since such an agency should have expertise in creating content that gets correctly targeted views and relevant links.

If you opt to create your content in-house, decide who will handle the content and who will handle the design aspects, and set deadlines.

Remember, link bait content is supposed to be more in-depth or generally interesting than your usual content.

Using a free graphic design tool like Canva allows you to create the graphic elements of your assets using an easy drag-and-drop system. This way, even if you don't have in-house designers, you can still create link bait assets for your law firm that are visually appealing. Just keep in mind, the better the quality and strategy, the more likely it will generate tangible interest.

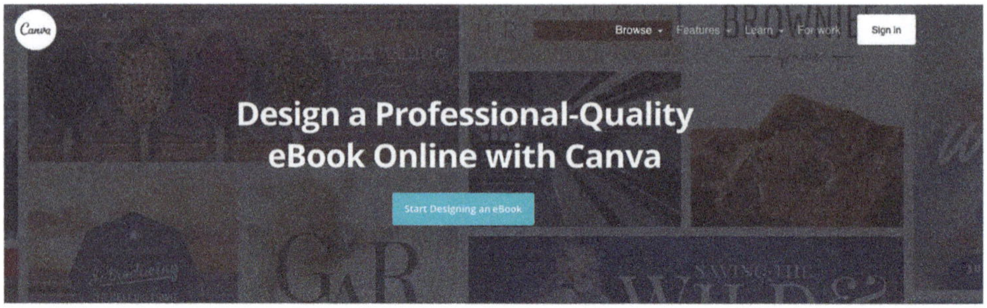

How to promote

You've chosen your topic, you've created your assets, and now it's time to promote them. After all, you want to use this content to generate new leads or acquire links for your firm.

There are a number of different places where you can promote your content, such as on social media, using ads, and hashtags on:

- Twitter
- LinkedIn
- Targeted Facebook groups
- Reddit

You can send email to your own mailing list.

You can do link outreach. Here's how:

3. Find likely linkers by using Ahrefs to see sites that link to similar content.
4. Use *Hunter.io* to find the email addresses of these sites.
5. Send an email like the one in the template below (adapted from Brian Dean of Backlinko).

"Hi [First Name],

I was looking for content on [Topic] today, when I came across on your article: [Article Title].

I especially enjoyed [Something specific from their article].

Also, I just published a new guide on [Your Topic]: [URL].

Since you are someone who writes about [Topic], I thought you'd enjoy it.

My guide may also make a nice addition to your page. Either way, keep up the great work with [Website]!

[Your Name]"

Notice how the template allows a degree of personalization without a whole lot of effort.

Takeaways

Link bait assets take time and effort to produce if you want to do them well, but once you get them right, it's possible that you'll have people all over the world linking back to your content.

From roundups of quotes from experts on your niche topic, to the types of content we shared in this guide, link bait can be very powerful in boosting the authority required for your other SEO efforts to kick into high gear. In turn, you'll generate loads of new leads from potential clients. Give your law firm the best possible chance to position itself as an industry expert and start creating link bait assets.

13. Law Firm Case Studies for Content Marketing

Now that people are coming to your site because of your impressive content, make sure to tell the stories of your best customers. Case studies are like testimonials on rocket fuel and can also increase your visibility, if you follow the steps outlined in this section. Your case studies can act as content marketing in the same way your blog posts do. In fact, case studies are an important element in your marketing arsenal that you can use to generate new leads for your business.

According to Nolo,[77] it is possible to avoid compliance issues and find appropriate things to share in a case study format:

> *"Avoid identifying details and stick to discussion of information that resides in the public record — for example, the summary of the case from the court's opinion.*
>
> *Not convinced that the case study approach works? Which of the following descriptions is more persuasive:*
>
> 1. Our firm's lawyers collectively have 50 years of appellate practice experience. We have a winning record before the XYZ Court of Appeals.
> 2. After our clients completed construction of their dream home, the County which had previously approved the plans claimed that the clients were in violation of zoning laws and directed them to move their entire house seven feet from the street curb. Our clients challenged the County's ruling in court, and lost. They came to our firm to handle the appeal after several firms advised them to accept a settlement which would partly compensate them for the costs of new construction but leave them without a place to live for at least a year. Instead, we appealed and secured a reversal of the County's decision as well as an award of attorneys' fees, thus enabling our clients to remain in the house of their dreams."

In this section, we'll look at what you should include in your legal case studies and explain how to present them on your website.

Start with a title

The title is what will entice your prospective clients to read your case study, so make sure it's descriptive. Ideally include a city and state to help with local SEO rankings.

If you have documented client permission, include their name in the case study, a short, distinct description of what you did for them, and the end results.

---

77 *https://blog.nolo.com/legalmarketing/2010/07/06/make-the-case-for-your-law-firm-with-case-studies/*

Consider using a template like this so you can create multiple case studies:

- Client description
- Client challenge
- Solution
- Results

If you don't have permission to use your client's name, use a phrase to describe the type of client you served.

In the example below from AzriaBruffettLaw.com, you can see this particular firm hasn't used the client's name but has included enough description so you know what the firm did for the client.

Gamechanging Settlement Creates New Case Law while Winning Attorney Fees and Allowing Client to Make Building Repairs

READ MORE ›

Adam Leitman Bailey, P.C. Saves a Mortgage from the Statute of Limitations by Using Innovative Acceleration Argument

READ MORE › **Mortgage Finance Practice Group**

Adam Leitman Bailey, P.C., Obtains Decision Clarifying Under New York Condominium/Co-Op Reserve Fund Law

READ MORE ›

Adam Leitman Bailey, P.C. Defeats Prior Owner's Motion to Vacate a Judgment of Foreclosure and Sale

READ MORE › **Title Insurance Claims Group**

Body copy

When it comes to your body copy (the text of the case study), there are a number of things you should include to make the most out of this content.

The first thing you need to state is the objective.

Readers want to see:

> Your client had a problem,
>> You thought of a solution,
>>> You delivered the results they wanted.

At the beginning of the case study, state the client's end goal. What did they want to accomplish, what results were they looking for, and what challenges did your firm face along the way?

You also want to highlight why this particular client chose to work with your firm. Was it something about the team that drew them in? Was it the fees? Was it the prior results? Highlighting these points helps others understand why they might want to make the same decision and engage your firm.

Next, discuss the process. If there's sensitive information that must be kept confidential, you can still outline the general steps your firm took to help the client achieve their initial goal.

Finally, describe the outcomes. What results did your work achieve? Emphasize how your firm's work played an important role in the client's success.

Craft it as a story and don't forget SEO

Every good story has a beginning, middle, and an end. Your case studies should be no different. Although a case study focuses on one specific client, you should use that client's story as an example to guide others on the journey.

Even as you're writing the case study, don't forget about SEO. If you host your case studies on your website (which you should), this could help your website rank better on Google.

In the following example, Chapman Law's case studies rank on Google, so if a client were looking for a health care attorney in Florida, this would be the perfect page to come to.

Case Studies Archive - Chapman Law Group: Health Care Attorneys ...
chapmanlawgroup.com/case_study/ ▾
Prison Medical Provider Indifferent to Chronic Issue Has **Case** Dismissed ... was suspended in Michigan due to a federal felony conviction in **Florida** for [...].

To improve your SEO, try the following tips:

1 Fill your case study with keywords, including keywords with city and state, but do it organically. Try not to go overboard as keyword overload will ruin the experience for your readers and you could be penalized by Google.

2 If you need to refer to other content on your website, like an FAQ page, blog post, or practice area page, you can use internal links. Internal linking helps Google understand how the content on your website is organized.

Case study analysis

Let's look at this sample *case study*[78] to understand exactly how a good law firm case study is put together.

Orlando Carbon Monoxide Lawsuit Case Study

Mar 5, 2018 | Personal Injury

You'll see in the image above that they've created a descriptive title, explaining what the case study will be about, and providing the location.

They've gone even further, tagging the case study with "personal injury."

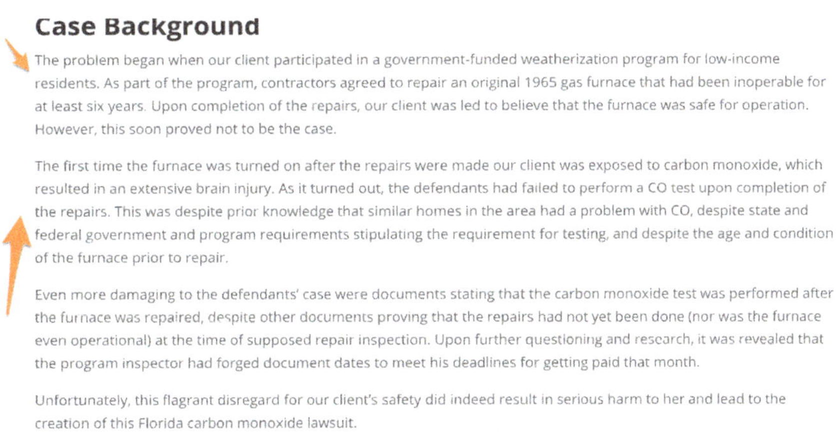

Case Background

The problem began when our client participated in a government-funded weatherization program for low-income residents. As part of the program, contractors agreed to repair an original 1965 gas furnace that had been inoperable for at least six years. Upon completion of the repairs, our client was led to believe that the furnace was safe for operation. However, this soon proved not to be the case.

The first time the furnace was turned on after the repairs were made our client was exposed to carbon monoxide, which resulted in an extensive brain injury. As it turned out, the defendants had failed to perform a CO test upon completion of the repairs. This was despite prior knowledge that similar homes in the area had a problem with CO, despite state and federal government and program requirements stipulating the requirement for testing, and despite the age and condition of the furnace prior to repair.

Even more damaging to the defendants' case were documents stating that the carbon monoxide test was performed after the furnace was repaired, despite other documents proving that the repairs had not yet been done (nor was the furnace even operational) at the time of supposed repair inspection. Upon further questioning and research, it was revealed that the program inspector had forged document dates to meet his deadlines for getting paid that month.

Unfortunately, this flagrant disregard for our client's safety did indeed result in serious harm to her and lead to the creation of this Florida carbon monoxide lawsuit.

78 *https://www.dwklaw.com/orlando-carbon-monoxide-lawsuit-case-study/*

The firm begins the case study by telling the story of how the client got into the situation that prompted the lawsuit. Adding this level of context helps frame the case study in the right way.

The Cost

The total known medical expenses to date are over $65,000.00. However, cases like this are about much more than the dollar cost of medical care. The victim's entire quality of life has been affected to the point of depression, an inability to accept her new reality, and feeling like a completely different person. Her entire social life has collapsed as she can no longer be as active as she once was. She has lost confidence in her ability to do things for herself and has given up her job at a library as well as volunteer positions as a result. Much of what made life enjoyable for her is now gone and she still suffers from ambulation difficulties, speech impairments, and headaches. Friends confirm that she is a very different person now.

The Arguments

This Florida carbon monoxide lawsuit brings forth several legal arguments.

- The defendants, the organization overseeing the program (program administrator), the inspector, the general contractor, and the property management firm, owed our client a duty of care to ensure that the furnace was repaired and safe to use.
- Responsibility for the duty of care cannot be transferred to another party or defendant.
- The program contract established a non-delegable duty to perform the repairs in such a manner that use of the furnace would be safe and such use would not create an unreasonably dangerous condition.
- The contractor also had a duty to ensure the furnace was repaired in a manner consistent with the safety protocols.
- The program administrator is liable for the acts of the program inspector who was acting as their agent.

Carbon monoxide has earned a reputation of being a silent killer because it is odorless, tasteless, and colorless. It's also highly poisonous and exposure to even the smallest of amounts can lead to traumatic circumstances very quickly. We often hear of carbon monoxide cases when a person has died, but that is far from the only danger.

The case study goes on to explain the cost and the various arguments brought up during the case. This level of authenticity helps position this particular law firm as one that other prospective clients feel they could trust.

The Outcome

Our Orlando carbon monoxide lawsuit attorney, Tony Sos, was able to secure a very favorable settlement for his client through his dedicated and detailed approach.

Finally, they end the case study by highlighting which attorney took the lead in the case and outlining the outcome. If they wanted to improve this case study, they could look at ways to expand the "outcome" section to provide readers with a more detailed view of the actual results (provided those details could be shared).

Where to promote your case studies

We've already mentioned that getting the SEO right in your case study helps it rank on search engines, but there are a number of ways to promote your case studies.

Case studies work well on social media

Case studies usually contain very specific and detailed content. Because of this, they usually last longer on social media and are more likely to be shared. What's more, because the information can be relevant at any time of the year, you can reshare your case study content multiple times, across multiple social channels.

You can also post long text-format case studies on Facebook and LinkedIn and promote them with paid social posts and/or ads.

Press releases are another way to share great customer success stories, especially if there's a current "news hook" or newsworthy trend to link them to.

Case studies can generate leads

If you spend enough time on your case studies, you'll often find they end up being fairly long pieces of content. These work as excellent lead magnets. You can put collections of your case studies behind a "gated wall" where people have to provide you with their email address in exchange for access to read them.

The benefit of doing this is that you know the leads that come through this way are specifically targeted. A website visitor is prepared to give you their email address in exchange for reading about the results you've generated for past clients.

Takeaways

Case studies are a valuable part of any law firm's content marketing strategy, even if you choose to use very short ones. They work to convert customers who are in the comparison stage of the sales funnel, those who understand they need lawyer and are now ready to evaluate their options before deciding who to hire.

Your case studies will help you build authority and trust with your audience because they get to see genuine results.

Again, make sure you're fully compliant with ethics rules, such as getting a client's consent before mentioning their case in any public forum.

PART 4

Increasing Conversions and Tracking ROI in Analytics

In this section we will explore a few extra ways your website marketing can get out-of-this-world results through persuasion tactics and using analytics data to inform your decisions about which changes you will make.

10 Things Great Law Firm Websites Do Right

Trying to keep your website functioning at its highest potential is no easy task with everything else you have on your plate. That's why this short list of important things to adjust can help you quickly home in on what's most important.

Most websites fail until they methodically test and correct the following:

1. Headlines and Taglines
2. Intro Text
3. SEO Copy
4. Unique Selling Position
5. Readability and Layout
6. Pictures (Images)

7 Usability and Navigation
8 Testimonials and Reviews
9 Calls to Action and Offers
10 Guarantees and/or Policies

Let's take these one at a time.

1. Headlines and Taglines

As mentioned earlier, magazines often have full-time headline writers. All they do is study the headlines that have increased sales consistently. If you are not A/B testing or at least trying different headlines on a regular basis to make them the best that they can be, your website will not stand out from the crowd.

Consider using the free Google Optimize A/B testing platform, Optimizely, or Visual Website Optimizer.

If you want to learn more about headline optimization, see the book *Advertising Headlines That Make You Rich* by David Garfinkel.

2. Intro Text

The introductory body copy of your website can make or break whether or not people continue to read on, or bounce off to another website.

Are you leading with empathy and addressing your customers' pain points or simply saying we do this great and we do that fantastic, etc. Make sure that you are writing in a way that is customer-centric and puts your customers' needs first.

3. SEO Copy

Search engines like to see important keyword phrases high up on the page and preferably at the beginning of the first sentence. So not only do you need to make a persuasive argument for why you should be hired, but you also need to think about other factors like search engine robots.

One of the best ways to figure out how much SEO-friendly text you should have on your homepage, practice area pages, and blog posts is to look at the top five or ten ranking websites in your field. See what they have for word counts on these pages and how they position their firms.

If your website fails at either intro text or SEO copy on any of your pages, both your rankings and conversions will go down.

4. Unique Selling Position

Are you clear on why you are better than your competitors? If not, do some thinking on what truly makes your law firm a better firm to hire.

If you describe your firm as "America's premier intellectual property law firm," can you back it up? Make sure that you not only add a value proposition or unique selling position, but that you back up your claim with some details so it is more persuasive.

You can mix these statements into headlines along with keywords to cover both important factors at the same time.

5. Readability and Layout

People don't always have time to read all of your text. Longer and more in-depth content can be both great for search engines and for convincing customers who need a lot of information, but it is really critical to make the text easy to scan and skim.

Try not to use too much industry jargon and use more conversational language instead. Keep sentences short and limit paragraphs to three to five sentences.

Using bullet lists and numbered lists is not only good for the user, but Google appreciates it as well.

6. Pictures (Images)

Having high-quality photographs shows that you care about the presentation of your firm and implies that you are more likely to care about your clients. Boring stock photos don't tend to work well, but they are better than poor-quality candid photos shot on the fly.

Make the investment in hiring a professional photographer to get high-quality photos of your key attorneys, a team photo, and even some quirky office photos to show a bit of the firm's personality. Good photos can go a long way toward warming the hearts of prospects.

7. Usability and Navigation

If your website is hard to use, people will exit quickly. Conversion experts agree that usability is often at the foundation of many big conversion wins.

The way that people navigate your pages and menus should be well-thought out. You can try UserTesting.com to have people review your website and give you feedback on what is working and what is not. HotJar can be used to figure out where people are clicking, moving their mouse, and scrolling as well as where they are having trouble filling out a form.

Don't leave your website improvements to chance. Go beyond the basics of looking at Google Analytics to improve your website.

8. Testimonials and Reviews

I recently read a great book called *Story Brand*, which says that the smiling faces of your customers are your best marketing. Most firms just have a few testimonials and don't spend much effort on getting more.

However, having testimonials specific to your firm's different practice areas can really increase the persuasiveness of those pages.

Adding video testimonials and case studies and getting positive reviews of your brand are the core components of making sure customers coming to your website from any marketing channel turn into leads.

9. Calls to Action and Offers

You need really clear calls to action to make a website win consistently. Remember, 95% of the people who visit your website are not ready to fill out your free legal consultation form or call you, so it's important that you offer downloadable guides like e-books or white papers. If you can, add a live chat option to interact with site visitors.

Having calls to action mapped out to the different stages of the sales funnel (awareness, consideration, and decision) will mean that you get considerably more leads.

If you want to learn more about this topic, see Brian Eisenberg's book, *Call To Action*.

10. Guarantees and/or Policies

If you offer a professional service guarantee or a customer satisfaction guarantee, it can go a long way in removing a prospect's resistance to working with you.

Let people know up front what your policies are and prospects will appreciate it.

Takeaways

Are you testing or guessing what elements on your website should be there? There is no sense in reinventing the wheel when it comes to making a website work better.

Conversion experts have long been studying how to turn visitors into customers, and if you follow these guidelines, you will be proud of your website and how fast your law firm will grow.

Everyone wants the best website, but did you know that conversion experts all use analytics and various types of tools to systematically improve lead flow? Read the next section on analytics and you will never again do marketing without first using data analysis.

Top 9 Things Law Firms Should Track in Google Analytics

Keeping focused with analytics will keep you on the fast track to getting more sales. Avoid getting overwhelmed by looking at too much web analytics data and focus instead on the key performance indicators (KPIs) that matter most to your law firm.

We like to collect the following in an Excel spreadsheet: key Google analytics data, user experience elements like pages with high bounce and exit rates, SEMrush ranking reports, and some important data from Google Search Console such as click-through rates and broken links. This helps us keep it all in one place so it can be tracked each month.

On the first spreadsheet tab you can list highlights like these:

Traffic and Rankings Overview

- Your site generated 1,976 organic visits in October 2018, up 10.02% from the previous month. Organic traffic is up 214.14% year-over-year and currently accounts for 75% of your overall site traffic.
- There are 63 keywords ranking in the top 30 search results of Google that we are currently tracking (with 36 keywords ranked on the first page of Google).
- The keyword "neighbor's dog bit me on my property" delivers about 16.73% of traffic to your site from organic search, according to SEMrush data, followed by "neighbor's dog bit me" (12.74%).
- Besides the podcasts dog-bite-example-URL, the home page was the most viewed page on the website in October, driving 461 visits.

Goals and Conversions Overview

- Your site generated a total of (35) organic leads during the month of October, up 105.88% from the previous month.

Technical/User Experience Overview

- 13 broken links have been identified that we recommend are fixed using 301 Permanent Redirects
- Your website home page bounce rate is at 58% with average time on site of 0:01:59.

Then we include some nice charts and graphs like these:

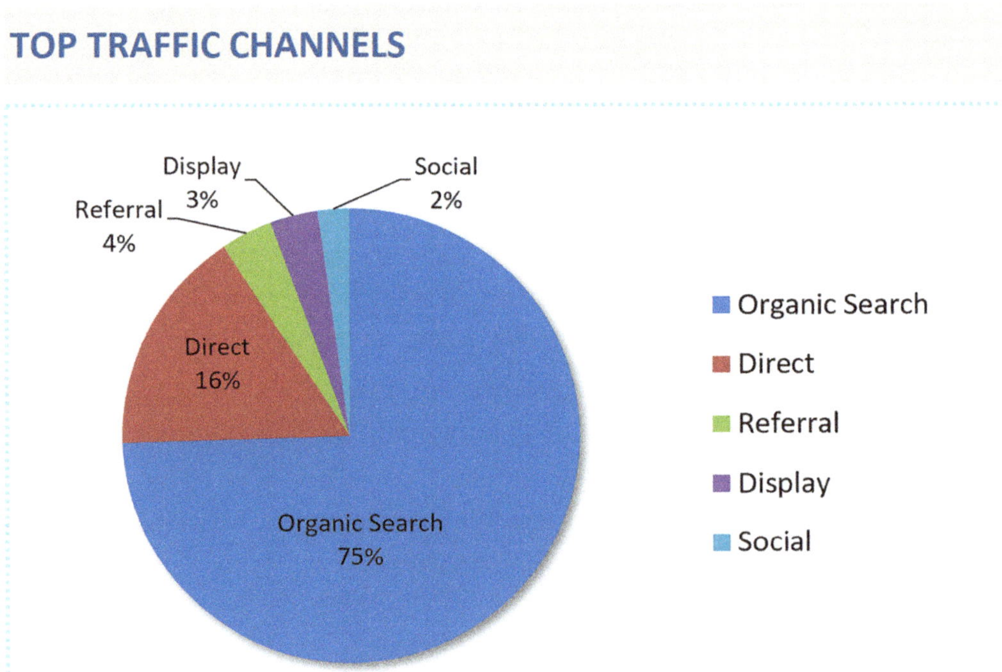

You can even customize a Google Analytics dashboard — if you want to keep it simple — to include these key performance indicators (KPI's) and get quick daily or weekly views of how your marketing efforts are performing. Here are our top nine KPIs for law firms.

1. Tracking Types of Leads/Total Number of Leads

Marketing for law firms is typically based on generating leads. This KPI tracks the total number of leads and should be broken out by the various channels with an associated conversion rate. The insight from this KPI will help you decide if increasing your attention (or spending) on a particular marketing channel will create more traffic and leads.

Here's how to get a full picture of where your leads are coming from. Make sure that you have tracking set up for each type of lead. Track phone calls with a tool like Call Rail, and form submissions via the amount of thank-you page visits. Consider adding live chat with a tool like Ngage Live (which is highly focused on law firms), and track email sign-ups and e-book downloads.

2. Cost Per Lead

If you have an unlimited marketing budget maybe you don't care how much each lead is costing you. For most firms, however, understanding the right marketing channel to focus on is using your marketing team's time and money wisely.

Google Analytics will even automatically link this data from their Google AdWords PPC to report the cost per lead as a summary report or by an individual campaign. And with a little customization you can even assign a specific lead value for organic search or other channels such as social media.

3. Types of Web Traffic/Channels

Much like a well-balanced diet, a good mix of the type of visitors to your website will also indicate a healthy marketing effort. Make sure to review the percentage of visitors coming from various sources such as organic search, direct, PPC, email, display ads, or social media.

4. Overall Website Conversion Rate

If you're actively doing conversion optimization projects for your website, an overall conversion rate KPI will help you see if your changes are improving sales. Even if you are not doing conversion rate optimization, it's important to track any upward or downward trends, as this affects your lead volume.

It's also not uncommon to see changes in various marketing channels such as PPC, where sudden drops or increases in the number of leads occurs without any changes made by you. Many businesses have seasonal aspects to their marketing efforts, so don't overreact to a dropping rate without considering other external factors.

5. Bounce Rate and Exit Rate

When somebody lands on an individual page right from the search engines and then never visits another page on the same site, that is considered a bounce. You need to look at the pages that have the highest bounce rates and figure out how to make them more engaging.

The same is true for exit rates. You need to look at the pages that people most commonly exit from and add something to keep them engaged. Again, adding links to and from blog posts and to multimedia content like video, infographics, and podcasts are great ways to keep people interested.

Google Analytics is only useful if you use it to take action, such as reducing the bounce rate of your pages.

6. Tracking Trends in Quality Visits with Average Page Views

Not all visits are created equal in the online world. A visitor who bounces by leaving the website after just looking at a single page is not a quality visit. If you are modifying or creating new content for your website, this KPI that compares average page views against website visits is a way to indicate improvements on your website relevancy as you improve it.

Having a blog with quality content broken out into categories by your different practice area experts is a great way to deepen site visitor engagement. You can highlight blog posts that people might enjoy when looking at practice area pages. Conversely, you can make links from blog posts about specific practice areas into the main service level pages.

7. Top Pages

Looking at the top content on your site will help you determine what content is getting viewed the most. Go to the "behavior" section in Google Analytics and click on "site content" and then click on "all pages." This will highlight all of your content and the total page views that content has received.

If your top content is not converting or driving people deeper into the site, here's your chance to know where to start adjusting to increase visitor engagement.

Consider repurposing content (such as a top-performing blog post) and spinning it off into videos, podcasts, or other types of additional content.

8. Traffic Growth or Decline from Organic Search

It's a joy to see on a month-to-month and year-over-year basis when we are dramatically increasing the number of visitors from organic search for our law firm customers. If you don't go into Google Analytics and look specifically at the segment of traffic coming from organic search, and compare different date ranges to rule out seasonal fluctuations, you won't know if your website is winning significant visitors from increases in total keywords ranking.

9. About Us and Bio Content

Look at the about us and bio pages on your website to see how many visits they get and what the bounce rate is. If the pages seem overly stiff or formal, add some personal images — like photos of you and your colleagues at a charity event — or thought leadership videos and podcasts to spice these pages up.

Your about us page and bio pages will often be the second- and third-most visited pages on your website. Leaving it up to chance whether or not these pages drive people deeper into your website is not a winning strategy.

Now that you have a few key performance indicators to review in your website analytics, make sure someone at your law firm and/or a subcontractor is assigned to check on these things at least on a monthly basis. Great websites are made through constant improvements based on analyzing critical data.

Creating dashboards is easy

Here is the information Google support provides on how to get started creating dashboards.

To create a dashboard

1. Sign in to Google Analytics.
2. Navigate to your view.
3. Open Reports.
4. Click CUSTOMIZATION > Dashboards.
5. Click +New Dashboard.
6. In the Create Dashboard dialog, select either Blank Canvas (no widgets) or Starter Dashboard (default set of widgets).

What your dashboard should contain

At the very least you need to track how many leads you are getting. Of course you want to look at the total number of visitors, the channels that are driving traffic, some metrics for organic search like the number of visitors, etc. But without looking at the number of leads on a monthly basis, you won't be tying your digital marketing directly to your business goals.

You can play around with different date ranges for your dashboard and send the results as often as you like to your email.

While analytics are critical to tracking ROI and website changes, having a sound strategy that factors in how all the tactics go together will take you to the moon and back. Here is where symbiotic relationships help make or break your ability to do the most with the time and budget you have.

11 Top Digital Marketing Tactics and How They Fit Together

Most law firms' digital marketing plans do not fail because of lack of information or desire. They fail because the execution of the tactics doesn't tie seamlessly into how the different tactics work together to be more efficient.

Below is an outline of the most critical digital marketing tactics and how you can better connect them so they work together effectively.

1. Branding

Building a brand is not just for traditional marketing. Building a brand online has direct consequences for your search engine optimization based on the ways Google looks at your expertise, authority, and trustworthiness.

If you have many people searching for your brand and positive reviews, your search rankings will go up. If your competitors are doing that better than you, it's used against you in organic ranking algorithms, which are an essential alternative to only paying extremely high costs per click in Google ads.

Having a clear set of branding guidelines for everything from the way that you use your logo, your colors, and fonts, to your mission statement and tagline, is imperative to make sure that your digital marketing doesn't go off the rails and send mixed messages.

Being positioned as a thought leader is critical for law firms that want to impress prospects and clients in general and niche practice areas. Having a plan to build your brand and protect it with reputation management, as well as building personal brands for your top attorneys, is much more strategic than just hiring someone to build a new website or run your social media without these key elements in place first.

2. SEO

Search engine optimization is tied to almost every other tactic directly or indirectly. If you are doing content marketing, you are doing SEO with the right frame of mind. If you are promoting your content with other tactics like social media and PR to get more links to your website, your SEO will benefit. When your SEO improves, more people see your brand and trust you more. That makes your visitors more likely to convert into leads because highly visible brands tend to have an easier time building trust.

3. Content Marketing

I believe that content marketing even has an impact on paid search. If you run Google ads and send people to a website with very basic information, is that as powerful as sending people to an information-rich website with an impressive blog and powerful resources? Given the very high cost per click in Google ads, you want to put your best foot forward and make sure your firm is positioned as a leader in your field.

There are plenty of content marketing experts out there these days, but did you know a lot of them just switched over from doing other things? Are you aware that many of them have no idea what a backlink is or how to handle technical website issues? If you are only relying on writers, you may get the best content, but if they don't understand how all the digital marketing pieces work together, that content will fail to be seen.

4. PPC and Paid Advertising

Google ads are one of the quickest ways to get leads. Google ads can be set up fairly quickly and even with a high cost per click, if you build landing pages with a very persuasive message (rather than just dumping people on your home page or an overly busy practice area page), you can make it work.

Running Google ads year-round even with a low budget for very niche topics with high "purchase" intent is a great way to ensure people are seeing your brand for key practice areas.

Paid search is a highly specialized process that includes conversion optimization, where you are A/B testing different headlines, value propositions, images, and calls to action.

If you leave this only in the hands of someone who is great at Google Adwords, you may be leaving a lot of leads on the table because you will be paying too much for each click due to your low conversion rate and low quality score.

5. Conversion Rate Optimization (CRO)

Conversion rate optimization (CRO) is the process of making your website win. You need to really think about marketing psychology and what will drive a customer to buy from you. CRO is a highly specialized art and I learned from Brian Eisenberg, the godfather of conversion optimization, that it can be taught and there are very specific methodologies that need to be followed.

Part of the conversion optimizer's arsenal is developing personas and mapping out the buyer's journey with the process your customers take when researching and then considering what firm to hire, as well as finally deciding who to hire.

Using tools like Unbounce or Lead Pages, conversion optimizers can often blow away the conversion rate of your main website, especially when they set up A/B testing software and prove what value propositions and headlines work to convert customers.

If you have a low conversion rate, your efforts, not only in paid search but in all of your other tactics, will be watered down to the point where you can't afford to do the same things that a competitor with a high conversion rate can do.

If you convert at 10% or 15%, you can afford to pay more than 10 times the cost per click of somebody with a 1% conversion rate. Don't leave this stuff to chance and just blindly start running paid ads or hoping your search and social traffic will convert because somebody managed to get you to the top of Google or in front of people on social media.

6. Email and Marketing Automation

Email marketing is one of the cheapest forms of digital marketing. Once you have the email list, it's almost free, yet people fail to build their lists. E-books and white papers can help you build your list but you must think strategically and set those up with landing pages to entice people to download them.

Once people download something from your website or fill out a form, you can put them into a marketing automation drip campaign and follow up many times with them in a way that gives them additional helpful information.

This nurtures them from being a weak lead into being a very engaged prospect. Buying placement in email newsletters that reach a large number of your customers can be one of the most effective ways to get new business, yet very few people understand it.

Building your email list enables you to promote the strong content you've created, and that will have a compounding effect on your search engine optimization and social media.

7. Online Public Relations

PR firms often charge $5,000 or $10,000 a month for their services. Did you know that, if you publish a book and have a niche blog, you can most likely get publicity yourself using PRleads.com or HelpAReporterOut.com?

Some of the best backlinks for search engine optimization come from public relations-style outreach.

If you have newsworthy content, submitting press releases to submission sites like BusinessWire and PR Web is fine, but if you really want your public relations to take off, you should tie it directly to outstanding pieces of content like industry surveys that you create.

If you are part of a trend, you can write a press release on the topic and also write a more evergreen version of the press release as a blog post. You can even do an infographic on the topic and tell journalists about it. Better yet, offer to do an infographic for a popular or high-traffic website like I did by creating the authority marketing infographic for the Huffington Post.[79]

---

[79] *https://www.huffingtonpost.com/jonha-revesencio/stand-out-with-this-9-ste_b_6643180.html*

Huffington Post Example

 80

Your brand will benefit from this type of visibility, and as we have discussed, your brand power will impact many digital marketing channels.

8. Social Media

Social media is here to stay, but it's important to understand that, according to BrightEdge and Conductor, only 2% to 5% of traffic to websites comes from social media, while more than 50% of traffic comes from search engine optimization.

So if you make them work together by having your social media be a powerful method of promoting content that Google will love, you will do much better than you would by just posting blurbs and graphics on your Facebook business page.

---

80 *http://authoritymarketing.com/wp-content/uploads/2015/02/authority-marketing-infographic.png*

LinkedIn publishing is one of the best ways to build thought leadership, but you need to be aware that you should only publish the first half of your already published post and then link back to your original post so people can read the rest. The search engine optimization geeks of the world understand why you need to do it this way (to avoid potential duplicate content issues), but the average social media expert doesn't necessarily know this.

9. Referrals Helped by Online Tactics

Getting referrals is one of the top ways your law firm can get business, but if your website is not persuasive, you might not close those deals. Referral prospects may also search for you to see if you are truly coming up as an authority. They may also kick the tires of your social media profiles, and if you look half-asleep, they will ask someone else for a referral to a better firm.

In the e-commerce world, many people do affiliate marketing and build pages on their websites to show referral partners how they can best promote for you. Consider making a page on your website for your best referring firms such as CPAs, real estate professionals, and medical professionals.

10. Design

One of the biggest mistakes you can make is to build your website just using the gut instincts of the highest-paid people in your firm and those of your web designer. Websites that improve their conversion rate do so by testing what works and doesn't work.

Before you design a website, you need to have a conversion optimization and search engine optimization strategy. Otherwise the content that you choose for your website may not be enough to move the needle in other areas.

11. Development

Time and time again we see companies relaunching their websites but failing to use 301 redirects. Suddenly their search engine optimization crashes and customers are getting 404 error pages instead of the proper website. Before you develop the code of your website, you need to understand what things could block the crawling of a search engine robot, slow down the load time of a page, or make a website less usable.

Conclusion

My first book was titled *Web Marketing on All Cylinders* because I wanted to make a roadmap for how all of these tactics fit together. It took 420 pages and three years, but it was well worth it. It became a college textbook (still in use after five years), landed me speaking gigs at Harvard University and Brandeis University, and brought my firm tons of new customers.

This book is significantly shorter and more to the point, but there is no way around the fact that digital marketing simply has an almost overwhelming amount of detail to it.

That is why you need a team. You need people who understand the strategy as well as highly specialized people who deeply understand each of these very specific tactics. If these tactics are not done deeply and correctly, you might as well not do them at all.

As I mentioned in the beginning, 67% of clicks go to the top five search engine results. If you want your digital marketing to succeed, in my opinion, at the very least you need an aggressive search engine optimization and content marketing program for your law firm.

When you set a budget and delegate specific tasks to the right people, like farming out the technical part of your search engine optimization and hiring a content writer who really understands your practice areas, you will be much better off.

You will feel good about your content and you will rest easy knowing the right technicians are working along with the most creative people who are using the most sophisticated tools — including artificial intelligence — to make a seamless process for getting high-quality leads on a regular basis.

Final Thoughts!

Marketing your law firm is difficult without a guide like Yoda or a guidebook like this.

Not only do you need to think about your search engine optimization (SEO), but you also need to plan your content and then increase your conversions and track them.

You now have a solid understanding of how SEO works from both a technical and an on-page perspective.

You understand that it's important to generate a range of high-quality content to attract new customers, generate links, and position yourself and your firm as an authority in your industry.

You and your law firm have a unique opportunity now to put this information into practice.

When you do, you'll find that you're able to:

1. Analyze your competition to see what they do well and how you can gain a competitive advantage.
2. Analyze your own website and content to see what could be improved.
3. Research your customers to see what sort of content resonates best with them.
4. Develop a content strategy that helps attract, engage, and convert customers.
5. Create a content strategy that uses a range of different publishing mediums, including podcasting, webinars, and e-books.
6. Understand the tools (paid and free) you can use to make your life easier and make your website win.

The world is ready to see your website and consume your content — are you ready to share it?

PART 5
SEO and Content Marketing Resources

Marketing tools, the best blogs, conferences, and techniques change all the time, so in addition to checking out these resources below, visit our blog download section for updated information.

https://www.legalmarketingreview.com/downloads

Here you will find tools to speed up your marketing process, including checklists and tools you can use to make your own legal content marketing and SEO workbook.

Checklists and Resources for Legal Marketing with the "On All Cylinders" System

1. Marketing Plan template
2. Web Marketing on All Cylinders checklist on how 11 tactics go together
3. Big Dog Authority Marketing checklist and online quiz
4. 10 things law firm websites should avoid checklist

5. 10 things law firm websites do right conversions checklist
6. Technical SEO checklist
7. On-page SEO checklist
8. Content marketing checklist/roundup methodology
9. User experience and user signals checklist
10. Link building checklist
11. Social signals checklist
12. Analytics checklist (Make sure code is installed, set up goal tracking, and dashboards)
13. Persona development guidelines
14. Buyer's journey mapping chart
15. Brand signals/engagement

The Big Dog Authority Marketing Checklist for Lawyers

Position yourself and your law firm as experts and thought leaders and you will be seen as the big dogs.

I started selling websites in the dark ages of 1995 at McDougall Associates Advertising. I drove around with a laptop and a phone jack and dialed up AOL in people's offices. One guy called me a snake oil salesman and said, "This internet thing isn't going anywhere, kid," and threw me out of his office. At times, I felt like a Chihuahua.

In spite of that, I quickly fell in love with the internet and search engine optimization.

I've built a multi-million dollar agency through hard work and long hours but knew there had to be a more streamlined way.

So I decided to write a book.

I hired an editor who told me to write a short first book but instead, I took three years to write a 420-page college textbook on the ever-changing world of digital marketing!

And yet I discovered a book is not nearly enough.

It got me many new customers, but I made a lot of mistakes along the way that I want to help other people avoid, so I created the Authority Marketing Roadmap.

The 6 essential steps to becoming a *visible* expert are

1. Pick a target market or practice area niche to narrow your focus.
2. Write yourself into existence.
3. Turn your blog into e-books and a short book.
4. Blog your way to *lasting* SEO, social media, PR, and link-building success.
5. Do regular public speaking.
6. Build an email marketing list.

Authority Marketing is the systematic process of building your personal brand in a way that positions you and your law firm as the big dogs for Google and your customers.

If you are feeling like a Chihuahua and you'd rather be seen in your industry as a Great Dane, then this checklist gives you a quick overview of the most important things you need to do build your thought leadership and authority.

You can also take the *Big Dog Authority Marketing Quiz*,[81] but it's important to keep this checklist handy as a reference.

Before we get started, let's expand the six essential steps into the 12 most important tactics.

1. Brand via specialization: Pick a niche practice area to call your own

One of the biggest mistakes people make in marketing is assuming that narrowing your focus will limit your results. It's usually the opposite. When you narrow your focus by selecting a niche or by targeting a specific industry, people want to work with you more, not less.

---

81 *http://authoritymarketing.com/quiz/*

2. Blog regularly

These days most thought leaders have a blog. If you want good search engine optimization success, a blog is in most cases a requirement. If you're not blogging regularly, how else will you regularly add fresh content to your website?

You can certainly add resource pages (which are fantastic) and an FAQ section, but having a popular blog can help skyrocket your website's traffic and the perception in your industry of you being an authority figure.

3. Write a book, even if it is very short

Nothing says that you are an expert better than being an author of a book. In addition, being a best-selling author of a book or even an e-book in a specific Amazon category makes you famous in your space.

The big mistake I made here in 2010 was not blogging my book first and then after three years of writing practically in a cave, expecting it to sell without a systematic book marketing process and platform.

4. Practice PR for media mentions

If you are seen on TV, interviewed on the radio, and featured in publications, people trust you and your firm more. Few people would argue with this and yet many experts don't put in the effort required to get regular media mentions.

Tools like HelpAReporterOut.com and PRleads.com, along with submitting meaningful press releases, can help you get started quickly.

5. Do public speaking and host events and seminars that show you are a dedicated thought leader

Some people fear public speaking more than death itself. If you are seen regularly as a prominent public speaker, people will line up to do business with you. If you study this tactic and prepare for your speaking engagements and webinars, you have a great chance of overcoming your anxieties and performing well.

6. Use SEO — "own" the keywords that are part of your positioning statement

If you're not popping up in organic search results for keywords relating to your topic, you are missing out on the largest media platform in the world. Google became much more complicated in 2011 with the Google Panda algorithm update that requires high-quality content, and in 2012 with the Google Penguin update that requires high-quality backlinks.

Now, you need to build engagement and show that people love your brand. Google now judges your website based on their EAT acronym. This stands for expertise, authoritativeness, and trustworthiness. Numerous Google patents elaborate on their ability to judge who your authors are and if your company is trustworthy. Having regular content is no longer good enough. It needs to be tied to specific people that they trust, and not just your company name.

7. Use social media — be deeply involved in online relationships, not just sharing content

Social media influence is no longer an optional part of becoming a persuasive attorney. If you want your writing and blog content to get a lot of attention from Google, then other people need to be sharing that content.

One of the biggest mistakes people make when doing modern search engine optimization is to assume that merely selecting long tail keywords for each piece of content is enough to drive traffic.

Today, your content needs to be highly shareable. Sharing photos of your company Christmas party and charitable events is certainly nice for your Facebook page, but if you want social media to work at a higher level, you need to tie it to your content promotion strategies.

This works best if you have a list of influencers that you regularly quote and for whom you regularly comment on their blog posts. If you do not build relationships and engagement with important influencers and people in your topical area, your social media efforts will be built on shifting sands.

8. *Practice link building with influencers via relationships*

Getting people to link to you is one of the hardest things to do in digital marketing. It becomes so much easier when you create relationships with journalists and influencers. Interviewing others in your space in a podcast and turning that into a survey with an infographic is a great way to build links.

If you don't have various types of link assets, you won't get the right type of links. And if you engage in low-level link building such as article submission sites or weak directories, you will trigger a Penguin manual penalty or algorithm problem that you will live to regret for years. Trust me, it's happened to me and you don't want to be in this situation.

9. *Seek sales influence — use the power of being a niche expert with content to persuade*

Cold calling isn't dead but it's not what it used to be. When you tie sales and marketing together — "smarketing" — you will have much better results. For example, having great content on your website that you can share with your prospects is a much better way to open a conversation than simply asking them to buy from you or meet with you.

The various factors in this checklist will help you to appear larger than life and increase the likelihood that people will want to work with you one-hundred fold. Your salespeople will love this, especially if they take part in the content development.

10. *Practice conversion optimization — have e-books, content offers, media mentions, and various trust signals*

If you do not have clear calls to action on your website, you will miss out on a large volume of leads. Many people simply expect customers to call them or fill out a long form after the first visit to their website.

Google has developed a highly sophisticated system of analyzing what they call the *buyer's journey*. In the early stage of the buyer's journey, customers are at the top of the sales funnel and will respond well to something along the lines of an e-book or a white paper download rather than a request to buy from or work with you. As they move down the funnel, they might download a case study or a comparison chart. Finally, at the bottom of the funnel, you can offer them a free consultation if they fill out a form or ask them to call you directly.

Improving the usability and quality of your website and having offers appropriate to the various stages of the marketing funnel will deeply improve your conversion rate.

Being an authority and visibly featuring the faces of your legal thought leaders on your website is also a great way to improve conversions. Videos, podcasts, and blog posts from your attorneys are a better way to get people to engage with you than just giving them sales material.

11. Build a platform and email marketing list

Top experts have large email marketing lists. When you have a large email list, you have an incredible amount of power, regardless of whether you get any traffic from Google or social media.

Building your email list should be one of your top priorities and it gets a lot easier when you have a substantial amount of "gated" content (content that prospects must provide a name and email in order to download). For example, HubSpot says that you get a massive increase in leads when you have 30 or more e-books. (Remember, e-books don't have to be long to be valuable.)

12. Use tracking and analytics to determine your new levels of influence

Recently I met with a company that said they want to go from making a couple hundred thousand dollars a year to $1 million a year in sales on their website. They not only did not have conversion tracking set up, but they also were not aware of what setting up goals in Google Analytics meant.

Examples of goal conversions and key things to set up for analytics tracking

- Email Subscribers
- E-book / Whitepaper Downloads
- Form Submissions
- Shopping Cart Orders

- Live Chat
- Phone Calls
- Event Tracking
- Attribution Tracking (HubSpot)

Not only do you need to get serious about tracking conversions, but you will also want to look at the various factors that relate to building your authority and then track them in your website analytics.

The following are just a few of those factors authorities should track beyond the standard goals:

- Unique Visitors
- Blog Visits
- Referrals
- Social Media Visits
- Domain / Link Authority
- Conversions from Content
- Bounce Rate
- Time on Site
- Conversion Paths
- Brand Mentions and Mentions of Team Member Names

Bringing it all together

While it is possible that you could succeed in life and in your business just fine using only a few of the tactics above, if you work on each of them, it will save you a lot of time because there are many interdependencies among them.

Never give up

One of the most common reasons people fail when building authority and blogging is to give up too soon. If you follow this roadmap and work on each of these categories, you will feel like a king and get the lion's share of the business in your niche practice area.

Passing the test

Judging authority is not an exact science. Google's PageRank, for example, can't tell if you are an authority offline, and even the best social authority tools like Klout are questionable.

That said, this checklist at the link below will give you a rough idea if you are a visible or invisible expert.

https://www.legalmarketingreview.com/downloads

We welcome your feedback. Feel free to email me at *jm@mcdia.com* (John D. McDougall) or connect on Twitter @mcdougalljohnd

10 Ways to Meet Ethical Obligations in Online Marketing for Law Firms

Attorneys must abide by the rules of professional conduct in their respective states when doing marketing. The American Bar Association's rules of professional conduct and the rules of your state are likely to be fairly similar, but not in all cases.

Therefore, you need to check your particular state's rules to make sure you abide by them.

Below is not a comprehensive list but rather a starting point to illustrate some of the ways you can avoid ethical issues.

1. Include a disclaimer on your website

Every single page of your website needs a disclaimer to comply with State Bar rules. It should contain statements such as:

- This website is an advertisement
- This website does not contain legal advice
- Using this website and its content does not form an attorney-client relationship
- Note that any verdict, settlements, testimonials, or case studies do not guarantee future results.

If you have pages translated into other languages, those pages need a disclaimer in that language.

You are responsible for the content on your website (not anyone you have hired to help you create it).

2. Be careful with what you claim on your bio

Your bio and even your business card could be used against you if you break the rules of ethics. If you are bragging about cases you have won, make sure you get your client's consent before adding this information to your bio.

3. Be ethical when naming your firm

Most states use the ABA Model Rule 7.5, which says that the names of law firms can't be false or misleading. If you are just a solo practitioner, don't include "and Associates" in your name. If you use a practice area in your name, make sure that you have experience in that area.

You should also avoid implying that you are connected to a government, public or charitable agency.

There are some states that have unique rules. Have you heard of the anti-AAArdvark rule? It is designed to dissuade lawyers from using silly names just to get a priority listing in directories.

Check with your state before going through the great expense of designing your logo, buying a domain name, and implementing all of your marketing.

4. Use social media, but use it carefully

Social media changes all the time and it's hard to keep up, but do not use commercial speech without a disclaimer, do not publish a client's information, and avoid comparative speech.

Social media should be more about engaging and highlighting your firm's personality versus aggressively giving sales pitches. When you are sharing team photos and helpful content, you are less likely to run into ethical issues than if you are directly selling your services.

5. Take ownership of your directory listings

When you claim a directory listing, you become responsible for it, but not claiming your listings will put you at a significant disadvantage because they are very powerful ways to market your firm.

Be careful not to call yourself an expert or specialist in your company description in directories. If you are recognized by your bar as an expert, then it's fine, but if not you could be committing an ethical violation. If you use commercial speech, make sure to add a disclaimer. Do not state that you practice in an area of law that you don't practice.

6. Manage your online reviews

When you have access to control reviews, you are responsible for them. You don't control them on Yelp and Google, so you shouldn't have issues with what people put up on those sites.

Make sure that when people review your firm, they don't use comparative speech, give any guarantees, or share any confidential details about cases.

Never pay for reviews, mainly because it's cheesy but also because the review sites might ban you. You also can't pay your clients to leave reviews for your firm. Making up fake profiles is a very bad idea.

7. Adjust the mobile-responsive version of your website to include a disclaimer

Make sure that the mobile version of your website doesn't fail to include your disclaimer. Sometimes things are omitted to make the mobile version cleaner and simpler, and your digital marketing agency might not be aware that you can't drop the disclaimer.

8. Avoid extraordinary claims

Don't claim to magically be able to guarantee results or that you are better than another firm if you can't back it up with proof.

9. Get consent for case studies

Ask for consent from a client before writing case studies or providing examples of where you have been successful.

10. Back up your website and all marketing materials

You are most likely responsible in your state to keep a copy of your marketing materials for a period between two and five years. Make sure you or your hosting company makes a backup of your website on a regular basis.

Conclusion

Digital marketing is here to stay and so it's wise to read about and implement the best practices for avoiding ethical issues and complying with your State Bar rules.

Once you know the key compliance areas, there is plenty of great work to be done, like sharing helpful content, raising your ranking in the search engines, and increasing the odds that people get to know and like your firm, as well as highlighting the practice areas you focus on the most.

Just because you can't make claims about being an expert or specialist doesn't mean you can't offer an incredible resource of helpful information around a practice area and become well-known for it.

Top Digital Marketing Tools for Law Firms

Making your law firm website noticeable to the masses can cost you a lot of money. Thankfully there is a wide range of free digital marketing tools that you can use to dramatically improve your process and make it far more strategic.

Google Analytics – *www.google.com/analytics*

Google Analytics helps you track multiple elements: the leads you get; the channels driving traffic such as organic search, paid ads, and social media; your conversion rate and bounce rate;, most visited pages: and more. Register for a free account with Google then add a snippet of code in your law firm's website header.

Google Search Console – *https://search.google.com/search-console/welcome*

Whereas Google Analytics shows you how customers use your site, GSC gives insights on how search engines interact with your site. Search Console tools and reports help you measure your site's search traffic and performance, fix tech issues, and according to Google "make your site shine in Google Search results." It is where you can see the keywords that are sending people to your site and the click-through rates, along with mobile performance by page. It is what you use to upload bad links to the disavow tool and more.

Google Keyword Planner – *https://ads.google.com/home/tools/keyword-planner*

A keyword planner is a specialized research tool that allows people with websites to identify the right keywords that they can use to target for display ads, video ads, app ads, and search ads but also for SEO. Find the right keywords with the right combination of search volume and competition.

Google Trends – *https://trends.google.com/trends/*

This tool will let you know what is trending around the world or near you right now. It's a tool that enables you to see the latest trends, visualizations from Google, and data. Explore topics using search keywords such as: "lawyer+ practice area" or "criminal defense lawyer." Comparing keywords helps you to understand the search demand for various keywords that are related to your practice area. There is a section known as "interest by subregion" where when you click on the state, you will be able to see how your search interest is broken down by metro area.

Think With Google – *https://www.thinkwithgoogle.com/*

Google has a website where they share all kinds of interesting marketing insights. One of the most important is the mobile load time tool. We use GTmetrix to check load time quite frequently but Google's tool is also excellent. Take a Saturday morning and explore Think With Google, and you will be pleasantly surprised at what they offer to help you improve your marketing and technical insights.

Ubersuggest – *https://neilpatel.com/ubersuggest/*

Ubersuggest is another tool that is considered by many to be the best option or substitute for Google's Keyword Planner. This tool will allow an individual to search for specific keywords that may fail to appear in Keyword Planner. Ubersuggest will also show you searches of newer keywords, unlike Google Keyword Planner.

SEMrush – *https://www.semrush.com*

Get insights into your competitors' strategies in display advertising, organic and paid search, and link building. You can uncover your competitors' ad strategies / budget, find the right keywords for SEO and PPC campaigns, see side-by-side domains comparisons of common and unique keywords, and switch from charts to spreadsheets. Do a site audit, so you can prioritize fixing SEO issues. Then you can do a social media audit and track against numerous competitors in terms of followers, reach and engagement. One of the newer things is topic research, where you can see a mind map of what keywords relate to a topic, along with the top headlines (by most linked to) and the top questions asked in relation to them. It's truly an amazing tool.

Screaming Frog – *https://www.screamingfrog.co.uk*

With Screaming Frog you can download all of the website page names or URLs of your site and competitors into Excel. It will show you the status codes, title and meta descriptions, and all kinds of information about the pages that you can use to determine the next steps to take for increasing your rankings. It is referred to by search engine optimization experts as a crawling tool or spider and is one of the foundational tools needed to properly do SEO.

HootSuite – *www.hootsuite.com*

HootSuite is a social scheduling tool. This tool allows people to write social media updates in advance and schedule the updates to be posted hours, days, or weeks later. This strategy will give you or your firm the appearance of always being active throughout the day. People are interested in sites that are always active, and with the HootSuite tool, your social media profile will be active even when you are not online. One drawback of social media is the fact that it can technically eat up almost all your time, which is why you need a good strategy and tools. Buffer is another social media management tool that deserves a look.

Unbounce – *https://unbounce.com/*

Unbounce is partially responsible for me and my team getting flown to Google headquarters four years in a row. Rather than sending people to the homepage or even a very busy sub-page of a website from Google ads, we often build landing pages using this tool to improve conversion rate optimization. We can make a page that is less cluttered than the main website and that has a multitude of persuasion elements built in that can be A/B tested, to prove what is making the website successful or not. Lead Pages is a similar and also extremely popular tool.

Ahrefs – *https://ahrefs.com/*

If you want to check your backlinks and clean up the bad ones, this tool is essential. There is a great common link option where you can see the backlinks that occur frequently between your competitors. That is a gold mine and a roadmap for getting more links for yourself. There are many link tools out there but this one has the best data. When you do comprehensive bad link cleanup you can also use Open Site Explorer, SEMrush, Majestic or other tools; *https://www.linkresearchtools.com* is a more expensive option. Then combine the data because each of these tools gives slightly different Interpretations of what links you have.

HotJar – *https://www.hotjar.com*

HotJar, unlike Google Analytics, is more concerned with where people are scrolling, moving, and clicking than what pages they are going to. You can set up heat maps, capture a user's actual session via screen recordings, surveys, ways to let customers give feedback, conversion funnels, form analytics, and make sure you are GDPR compliant. Hotjar Connecticator is a WordPress plugin that sets up on your website very easily. Similar and often more expensive tools include Crazy Egg and ClickTail.

Google Optimize – *https://optimize.google.com/optimize/home/*

Forty-five percent of small and medium businesses don't optimize their websites through A/B testing, according to a recent survey. Yet all high-end conversion optimization companies make it a staple of how they improve websites. You can set up simple A/B tests to figure out things like which headline performs better than another or use multi-variant testing to examine the impact of multiple persuasion changes together. For smaller sites with limited traffic, it can be difficult to get statistical accuracy, so UserTesting.com and HotJar can be great alternatives. If you don't have the money to pay for Visual Website Optimizer or Optimizely and are afraid of the learning curve, get started with Google's own tool.

Smartsheet – *https://www.smartsheet.com*

My team used BaseCamp for many years with mixed results. It's almost too sophisticated and cumbersome to get complete buy-in. Even if you get your team to buy in, then your customers get freaked out having to do anything but just use email to keep track of things. In comes Smartsheet at the suggestion of one of my customers. It's like Microsoft Excel on steroids, where you can insert comments next to line items, designate the status of a to-do list item as well as who is responsible for it, and you can upload files and run a crazy amount of reports without having to keep multiple spreadsheets, if you set it up right. You can also create collapsible menus to show top-level detail versus all of the detail on a list of things such as every type of content you are producing or a list of blog posts. Sure it has Gantt charts and all of that, but if you just want to show everybody on your team a list of what is being worked on, it's perfect.

HubSpot – *https://www.hubspot.com/*

HubSpot is like a Swiss Army knife. It is perhaps the most well-known and comprehensive digital marketing suite. It has tools for improving your content marketing that range from helping you do a better job blogging to setting up marketing automation workflows. It has advanced analytics that do some things like longer-range attribution tracking that Google Analytics doesn't have out of the box. It has suites for sales and marketing and even a free CRM system. They wrote a chapter in my last book and they have also included a nice bit of information below.

9 HubSpot Tools That Can Help Law Firms Rev Up Their Digital Marketing

By Anna Norregaard, Partner Executive at HubSpot

HubSpot is an inbound marketing software and sales software to help you increase your visibility online, convert traffic into leads, and manage business development opportunities. It is a software platform that includes many integrated tools to help you grow your firm. Here are some of the sales and marketing tools at a 30-thousand-foot view.

Tools to help your law firm get found

1. Website making tool – HubSpot has a content management system that combines the power of website creation with CRM to customize the entire buying journey, streamline marketing and sales alignment, and deliver true closed-loop reporting.
    a. You can create a beautiful website with HubSpot as your platform — like how you would use WordPress — or just use it on your existing website.
    b. If you choose the HubSpot CMS as your platform: It is the only solution that is directly integrated with CRM, so you can take all your contact data and create rich experiences that are relevant to your visitors. No importing or technical integrations required.
2. Blogging Tool – Write high-quality blog posts that help you get found in search, social media, and beyond.

a You can build your sites blog with HubSpot, even if it is not the platform for your whole site. Alternatively, you can use it with your existing blog for advanced optimization.

b Draft and publish blog posts from scratch or start with a pre-made blog post blueprint. Quickly insert images, format headers, and add links with the on-page editor.

a Use the composer to streamline the editing process by adding comments, sharing feedback, and collaborating with authors. Preview how your post will look on any device, then publish content your visitors will want to read from beginning to end.

3 Content Strategy/SEO Tool – Easily follow the proven best content methodology practices to identify the best keywords to pursue, and then execute, optimize, and report on content that generates results.

a HubSpot provides topic suggestions based on relevance, competition, and popularity, as well as access to monthly search data so you can estimate how ranking for specific topics will translate to organic traffic gains. Then, use HubSpot's integrated content tools to create clusters of web pages and blog content around each of your core topics.

b With HubSpot's integrated SEO tools, get on-page SEO advice in the same place you're creating blog posts, landing pages, and site pages. Easily monitor the performance of your content to identify the topics that are working the hardest for you — and the ones that aren't.

4 Social media --Publish updates, monitor terms, and analyze performance across Facebook, LinkedIn, and other social platforms.

a Publish content directly to LinkedIn, Facebook, Instagram, Twitter, and Google+, or connect your social accounts to your blog and automatically share new content as it gets published.

b HubSpot links social interactions to real people in your database, so you can see deep context and prioritize conversations with the people who matter.

Tools to help convert leads

5 Calls to Action – Easily build call-to-action buttons in HubSpot.

CTAs are among the most important elements of a website. They have the mighty job of catching your visitors' attention and guiding them to take that next important step.

a Use the button generator and have fast-loading CSS buttons for your site with alt-text already enabled. Or upload an image to get even more creative with your CTAs.

b Create a unified campaign by using the same CTA across your webpages, blog posts, and email campaigns. Because HubSpot is an all-in-one platform, integrating your channels around a single call to action or campaign becomes a breeze.

c Centralized CTA manager lets you track your CTAs in one place, regardless of how many you have or where they appear on your site, blog, or emails.

6 Landing pages – Create and test beautiful landing pages that generate leads and look great on any device without designers or IT.

a Create and publish new landing pages in no time even if your site is built in another platform like WordPress. Choose from a robust library of built-in mobile optimized templates that are proven to convert or build pages from the ground-up. With HubSpot you can add copy, inset images, and build conversion forms in minutes.

b Personalize landing page content for individual visitors. Dynamically show different content based on a visitor's location, source, device, buying stage, or any other contact details stored in your CRM.

c Easily analyze, test, and optimize landing page performance. Easily identify your best converting landing pages in a centralized dashboard. Then dig deeper to see how many visits, contacts, and clients each page is generating. A/B test pages that are not performing, and automatically see which version works best.

Tools to help convert leads to sales

7 Integrated CRM –Track your contacts' every move across your website, social, email, and business development interactions.

  a Segment, score, and report on the contacts in your database.

  b Remove manual list building through setting rules to auto-update lists based on CRM data or contact behavioral engagement measured across channels.

  c Identify business development opportunities and customize a pipeline in HubSpot with stages to keep track of them.

8 Email – HubSpot Email helps growth teams send beautiful, optimized emails quickly and easily, without ever touching a line of code.

  a From your website to your CRM system, use deep connections to every other part of your growth stack to help you send deeply. Personalized messages will feel like a one-on-one conversation.

  b Create professional emails from dozens of templates available, create custom coded emails, or purchase templates from HubSpot's marketplace to build emails.

  c Optimize every detail of your send. Use HubSpot's dynamic deliverability and engagement checker as you write your copy into your template and use A/B testing to home in on the best content.

9 Workflows – Nurture your high-quality leads with marketing automation.

Workflows allows marketers to automate many important yet mundane tasks, saving you time and allowing you to do things that you couldn't accomplish without marketing automation.

  a Workflows allow you do things like automatically send a series of emails after someone takes an action. After sending a thank you for downloading our ebook email, you can then send a series of emails like the following: Four days after an initial ebook download, send a link to some related blog content; four days later, send a link to a case study; and four days after that, send a request to chat on the phone or offer to give a free quote. This nurtures prospects from the top, to the middle and finally to the bottom of the marketing funnel.

b You can use HubSpot to send internal notifications, score leads, and personalize the content on your website to each viewer.

c Easily build drip nurture lists of certain people, or use contact behavior to trigger nurture emails automatically.

HubSpot provides many tools to help manage all the components of your sales and marketing strategy and then automate manual processes to help you become more efficient and effective.

By using HubSpot to manage these activities, the platform automatically tracks the performance of all aspects of your website and communication strategy. In doing so, you can better assess how each activity and campaign compare to one another in increasing your firm's thought leadership and its ability to generate more cases.

Conclusion

These are some of the tools I use every month, if not every day. Chiefmartec.com has almost 7,000 tools in its yearly review of the marketing and technology landscape. With the advent of artificial intelligence, big data, and lots of venture capital money going into this space, you can expect to see even more tools and ones that will make or break your campaigns.

Top Digital Marketing Blogs for Law Firms to Follow

As a lawyer, you know it's important to always stay ahead of the trends when it comes to news about the law and how to best market your law firm.

In this final section of this guide, we list a handful of top blogs you need to follow to make sure you're always at the top of your legal game and also that you always have the most up-to-date knowledge about how to market your law firm in the most effective way.

Although many of the sites are not just for law firms, it's important to reach beyond your own industry to see what the marketing community is doing. The knowledge and wisdom each post has can be transferred to your own law firm site.

Legal Marketing Review – *https://www.legalmarketingreview.com/*

Legal Marketing Review is run by none other than me, John McDougall, CEO of McDougall Interactive, an authority on digital marketing for law firms. This site specifically helps a large number of law firms understand how they can create a comprehensive internet marketing strategy through content marketing, SEO, paid search, and social media to generate more and better leads.

Neil Patel – *https://neilpatel.com/blog/*

Neil Patel's blog is a great resource if you want to learn in depth about different marketing tactics. The content goes incredibly deep and is based on an advanced knowledge of how search engine optimization and social media go together. It's also presented in a fun-to-read format, despite covering subjects comprehensively.

HubSpot's Blog – *https://blog.hubspot.com/*

HubSpot has one of the most visited websites about digital marketing, sales, agency, and customer success online. It's a must-read resource. HubSpot's Blog has more than 400,000 subscribers and attracts over 4.5 million visitors monthly.

Search Engine Land – *https://searchengineland.com*

This is where you go if you want to find out the latest news about the search engines. They cover algorithm changes in detail and are the top site for this topic when it comes to changing search trends.

Above the Law – *https://abovethelaw.com/*

Above the Law is a great site for all things law. They cover a number of key categories and offer information useful to students of law as well as law firms.

FindLaw – *https://www.lawyermarketing.com/blog/*

FindLaw caused some issues for my clients over the years, like adding duplicate content, but I think it's fair to give credit where credit is due in regard to the amount of their legal content indexed in Google.

Copy Blogger – *https://www.copyblogger.com*

Copy Blogger and Pro Blogger are two of the top websites for learning about writing and content marketing. Refine your craft and creativity that is central to increased engagement.

Social Media Examiner – *https://www.socialmediaexaminer.com*

Social Media Examiner is one of the top sites focused specifically on social platforms, but of course dovetails into content marketing, etc.

Takeaway

There are many blogs that you can (and should) follow; however, the best thing you can do is to find a small number of blogs that provide you with tangible value with every post. That way you can be sure you won't be wasting time and will be able to take action on what you have learned.

About the Author

My name is John McDougall, and I am the CEO of McDougall Interactive, publisher of The Legal Marketing Review, and an authority on internet marketing for law firms.

My father owned the sixth-largest ad agency in New England from the 1980s to the early 2000s, so advertising is in my blood. I switched from media planning to web marketing in 1995 and never looked back. I took a class on search engine optimization in 1996, so I am among the earliest adopters of SEO.

After providing internet marketing consulting services for a variety of industries (with clients such as Philips Medical, Arrow Electronics, Hearing Planet, MIT, and numerous law firms, banks, retailers, and colleges), I realized we could have a greater impact if we focused on one type of client. Our strongest category, where we have driven tens of millions of dollars in leads, is law firms, so I decided to create a blog — and now this book —- to share my extensive knowledge.

My team of over a dozen people helps law firms understand how to create a comprehensive internet marketing strategy and how to use SEO, paid search, and social media to generate more, and better, leads.

We know how to develop legal content for you and with you. We know the sites you want links from, the journalists in your space, how to produce legal video marketing that drives leads, and what it takes for a law firm to transform their web marketing into a powerful branding experience that is helpful to potential clients.

I hope that my blog, this guide, and my passion for marketing and creativity will help counsel you as you extend your networking skills from word-of-mouth to the web.

About McDougall Interactive and Our Services

Founded in 1995, McDougall Interactive is a full-service internet marketing company that has worked on hundreds of successful website marketing campaigns.

It all started when John McDougall was working as a media planner in 1995 at McDougall Associates, where his father asked him to start the internet marketing and website design division.

After taking an online SEO class in the 1990s (one of the first ever, around 1996), John fell head over heels in love with all things SEO and digital marketing. Here's one of his fonder memories:

> *"In 1995, I would drive around with a laptop in my blue on blue Ford Bronco and show prospects the internet by dialing up on AOL. Maybe it was the crazy sound of the 56k modem, but one guy called me the modern version of a snake oil salesman and said, 'This internet thing isn't going anywhere, kid...'"*

Well, as we all know, the web has put on some serious big boy/girl pants and companies like Google and Apple are some of the largest in the world. Not to mention that the "internet of things" is about to send marketers on another wild ride.

A few of our agency highlights

- Our award winning book, *Web Marketing on All Cylinders*, is now a college textbook!
- Our writing and thought leadership has been featured on sites like The Huffington Post, HubSpot, eContent Magazine, Wordtracker University, National Law Review, LinkedIn Pulse, Writers Access, and more.

- Our seminars on digital marketing have been featured in *The New York Times*, and Google holds regular events at our office.
- We have been featured in numerous local publications such as the *Boston Globe, Boston Herald, North Shore Magazine, Salem Evening News*, and more.
- We are a HubSpot Partner / Value-added reseller. (HubSpot contributed a section to Part 5 of this guide.)
- Google Adwords and Analytics certified.
- Conversion optimization certified by industry leader Market Motive.
- Multiple authors on staff.
- We produce creative videos, including a viral one with 12 million views.
- Our blog and focus on thought leadership is at *authoritymarketing.com*.

Mini case study highlights

- We won the "best of show" at the 2014 New England Financial Marketing Awards — and best for deposits in the 2015 NEFMA awards for driving tens of millions of dollars in deposits to an online-only bank we *designed and marketed*[82] for Bank5Connect. It has now been designated the second-best online-only bank, and we did all the design and marketing.
- We made over $15 million dollars in two years for a mesothelioma attorney by using a combination of content marketing and Google Ads.
- We generated $500k in additional revenue — in just six months — for a golf e-tailer, using conversion rate optimization and A/B testing.
- We have many B2B and professional services marketing success stories for companies like Koch Membranes, Arrow, and Phillips Medical.
- Among our B2B case studies is getting a company ranked so well for "hearing aids" (#1) and related terms that they got bought out by a competitor (Hearing Planet), and we got rankings of #3 in Google for "golf clubs" for Rock Bottom Golf, which got us featured on *Internet Retailer*.[83]

---

82 *https://www.mcdougallinteractive.com/our-work/bank-marketing-financial-services-marketing-case-study/*

83 *https://www.mcdougallinteractive.com/our-work/ecommerce-marketing-case-study-rock-bottom-golf/*

Our first book

A college textbook and IPPY gold award winner.

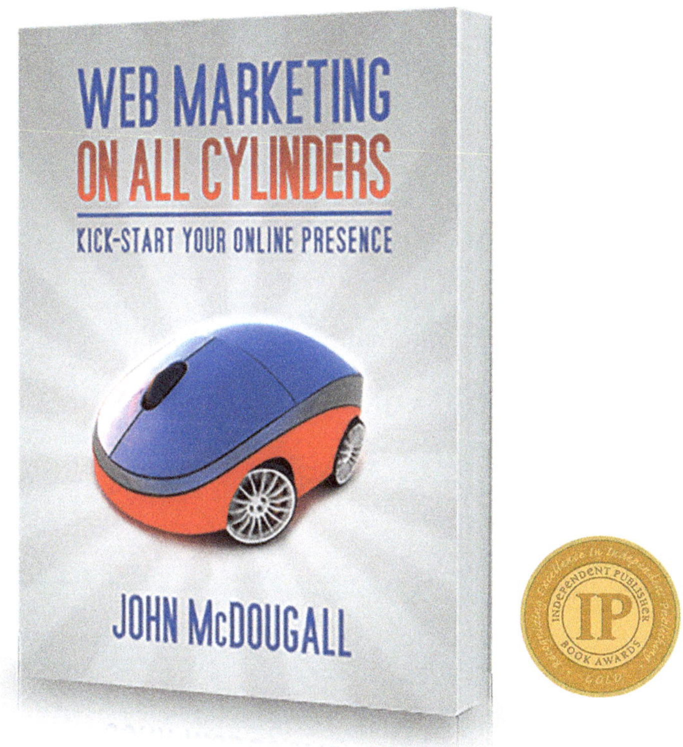

Digital Marketing based in Massachusetts

McDougall Interactive is based in Gloucester, Massachusetts, and employs a talented lineup of digital marketing experts on search engine optimization, paid search, social media, and pay-per-click (PPC); published writers and prolific bloggers; and dedicated link builders. We work in concert to help your business generate more leads and sales by increasing both inquiries and conversions.

Our agency-level background in traditional web design and development means we are at our best when handling integrative marketing campaigns designed to attract not only search engines but people.

A Multifaceted Approach to Internet Marketing

At McDougall Interactive, we believe that it takes a persuasive online presence to succeed in business, which is why our internet marketing campaigns can include, among other strategies.

1. Branding
2. SEO
3. Content Marketing
4. PPC and Paid Advertising
5. Conversion Rate Optimization (CRO)
6. Email and Marketing Automation
7. Online Public Relations
8. Social Media
9. Referrals (helped by Online tactics)
10. Design
11. Development

We're an Elite Google Partner

In 2012, 2013, 2014 and 2015, we were honored to be invited to Google headquarters, all expenses paid. Only 110 other agencies in the United States got this honor each year and likely only a handful got it four years in a row.

John McDougall, our founder, couldn't resist trying one of the Google bikes to see if it would somehow help our search rankings!

And here is John (and our paid search director at the time, Bob Rustici) taking the obligatory photo in front of the Google logo.

Work with Us

If you like what you see, give us a call at 978-750-8000 or email us. We would be more than happy to hear what keeps you up at night and help solve your marketing problems.